LIBRARY OF HEBREW BIBLE/ OLD TESTAMENT STUDIES

539

Formerly Journal for the Study of the Old Testament Supplement Series

Editors
Claudia V. Camp, Texas Christian University
Andrew Mein, Westcott House, Cambridge

Founding Editors
David J. A. Clines, Philip R. Davies and David M. Gunn

Editorial Board
Alan Cooper, John Goldingay, Susan E. Gillingham, Norman K. Gottwald,
James E. Harding, John Jarick, Carol Meyers,
Daniel L. Smith-Christopher, Francesca Stavrakopoulou,
James W. Watts

BODY, GENDER AND PURITY IN LEVITICUS 12 AND 15

Dorothea Erbele-Küster

LONDON • NEW YORK • OXFORD • NEW DELHI • SYDNEY

T&T CLARK
Bloomsbury Publishing Inc
1385 Broadway, New York, NY 10018, USA
50 Bedford Square, London, WC1B 3DP, UK
29 Earlsfort Terrace, Dublin 2, Ireland

BLOOMSBURY, T&T CLARK and the T&T Clark logo
are trademarks of Bloomsbury Publishing Plc

First published in 2017
This paperback edition published in 2022

Copyright © Dorothea Erbele-Küster, 2017

Dorothea Erbele-Küster has asserted her right under the Copyright,
Designs and Patents Act, 1988, to be identified as Author of this work.

All rights reserved. No part of this publication may be reproduced or
transmitted in any form or by any means, electronic or mechanical,
including photocopying, recording, or any information storage or retrieval
system, without prior permission in writing from the publishers.

Bloomsbury Publishing Inc does not have any control over, or responsibility for,
any third-party websites referred to or in this book. All internet addresses given
in this book were correct at the time of going to press. The author and publisher
regret any inconvenience caused if addresses have changed or sites have
ceased to exist, but can accept no responsibility for any such changes.

A catalogue record for this book is available from the British Library

A catalog record for this book is available from the Library of Congress

ISBN: HB: 978-0-5672-4656-1
PB: 978-0-5677-0876-2
ePDF: 978-0-5674-9665-2

Series: Library of Hebrew Bible/Old Testament Studies, volume 539

Typeset by Forthcoming Publications (www.forthpub.com)

To find out more about our authors and books visit
www.bloomsbury.com and sign up for our newsletters.

Contents

Preface	vii
Abbreviations	ix

Chapter 1
MAPPING 1
I. Language, Body and Gender 1
II. Discourse History 3
   a. Discourse Analysis of the Body from the Perspective of Gender 3
   b. Translation as Part of Discourse and Interpretation History 5
III. Survey of Research 6
   a. Source-critical and Form-critical Classification 7
   b. Correlations of Text and Practice 11
   c. Interpretive Models of Purity 15
   d. Perceptions of the Body and (Its) Gender 20
IV. Outline 22

Part I
EXEGETICAL ANALYSIS

Chapter 2
LEVITICUS 12 27
I. Translation (MT) 27
II. Two Gendered Cases 28
III. Microstructure 30
   a. Israel's Descendants 30
   b. The Woman Who Produces Seed 33
   c. Male and Female Descendants 34
   d. As During the Days of Her Menstruation 36
   e. Foreskin of His Member 36
   f. Remaining in Accordance with the Blood of Purification 37
   g. At the Entrance to the Tent of Meeting 39
   h. She Shall Present a Yearling Sheep as a Burnt Offering 42
   i. He Completes the Purification Ritual 45
   j. She Is Pure as a Result of the Source of Her Blood 47

IV.	The LXX Rendering		49
	a.	Translation	49
	b.	Coining New Words	50
	c.	Remaining in Her Impure Blood	50
	d.	According to the Days of Her Menstrual Separation	51
	e.	The Priest Shall Complete the Atonement Ritual	52
V.	The Origin of Cultic (Dis)ability and of the Gendered Body		53

Chapter 3
LEVITICUS 15 — 56

I.	Translation (Masoretic Text)		56
II.	Structural Symmetry as Gender Symmetry?		58
	a.	Is the Introduction Gender-inclusive or Gender-specific?	59
	b.	Does the Chapter's Structure Imply Equality of the Sexes?	61
III.	Microstructure		63
	a.	YHWH Spoke to Moses and to Aaron	63
	b.	A Man Who Has a Discharge	63
	c.	A Woman, When She Has a Discharge	64
	d.	A Man Who Has a Seminal Emission	65
	e.	Bleeding Beyond the Period of Niddah	66
	f.	Whoever Touches Something…Shall Be Ritually Impure	67
	g.	Every Person, Who…, Shall Wash His or Her Clothes	73
	h.	A Woman Who Lies with a Man	74
	i.	You [pl.] Shall Separate Israel's Descendants	76
	j.	This Is the Instruction	77
IV.	The LXX Rendering		78
	a.	Translation	78
	b.	Hebraisms in the Greek Text	81
	c.	Genital Discharges	81
V.	Gender Neutral and Gender Specific Language of the Body		84

Part II
BIBLICAL ANTHROPOLOGY AS DISCOURSE OF THE BODY

Chapter 4
FLESH — 89

I.	The One-Gender Model		89
II.	Circumcision of the Flesh		91
	a.	Circumcision as a Surgical Procedure	92
	b.	Circumcision as Rite	93
	c.	Circumcision as Covenant Sign	96
	d.	Circumcision as Identity Marker	97
	e.	Circumcision as the Fixing of Gender	98
	f.	Circumcision of the Heart	99
	g.	A Distinguishing Mark on the (Male) Body	101

Chapter 5
BODILY FLUIDS — 103
I. Genital Discharge — 103
II. Seed — 106
    a. The Female Seed — 107
    b. Seminal Ejaculation — 109
III. Blood — 111
    a. The Life Is in the Blood — 113
    b. Physiology and Symbolic System — 115

Chapter 6
MENSTRUATION — 117
I. Menstruation as Separation — 117
    a. What Do Menstruating Women and the Land of Israel Have in Common? — 117
    b. Bodily, Social, or Cultic Separation? — 119
    c. *Niddah* as a Cultic Term — 120
    d. *Niddah* as a Socio-religious Term — 121
    e. *Niddah* as Pejorative and Polemical Term — 122
    f. Discourse on Menstruation as a Boundary Marker — 124
II. Menstruation as Destabilization — 127
    a. What Do Menstruation and Sickness Have in Common? — 127
    b. Destabilization of Physical, Emotional, and Mental Balance — 129
    c. Destabilization of Cultic Status — 131
    d. Destabilization of Aesthetic and Religious Sensibilities — 131
    e. Women's Experiences? — 132
III. Menstruation in Narrative Texts — 133
    a. 'The way of women is upon me' (Genesis 31.35) — 134
    b. 'The way corresponding to women' (Genesis 18.11) — 135
    c. 'She was purifying herself from her impurity' (2 Samuel 11.4) — 135
    d. Narrative Texts Beyond the Conceptual World of the Purity-torot — 136

Chapter 7
THE CULTIC PERSPECTIVE — 138
I. Impurity as Cultic Disability — 140
    a. Is Impurity Material? — 140
    b. Impurity as a Technical Cultic Term — 142
    c. Impurity as a Marker of the Gender Boundary — 142
II. Purity as Cultic Ability — 145
    a. Is Purity Material? — 145
    b. Purification or Purity? — 146
    c. Declarative Formulae — 148

Chapter 8
PROSPECTS ... 151
I. Textual Conceptions and Their Performative Practices ... 151
    a. Discourse and Translation History ... 151
    b. Leviticus 12 and 15 as Performative Regulations Creating Body, Gender and Purity ... 153
    c. From Practice to Theory of the Purity-*torot* and Back ... 156
II. Leviticus and Body Practices as Survival Space in Exilic and Persian Times ... 159
    a. Fictionality and Normativity ... 159
    b. Leviticus as a Reading Space ... 160

Bibliography ... 164
Index of References ... 176
Index of Authors ... 184

Preface

The book at hand is the outcome of a long and fascinating journey, one moving between different languages and countries. Long ago the journey into the heart of the Torah, more precisely the regulations concerning the gendered body in Lev 12 and 15, began as a postdoctoral project at the Graduate School at the University in Heidelberg/Germany and the Protestant Theological Faculty in Kampen/NL. Its first fruits were published in German under the title 'Körper und Geschlecht. Studien zur Anthropologie von Leviticus 12 and 15' in 2008 in the series WMANT, and were later accepted as Habilitationsschrift at the Johannes Gutenberg University Mainz/Germany.

The present English monograph has built on the original work, mainly due to continuous research and discussions on the subject. In order to stress the observation that 'purity' and 'impurity' come into being only as a result of the use of specific (gendered) language and intersect with the construction of body and gender, the term 'purity' has been purposefully included to the book's title. Attention is given to the way the textuality of body and gender unfolds in the non-argumentative style of the regulations; this is done by making use of recent research in ritual studies taking into account the textuality of the rituals in Leviticus. The former German subtitle has been removed, as in English 'anthropology' implies different notions in the Anglophone academic discourse.

The changes made in this English work go beyond adjustments to the title – other important additions and modifications have been made. As a result of my having taught in different languages and having engaged in various translation projects, I am acutely aware that translating – in the case of this study from German into English – does imply interpretation as well. Luckily I had valuable hermeneutical guidance as I prepared my English presentation: Brian Kelly and Andrej Verheij helped with the translation and suggested useful corrections, while my copy-editor, Duncan Burns, helped me along the finishing straight with diligence.

I am grateful to Athalya Brenner for introducing me to one of the editors of the LHBOTS series, Claudia Camp. Claudia challenged me to clarify my arguments for prospective readers. In recent years, the Annual Meetings of the SBL provided the forum in which the arguments offered in this English version could be honed and refined. With diligent and sharp eyes, Claudia read through the chapters and commented on them. Miriam Cantwell from Bloomsbury T&T Clark reminded me with kind tenacity to deliver the manuscript. I would like to express my gratitude to the members of the LHBOTS editorial board for accepting the manuscript for publication.

And so, finally, you as readers have the product at hand. My hope is that this work will prove insightful, and perhaps also enjoyable.

There have been a lot of encounters on this way with persons (mentioned and unmentioned ones) who encouraged me and shared their insights with me. Volker Küster has been a constant co-traveler through the turn of the tide.

I would like to express my gratitude to all of them.

Heidelberg, Advent 2016
Dorothea Erbele-Küster

Abbreviations

AB	Anchor Bible
ABD	*Anchor Bible Dictionary*. Edited by David Noel Freedman. 6 vols. New York: Doubleday, 1992
AHw	*Akkadisches Handwörterbuch*. Wolfram von Soden. 3 vols. Wiesbaden, 1965–1981
ATD	Das Alte Testament Deutsch
BBB	Bonner biblische Beiträge
BBRS	Bulletin for Biblical Research, Supplements
BDB	Brown, Francis, S. R. Driver, and Charles A. Briggs. *A Hebrew and English Lexicon of the Old Testament*
BETL	Bibliotheca Ephemeridum Theologicarum Lovaniensium
Bib	*Biblica*
BIS	Biblical Interpretation Series
BKAT	Biblischer Kommentar, Altes Testament
BN	*Biblische Notizen*
BZAW	Beihefte zur Zeitschrift für die alttestamentliche Wissenschaft
CAD	*The Assyrian Dictionary of the Oriental Institute of the University of Chicago*. Chicago: The Oriental Institute of the University of Chicago, 1956–2006
CAT	Commentaire de l'Ancien Testament
CBET	Contributions to Biblical Exegesis and Theology
COT	Commentaar op het Oude Testament
DCH	*Dictionary of Classical Hebrew*. Edited by David J. A. Clines. 9 vols. Sheffield: Sheffield Phoenix Press, 1993–2014
DSD	*Dead Sea Discoveries*
FAT	Forschungen zum Alten Testament
FRLANT	Forschungen zur Religion und Literatur des Alten und Neuen Testaments
Ges[18]	Gesenius, Wilhelm. *Hebräisches und Aramäisches Handwörterbuch zum Alten Testament*. Edited by Rudolf Meyer and Herbert Donner. 18th ed. Berlin: Springer, 1987
GesB[17]	Gesenius, Wilhelm. *Hebräisches und Aramäisches Wörterbuch zum Alten Testament*. Edited by Frants Buhl. 17th ed. Berlin: de Gruyter, 1959
GK	Gesenius, Wilhelm. *Hebräische Grammatik*. Edited by Emil Kautzsch. 28th ed. Leipzig: Vogel, 1909

HAL	*Hebräisches und aramäisches Lexikon zum Alten Testament.* Ludwig Koehler, Walter Baumgartner, and Johann J. Stamm. 3rd ed. Leiden: Brill, 1995, 2004
HALOT	*The Hebrew and Aramaic Lexicon of the Old Testament.* Ludwig Koehler, Walter Baumgartner, and Johann J. Stamm. Translated and edited under the supervision of Mervyn E. J. Richardson. 4 vols. Leiden: Brill, 1994–1999
HAT	Handbuch zum Alten Testament
HCOT	Historical Commentary on the Old Testament
HthKAT	Herders Theologischer Kommentar zum Alten Testament
JANES	*Journal of the Ancient Near Eastern Society*
JBL	*Journal of Biblical Literature*
JBT	*Jahrbuch für Biblische Theologie*
JCP	Jewish and Christian Perspectives
JJS	*Journal of Jewish Studies*
JPS	The Jewish Publication Society
JSJ	*Journal for the Study of Judaism in the Persian, Hellenistic, and Roman Periods*
JSOT	*Journal for the Study of the Old Testament*
JSOTSup	Journal for the Study of the Old Testament Supplement Series
KBL^3	Koehler, Ludwig, and Walter Baumgartner. *Lexicon in Veteris Testamenti libros*. Ed. B. Hartmann, P. Reymond and J. J. Stamm. 3rd ed. Leiden: Brill, 1974
KTU	*Die keilalphabetischen Texte aus Ugarit.* Edited by Manfried Dietrich, Oswald Loretz, and Joaquín Sanmartín. Münster: Ugarit-Verlag, 2013. 3rd enl. ed. of *KTU: The Cuneiform Alphabetic Texts from Ugarit, Ras Ibn Hani, and Other Places.* Edited by Manfried Dietrich, Oswald Loretz, and Joaquín Sanmartín. Münster: Ugarit-Verlag, 1995 (= *CTU*)
LHBOTS	The Library of Hebrew Bible/Old Testament Studies
Liddell/Scott	Liddell, Henry George, Robert Scott, Henry Stuart Jones. *A Greek–English Lexicon. 9th ed. with revised supplement.* Oxford: Clarendon, 1996
Littré	*Œuvres complètes d'Hippocrate. Traduction nouvelle avec le texte grec par Emile Littré.* 10 vols. Paris: Bailliere, 1839–61
NBL	*Neues Bibel-Lexikon.* Edited by Manfred Görg and Bernhard Lang. 3 vols. Zurich: Benzinger, 1991–2001
NRSV	New Revised Standard Version
NSKAT	Neuer Stuttgarter Kommentar, Altes Testament
OBC	Orientalia Biblica et Christiana
OBO	Orbis Biblicus et Orientalis
OLA	Orientalia Lovaniensia Analecta
ORA	Orientalische Religionen in der Antike
OTL	Old Testament Library
QD	Quaestiones Disputatae
RB	*Revue biblique*
SBL	Society of Biblical Literature
SBLDS	Society of Biblical Literature Dissertation Series

SBS	Stuttgarter Bibelstudien
SJOT	*Scandinavian Journal of the Old Testament*
TANZ	Texte und Arbeiten zum neutestamentlichen Zeitalter
THAT	*Theologisches Handwörterbuch zum Alten Testament*. Edited by Ernst Jenni, with assistance from Claus Westermann. 2 vols. Munich: Chr. Kaiser Verlag; Zurich: Theologischer Verlag, 1971–1976
ThWAT	*Theologisches Wörterbuch zum Alten Testament*. Edited by G. Johannes Botterweck and Helmer Ringgren. Stuttgart: Kohlhammer, 1970–
TRu	*Theologische Rundschau*
VT	*Vetus Testamentum*
VTSup	Supplements to Vetus Testamentum
WMANT	Wissenschaftliche Monographien zum Alten und Neuen Testament
WUNT	Wissenschaftliche Untersuchungen zum Neuen Testament
ZAW	*Zeitschrift für die alttestamentliche Wissenschaft*
ZDPV	*Zeitschrift des deutschen Palästina-Vereins*
ZTK	*Zeitschrift für Theologie und Kirche*

Chapter 1

MAPPING

I. *Language, Body and Gender*

Two contradictory phenomena attract attention in the regulations on childbirth in Leviticus 12 and on genital fluids in Leviticus 15, namely gender duality versus gender-neutral formulations for the sexual body. Dealing with bodies and bodily processes the reader is struck by the paucity of concrete depictions of them. For example, the regulations for the post-partum woman do not refer to the actual birth as a social reality characterized by several dangers: miscarriage, stillbirth, and infant mortality, not to mention the possible death of the mother. This lack raises questions: From which perspective are these texts written? What body images do they convey? How do they perceive and effect gender?

With respect to these questions, this book highlights the discursive structure of the purity regulations in Leviticus 12 and 15 dealing with the gendered body mainly with respect to sexuality and reproductivity from a gender perspective:[1] a subject to which Hebrew Bible scholars (mostly female) have only recently begun to pay attention[2] – mainly focusing on women (as a category focalized by the text).

---

1. On this issue in general in the Hebrew Bible, cf. exemplarily, A. Brenner, *Intercourse of Knowledge*: *On Gendering Desire and Sexuality in the Hebrew Bible*, BIS 26 (Leiden: Brill, 1997).

2. Cf. V. Bachmann, 'Die biblische Vorstellungswelt und deren geschlechterpolitische Dimension methodologische Überlegungen am Beispiel der ersttestamentlichen Kategorien "rein" und "unrein"', in *lectio difficilior* 2 (2003), online: http://www.lectio.unibe.ch; H. Eilberg-Schwartz, *The Savage in Judaism: An Anthropology of Israelite and Ancient Judaism* (Bloomington: Indiana University Press, 1990); D. Ellens, *Women in the Sex Texts of Leviticus and Deuteronomy: A Comparative Conceptual Analysis*, LHBOTS 458 (New York: T&T Clark International, 2008); D. Erbele-Küster, *Körper und Geschlecht. Studien zur Anthropologie von Lev 12 und 15*, WMANT 121 (Neukirchen-Vluyn: Neukirchener, 2008); T. Philip, *Menstruation and Childbirth in the Bible: Fertility and Impurity*, Studies in Biblical Literature 88 (New York: Lang, 2006); U. Rapp, 'The Heritage of Old Testament Impurity Laws:

However, my study undertakes for the first time a detailed exegetical analysis in the classical sense of the two chapters from Leviticus of the Hebrew and the Greek text and by doing so opens up the possibility to show how the text is effecting sex, gender and body. Whereas the classificatory system of purity of Leviticus has been in the focus of many studies, here I shall explore how the constructions of the gendered body and im/purity intersect.[3] The term 'body' serves as a heuristic category to highlight the diverse bodily practices and terms described in Leviticus 11–15 that establish and mark differences in sexual, social and cultic perspective.

Leviticus 12 and 15 form part of a larger collection of purity rules that extends from chs. 11 through 15. The contents cover such themes as animals permissible for eating (ch. 11), skin diseases and mildew on textiles and houses (chs. 13–14), birth (ch. 12), and genital discharges (ch. 15). Together with Leviticus 15, the material on the post-partum woman in Leviticus 12 forms a bracket around the regulations about surface eruptions (chs. 13–14).[4] Chapters 11–15 in turn form part of a larger section (Lev. 11–26) that deals with purity and sanctification. The (sexual) body must be pure in cultic respects in order to be brought near to God. God's holiness must be capable of reflection in such a body (Lev. 11.44; cf. Lev. 19.2). Literary texts like the ones in Leviticus portraying the human body are not simply reproductions of some natural body; rather, they are images that one makes of the body. The human body is not a natural entity. Body and gender are mediated by language and culture.

Gender as a Question of How to Focus on Women', in *Gender and Religion*, ed. Kari E. Børresen, Sara Cabibbo and Edith Specht, European Studies, Università degli studi roma, 3 (Rome: Carocci, 2001), 29–40; N. J. Ruane, *Sacrifice and Gender in Biblical Law* (Cambridge: Cambridge University Press, 2013). The German version of the present volume listed in this note represents an earlier stage of my thinking. The present monograph, due to my continuous research and discussions on the subject (see the Preface), offers a more developed discussion.

3. Ruane, *Sacrifice and Gender in Biblical Law*, examines the intersection of gender and sacrifice in (priestly) law.

4. See below for the source-critical discussion in general. For the structure of Lev. 11–15 as a whole, cf. D. Erbele-Küster, 'Die Körperbestimmungen in Lev 11–15', in *Menschenbilder und Körperkonzepte im Alten Israel, in Ägypten und im Alten Orient*, ed. A. Berlejung, J. Dietrich and J. F. Quack, ORA 9 (Tübingen: Mohr Siebeck, 2012), 209–24. According to K. Elliger, *Leviticus*, HAT 4 (Tübingen: Mohr Siebeck, 1966), 13, 157, Lev. 12 is a later insertion. C. Nihan, *From Priestly Torah to Pentateuch: A Study in the Composition of the Book of Leviticus*, FAT 2/25 (Tübingen: Mohr Siebeck, 2007), 301, holds that 'Lev 12 probably belonged initially together with Lev 15'.

Body and gender identity emerge from and within the ongoing process of socio-religious norming through ritualized processes.[5] The so-called performative turn in ritual studies suggests further lines of inquiry. Certain forms of speaking, writing, and quoting are performative actions which create and maintain gender and body.

The present work aims to unfold this discourse of Leviticus 12 and 15 within the Hebrew Bible and beyond, especially in its first translations into Greek. Methodologically it is a close reading of Leviticus 12 and 15 underpinned by gender studies, semantics, discourse analysis, translation studies and ritual studies. These methods will be briefly introduced as a first step.

II. *Discourse History*

a. *Discourse Analysis of the Body from the Perspective of Gender*
Discourse manifests a symbolic system, as Mary Douglas, Judith Butler and others state.[6] The body, its boundaries and its gender are established through discourse. Body is neither a 'being' nor a given, but is established and marked by certain cultural codes. Butler outlines the issue in her introduction of *Bodies Matters* as follows: 'Consider first that sexual difference is often invoked as an issue of material differences. Sexual difference, however, is never simply a function of material differences which are in some way both marked and formed by discursive practices. Further, to claim that sexual differences are indissociable from discursive demarcations is not the same as claiming that discourse causes sexual difference.'[7]

---

5. Cf. J. Butler, *Bodies That Matter: On the Discursive Limits of 'Sex'* (New York: Routledge, 1993); P. Sarasin, *Reizbare Maschinen. Eine Geschichte des Körpers 1765–1914* (Frankfurt am Main: Suhrkamp, 2001); C. Benthien and C. Wulf, eds., *Körperteile. Eine kulturelle Anatomie* (Reinbek bei Hamburg: Rowohlt Taschenbuch, 2001); B. Duden, *Geschichte unter der Haut. Ein Eisenacher Arzt und seine Patientinnen um 1730* (Stuttgart: Klett-Cotta, 1970); A. Koch, 'Reasons for the Boom of Body Discourses in the Humanities and the Social Sciences Since the 1980s: A Chapter in European History of Religion', in Berlejung, Dietrich, and Quack, eds., *Menschenbilder und Körperkonzepte im Alten Israel*, 3–42; T. Laqueur, *Making Sex: Body and Gender from the Greeks to Freud* (Cambridge, MA: Harvard University Press, 1990); M. Lorenz, *Leibhaftige Vergangenheit. Einführung in die Körpergeschichte* (Tübingen: Diskord, 2000).

6. Cf. M. Douglas, *Purity and Danger: An Analysis of the Concepts of Pollution and Taboo* (London: Routledge & Kegan, 1966); J. Butler, *Gender Trouble: Feminism and the Subversion of Identity* (New York: Routledge, 1990), 128–32.

7. Cf. Butler, *Bodies Matter*, 1.

A gender-oriented discourse-analytic approach calls likewise for attention to the texts' communicative structure(s), asking questions like:[8] How do these texts discuss and manufacture female and male bodies? How are sex differences and similarities conceived of through the language?[9] How do they inscribe gender hierarchies? Can female voices[10] be detected in texts that were transmitted in the names of Moses and Aaron to Israel's progeny? Finally, what was their rhetorical function?

Focusing upon the regulations' discursive role means not to suspend the question of their supposed legal practices in ancient Israel completely. The perspectives gets changed as the purity regulations as discourse need not directly reflect historical or social conditions. The legal practices, however, do draft and codify norms and structures. Literary texts both reflect and constitute a specific culture and language. The discourse-analytical approach clarifies these processes and might be considered an exploration in the discursive structure of categories such as body, gender and impurity.

In earlier (feminist) studies on these chapters from Leviticus, the decisive issue was often the texts' practical relevance either for the shaping of everyday lives of men and women in ancient Israel or for the interpreters' background. Beyond the scholarly discourse Leviticus 12 and 15 have had a significant impact on the perception of the body in Judaism and Christianity. Initiatory rites such as circumcision and the pre-Vatican II Catholic custom of 'the churching of women' have played a major role.[11] For Jewish women, cultural and religious identity came into play, whereas feminist Christian scholars were forced to face the anti-Judaism debate. The interpreters reached widely varying conclusions about the texts' significance for gender politics, which is not surprising given the absence of clearly defined criteria for judging this. Thus Christian interpreters tended to see the purity regulations as an expression of misogyny, an attitude that Jesus and his followers supposedly overcame, while Jewish women emphasized the regulations' role in providing a space in which women could freely define their identities.[12] But the method of counting up rules and weighing them against each other cannot do justice to the texts.

8. Along with Brenner, *Intercourse of Knowledge*, 1–2.
9. Cf. Laqueur, *Making Sex*, 17: 'texts generate sexual difference'.
10. For the term fe/male voices, cf. F. van Dijk-Hemmes and A. Brenner, *On Gendering Texts: Female and Male Voices in the Hebrew Bible* (Leiden: Brill, 1996).
11. For a more general influence on Western cultures, cf. M. Marzana, *Philosophie du corps*, Que sais-je? 3777 (Paris: Puf, 2007), 89–92.
12. Cf. the overview of positions in Bachman, 'Die biblische Vorstellungswelt'.

A different heuristic and more fruitful approach is to uncover, by means of discourse analysis, how the texts establish their claims to construct body, gender and purity. To this end, this book investigates the interpretation history of the language concerning the body of Leviticus 12 and 15, starting from the effect of these chapters on other parts of the book of Leviticus and on the larger corpus – the Hebrew Bible – and then proceeding to translations, from the Septuagint (LXX) on down to our late-modern translations.

b. *Translation as Part of Discourse and Interpretation History*
Translations provide the basis for understanding texts from different times and cultures, but they can also encourage misunderstandings. Accordingly, I shall examine translation as a process of transmission and interpretation. In the case of the purity regulations, the difficulties center on cultic language concerning the body. This becomes apparent already in the Greek translations, as the first recipients struggled with the Hebrew text's understanding of the body, which was alien to them. My current translation work is not exempt from that struggle,[13] as our modern translations are part of the interpretation history. Therefore I shall give a translation with commentary of most of the texts under discussion, pointing out critical issues in modern translations.

This study will focus likewise on the first Greek translations; in doing so it will offer a glimpse into the discursive practices of the manufacturing of body and gender in Greek-speaking circles. The inclusion of the LXX text at length and its extensive discussion has not been done before now.[14] It serves a twofold purpose: first, to highlight the specificity of the LXX and, second, to show the linguistic and cultural constructedness of body and gender, in both, the Greek and the Hebrew text. It allows one to trace back the LXX's impact on the history of interpretation up to now. The comparison of the Greek translations to the Hebrew Masoretic Text (MT), a different text than that referred to by the first translators, provides an illuminating example of how language serves the specific

---

13. Two recent commentaries pay attention to the issue of translation; cf. J. Watts, *Leviticus 1–10*, HCOT (Leuven: Peeters, 2013) and T. Hieke, *Levitikus*, HthKAT, 2 vols. (Freiburg im Breisgau: Herder, 2014).

14. For an earlier study on some issues of the Greek text, see K. de Troyer, 'Blood: A Threat to Holiness or toward (Another) Holiness?', in *Wholly Woman – Holy Blood: A Feminist Critique of Purity and Impurity*, ed. Kristin de Troyer, et al. (London: T&T Clark International, 2003), 45–64. For Leviticus in general, see J. Wevers, *Notes on the Greek Text of Leviticus*, Septuagint and Cognate Studies 44 (Atlanta: Scholars Press, 1997).

cultural construction of bodies. Analyzing the similarities and differences in the LXX, rather than using it to emend the Hebrew text or to construct the translator's Hebrew *Vorlage*, as has been often the case in textual criticism, will provide insight into an early Second Temple period reception of the pre-Masoretic Hebrew text, namely, that of a third-century BCE Greek-speaking circle geographically removed from the Jerusalem Temple (Chapter 2 and 3).

In understanding the Hebrew concept of purity a major issue is how the translation into Greek has played on the understanding of the concept. The argument for translating the Hebrew roots טמא/טהר as '(not) in compliance with the cult' or 'cultic (dis-)ability' will be unfolded in Chapter 7.

The challenge each translation as an intercultural process faces is to use comprehensible language while preserving the original's strangeness, thus providing the opportunity to enrich one's linguistic and conceptual universe.[15] Accordingly, the translation confronts cultural differences while encouraging understanding and mediating between cultures. For this task, insights that emerged from the translational turn,[16] such as translation as negotiation between cultures, will be applied to the manifold translational processes of biblical texts from Hebrew into Greek and up to modern languages, especially English and German, including the translation which is presented in this study.

III. *Survey of Research*

Until recently the source-critical approach, which long dominated the interpretation of Leviticus, particularly among scholars rooted in German-speaking scholarship, was not receptive to such questions as discourse and translation history. Nevertheless, they have made their contribution, something which is neglected often in more recent studies dealing with the body in Leviticus 12 and 15. In this study I will link them. The following research areas in relation to the proposed

---

15. Cf. D. Erbele-Küster, 'Ungerechte Texte und gerechte Sprache: Überlegungen zur Hermeneutik des Bibelübersetzens', in *Die Bibel – übersetzt in gerechte Sprache? Grundlagen einer neuen Übersetzung*, ed. H. Kuhlmann (Gütersloh: Gütersloher, 2005), 222–34.

16. Cf. S. Bassnett and A. Lefevere, eds., *Translation: Theory and Practice* (London: Pinter, 1990). For the reception within German speaking research, see D. Bachmann-Medick, *Cultural Turns: Neuorientierungen in den Kulturwissenschaften* (Reinbeck bei Hamburg: Rowohlt Taschenbuch-Verlag, 2006), 238–84.

topic shall be briefly characterized: (a) source-critical and form-critical classification, (b) determination of the relationship between texts and practices, (c) attempts to classify the concept of impurity, (d) the construction of (sexual) bodies, and (e) the question of gender. Finally, in section IV of this chapter, follows a sketch of our subsequent investigation.

a. *Source-critical and Form-critical Classification*
Leviticus 12 and 15 form part of the so-called purity code from Leviticus 11–15. Classical form-historical examinations of the literary character of these chapters have stated that they are casuistic combinations of 'rituals, priestly instructions, and apodictic laws'.[17] In this line of interpretation, Leviticus is regarded as an instruction manual on cult issues.[18] The purity regulations in Leviticus 11–15 are assigned within the documentary hypothesis to the Priestly legal corpus starting from Exodus 25 and ending in Numbers 10.[19] Researchers who identify more than one literary layer in this source tend to characterize chs. 11–15 as secondary.[20] The premise that the legal texts in Leviticus 11–15 were added to an existing Priestly narrative implies several presuppositions: first, that there is a distinction between narrative (primary) and legal/ritual (secondary) texts; secondly, there is an acceptance that the latter could not have existed outside of a narrative framework.[21] There is also a question of the intention of the Priestly writers: Did they intend

---

17. Cf. K. Koch, *Die Priesterschrift von Exodus 25 bis Leviticus 16. Eine überlieferungsgeschichtliche und literarkritische Untersuchung*, FRLANT NF 53 (Göttingen: Vandenhoeck & Ruprecht, 1959), 100. The difficulty of this form-historical characterization is discussed by Knierim in his methodological study: R. Knierim, *Text and Concept in Leviticus 1:1–9*, FAT 2 (Tübingen: Mohr Siebeck, 1992).

18. Cf. R. Rendtorff, *Die Gesetze in der Priesterschrift. Eine gattungsgeschichtliche Untersuchung* (Göttingen: Vandenhoeck & Ruprecht, 1954), 1–2, 38–56, 77.

19. For a recent overview and discussion, cf. Nihan, *From Priestly Torah to Pentateuch*, 11–17; he himself discerned in chs. 11–15 pre-P traditions (pp. 270–301). For a short evaluation on recent historical reconstructions of Leviticus' composition, see Watts, *Leviticus 1–10*, §2.3.1, 'Compositional histories'.

20. Cf. Rendtorff, *Die Gesetze in der Priesterschrift*, 38, and Elliger, *Leviticus*, 8–9, 12–13. The conclusion that E. Otto, 'Forschungen zur Priesterschrift', *TRu* 60 (1995): 1–50, draws in his review article on studies of the Priestly work is similar; he speaks of 'post-Priestly layers' in Lev. 11–15 (p. 36).

21. Cf. A. Noth, *Das dritte Buch Mose*, ATD 6 (Göttingen: Vandenhoeck & Ruprecht, 1962), 4.

their work as a history whose goal was the giving of the land?[22] Or is the stress on the laws given at Sinai representing a ritual code meant to establish the sanctuary and the cult?[23]

As early as 1893, however, Heinrich Holzinger characterized the Priestly work, conceived as an organic unity, as 'an historic-legislative text'.[24] After the Colloquium Biblicum Lovaniense dedicated to the books of Leviticus and Numbers in 2006, the consensus seemed to shift to this view that Leviticus 1–16 constitutes a basic Priestly text.[25] Among writers who no longer view the Priestly (narrative) text as an independent source,[26] new possibilities have emerged for evaluating the literary place of the legal texts, as for example when the narrative and the legal parts are seen as a unity. 'Therefore, despite much editing in antiquity, P is best interpreted as unified composition that includes laws and instructions together with narratives.'[27] Accordingly, in recent times scholars have shown increasing interest in analysis of the structure of the book as a whole, which presupposes that Leviticus is a literary unity.[28] This approach has

22. Cf. K. Elliger, 'Sinn und Ursprung der priesterlichen Geschichtserzählung', *ZTK* 49 (1952): 121–43; in contrast, E. Zenger, *Gottes Bogen in den Wolken. Untersuchungen zu Komposition und Theologie der priesterlichen Urgeschichte*, SBS 112 (Stuttgart: Kohlhammer, 1983), 45, holds that divine proximity is the most important end in the Priestly work, not the land; cf. E. Blum, *Studien zur Komposition des Pentateuch*, BZAW 189 (Berlin: de Gruyter, 1990), 278–332.

23. Cf. Koch, *Priesterschrift*, and H. Utzschneider, *Das Heiligtum und das Gesetz. Studien zur Bedeutung der sinaitischen Heiligtumstexte (Ex 25–40; Lev 8–9)*, OBO 77 (Freiburg: Universitätsverlag, 1988). M. Köckert, 'Leben in Gottes Gegenwart. Zum Verständnis des Gesetzes in der priesterschriftlichen Literatur', *JBT* 4 (1989): 29–61, sees the interrelation of law and cult as decisive.

24. H. Holzinger, *Einleitung in den Hexateuch. Mit Tabellen über die Quellenscheidung* (Freiburg/Leipzig: Mohr Siebeck, 1893), 334, and A. Kuenen, *Historisch-kritische Einleitung in die Bücher des Alten Testaments hinsichtlich ihrer Entstehung und Sammlung. Die Entstehung des Hexateuch*, I/1, Autorisierte deutsche Ausgabe (Leipzig: Schulze, 1887), 78.

25. Cf. T. Römer, 'De la périphérie au centre. Les livres du Lévitique et des Nombres dans le débat actuel sur le Pentateuque', in *The Books of Leviticus and Numbers*, ed. T. Römer (Leuven: Peeters, 2008), 3–34. Koch, *Priesterschrift*, 98, reached the same conclusion earlier. M. Douglas, 'The Forbidden Animals in Leviticus', *JSOT* 59 (1992): 3–23, reads chs. 11–16 as a unity.

26. For example, R. Rendtorff, 'Two Kinds of P: Some Reflections on the Occasion of the Publishing of Jacob Milgrom's Commentary on Leviticus 1–16', *JSOT* 60 (1993): 75–81, and Blum, *Komposition des Pentateuch*.

27. Watts, *Leviticus 1–10*, p. 42.

28. Cf. H. J. Fabry and H. W. Jüngling, eds., *Levitikus als Buch*, BBB 119 (Berlin: Philo, 1999); D. Luciani, *Sainteté et Pardon I. Structure littéraire du Lévitique*,

yielded insights into the relationship between narrative texts and ritual texts.[29] Leviticus 'integrates ritual and narrative to create a unique genre of 'narrative ritual'.[30]

Determining the relationship between narratives and laws is not only a source-critical but also a form-critical issue, as the historical context, intention, genre and composition are interrelated.

Since source criticism began, a broad consensus has held that the Priestly work and its addenda date from the post-exilic period.[31] In this view, the work is best understood against the background of the religious, social, and political changes that accompanied the transition from the Babylonian to the Persian period in Judea (and Samaria). So, for example, Frank Crüsemann: 'Independently of the extent to which older material has been re-worked in it, there can be no doubt that the Priestly work presupposes the exile and everywhere reacts to it'.[32] This background supposedly explains the work's character of envisioning postexilic life. Several observations have been pointed out which reflect the imperial ideology of the Persian rulers as 'the identification of the

---

BETL 175A (Leuven: Peeters, 2005); Nihan, *From Priestly Torah to Pentateuch*; E. Zenger and C. Frevel, 'Die Bücher Levitikus und Numeri als Teile der Pentateuchkomposition', in *The Books of Leviticus and Numbers*, ed. Thomas Römer (Leuven: Peeters, 2008), 35–74.

29. Cf. R. Rendtorff, 'Is It Possible to Read Leviticus as a Separate Book?', in *Reading Leviticus: A Conversation with Mary Douglas*, ed. John F. A. Sawyer, JSOTSup 227 (Sheffield: Sheffield Academic, 1996), 22–35; J. Watts, *Reading Law: The Rhetorical Shaping of the Pentateuch* (Sheffield: Sheffield Academic, 1999), and *Ritual and Rhetoric in Leviticus: From Sacrifice to Scripture* (Cambridge: Cambridge University Press, 2007); F. Gorman, *The Ideology of Ritual: Space, Time and Status in the Priestly Theology*, JSOTSup 91 (Sheffield: JSOT, 1991); A. Bartor, *Reading Law as Narrative: A Study in the Casuistic Laws of the Pentateuch*, Ancient Israel and Its Literature 5 (Atlanta: Society of Biblical Literature, 2010), proposes 'narrative reading' as a methodology that takes into account the aesthetical structure of the law, focusing on the characters and situations it depicts (see esp. the introduction).

30. Cf. Bryan D. Bibb, *Ritual Words and Narrative Worlds in the Book of Leviticus*, LHBOTS 480 (London: Bloomsbury T&T Clark, 2008), 6. Cf. the present author's review in: *Review of Biblical Literature* (http://www.bookreviews.org).

31. Zenger, *Gottes Bogen*, 43–44, refers to a majority view that the *Grundschrift* of the Priestly work responds to the collapse of the state; R. Kratz, *Die Komposition der erzählenden Bücher des Alten Testaments. Grundwissen der Bibelkritik* (Göttingen: Vandenhoeck & Ruprecht, 2000), 117, takes the Second Temple as the earliest possible date for the *Grundschrift*.

32. Crüsemann, *Die Tora*, 329.

nations according to their ethnic origin...and their common language (Gen 10:5, 20, 31)'.[33] Opinions differ as to whether the Priestly work pre- or postdates the building of the Second Temple.

Those scholars who would place the composition of the Priestly work before the exile, maintain that the work does not presuppose the Deuteronomist. Another argument sees the Priestly work serving the concern for the cult of the laws.[34]

All these attempts to date the biblical text presuppose a close correspondence between the texts and contemporary events and conditions. Such exegesis run the risk of being circular,[35] i.e., inferring a supposed historical context from the texts and then dating the texts based on that inference. One of the fathers of Pentateuchal source criticism, Karl Heinrich Graf, expressed the difficulty of correlating laws with particular situations as follows: 'The laws in Leviticus date from the time of Ezra, that is, the post-exilic period; hence one searches the other historical books in vain for evidence of how the laws might have been practised'.[36] It may be not only because of its late date that we find so little about the application of the instructions in Leviticus 11–15 in the Hebrew Bible. It could equally well be due to the programmatic character of these chapters. Even such an interpreter as Jacob Milgrom, for whom the material in Leviticus 1–16 provides insight into actual sacrificial and purity practices, writes that the regulations make sense only in the context of a symbolic system:[37] 'Theology is what Leviticus is all about'.[38] Through its literary form the book of Leviticus subjected the purity customs to a coherent symbolic system. The issue of how we should understand the practices indicated by the texts will now be addressed.

33. Nihan, *From Priestly Torah to Pentateuch*, 383.
34. Cf. J. Kaufmann, 'Probleme der israelitisch-jüdischen Religionsgeschichte', *ZAW* 48 (1930): 23–42. Further developments of this view may be found in M. Haran, *Temples and Temple-Services in Ancient Israel* (Oxford: Clarendon, 1978), and J. Milgrom, *Leviticus 1–16: A New Translation with Introduction and Commentary*, AB 3 (New York: Doubleday, 1991).
35. H. Liss, 'Kanon und Fiktion. Zur literarischen Funktion biblischer Rechtstexte', *BN* NF 121 (2004): 7–38 (8–9). For C. Houtman, *Der Pentateuch. Die Geschichte seiner Erforschung neben einer Auswertung*, CBET 9 (Kampen: Kok, 1994), §115, 432–37 (see also §100), the dating of variously inferred layers merely expresses the interpreters' preconceived notions.
36. K. H. Graf, *Die geschichtlichen Bücher des Alten Testament. Zwei literarisch-kritische Untersuchungen* (Leipzig: Weigel, 1866), 2.
37. Cf. Milgrom, *Leviticus 1–16*, 45–46.
38. Ibid., 42.

b. *Correlations of Text and Practice*
Generally speaking, the way in which texts and practices interact is complex and has triggered a methodological discussion which has led to the rise of ritual studies – likewise in biblical studies.[39] The designation 'ritual' implies religious-historical, ethnological and form-historical aspects, as we shall see.[40] The exegetical literature on the cultic laws of Exodus and Leviticus characterizes those laws in conflicting ways. The laws are seen on the one hand as a reflection of an actual cultic practice[41] and as a means to instruct about that practice;[42] on the other hand, the ritual laws are characterized as programmatic and incorporated into the narrative structure (see above). In Leviticus we find a 'nostalgic and utopian evocation of Israel'.[43]

If the laws were not practiced, in what sense are they laws?[44] Even a scholar like Klaus Koch, whose form-historical investigation points to the texts' ritual style, highlights their programmatic character: 'P's text is programmatic… It is not the cultic etiology of an existing sanctuary.'[45]

---

39. Cf. C. Bell, *Ritual: Perspectives and Dimensions* (New York: Oxford University Press, 1997). Watts gives an overview in his recent commentary on Ritual studies and Leviticus (*Leviticus 1–10*, §2.3.6, 'Ritual Theories and Interpretations').

40. Cf. Rendtorff, *Die Gesetze in der Priesterschrift*, 77, and Knierim, *Text and Concept*, 98–106.

41. Cf. B. Levine, *Leviticus*, The JPS Torah Commentary (Philadelphia: The Jewish Publication Society, 1989), xxxvii: 'There is every reason to accept the cultic practice presented in Leviticus as essentially realistic'. Likewise L. Grabbe, *Leviticus*, Old Testament Guides (Sheffield: Sheffield Academic, 1993), 22–23.

42. Cf. Rendtorff, *Die Gesetze in der Priesterschrift*, 77, and Koch, *Priesterschrift*.

43. J. Watts, 'Ritual Rhetoric in the Pentateuch: The Case of Leviticus 1–16', in Römer, ed., *The Books of Leviticus and Numbers*, 307–18 (317). A. Marx, 'Les recherches sur le Lévitique et leur impact théologique', *Bib* 88 (2007): 415–33, underlines the utopian eschatological character of Leviticus.

44. For the ancient Near East, cf. M. Roth, *Law Collections from Mesopotamia and Asia Minor*, SBL Writings from the Ancient World 6 (Atlanta, GA: Scholars Press, 1995), 4–7. As with the Priestly texts, there are no indications that the Hammurabi Code reflects actual legal practice. Rather, copies of it were used for pedagogical purposes; cf. P. Bienkowski, 'Law', in *Dictionary of the Ancient Near East*, ed. P. Bienkowski (London: British Museum Press, 2000), 175–76 (176).

45. Koch, *Priesterschrift*, 89, regarding Lev. 15: 'The directions…do not give hints to reconstruct an underlying ritual, but rather display throughout a contrived style'. Cf. K. Koch, 'Die Eigenart der priesterschriftlichen Sinaigesetzgebung', *ZTK* 55 (1958): 36–51 (36, 51). Kratz, *Komposition der erzählenden Bücher*, 114–15, notes a pervasive stylization.

And yet, at the same time, he does not rule out that the texts may preserve remnants of ancient cultic practice. This twofold characterization of the *torot* in Leviticus seems common: 'Even if the prescriptive texts served as a priestly manual in the Second Temple period, these foundational ritual texts probably served primarily a theological and literary (rhetorical) purpose'.[46] One key question in this setting concerns the intended audience (or readership). Baruch Levine writes similarly in the introduction to his commentary: 'Leviticus is an important source of information on the realistic functions of the priesthood'.[47] We have then to ask: What practices, if any, are reflected in the cultic laws? Is providing instructions for behavior part of their actual concern?[48]

Those who regard Leviticus 11–15 as a manual view its *Sitz im Leben* 'within the framework of an early Jewish (post-exilic) worship service centered either on reading or preaching'.[49] However, the social-historical contextualization within Second Temple period may explain even better the programmatic character of chs. 11–15. These chapters, along with the *offering-torot* in Leviticus 1–7, could have served to validate the only institution in the Second Temple period: the (Aaronide) priesthood. According to this view, they have served as a 'priestly manual' in order to train the new Second Temple priestly class and to claim their authority.[50] In turn the priests elevated the authority of the text. Thus even the form-historical determination as manual says in this case more about the text's literary *Sitz im Leben* and its social function in affirming priestly authority than it does about the text's role in cultic procedures or in everyday life.

The purity chapters can therefore be described as possessing a frame of reference that transcends the actual practices[51] in the same way that

---

46. Bibb, *Ritual Words*, 44. For a critique of such a dual characterization, cf. Liss, 'Kanon und Fiktion', 9.

47. Levine, *Leviticus*, xxxv. Noth, *Das dritte Buch Mose*, 81, characterizes Lev. 12 as formulation of 'professional priestly knowledge'.

48. Cf. D. Erbele-Küster, 'Reading as an Act of Offering: Reconsidering the Genre of Leviticus 1', in *The Actuality of Sacrifice: Past and Present*, ed. A. Houtman et al., JCP 28 (Leiden: Brill 2014), 34–46.

49. E. S. Gerstenberger, *Leviticus: A Commentary* (Louisville: Westminster John Knox, 1996), 4.

50. Cf. Nihan, *From Priestly Torah to Pentateuch*, esp. 300, 390–94.

51. Cf. Kratz, *Komposition*, 117. Likewise Crüsemann, *Die Tora: Theologie und Sozialgeschichte des alttestamentlichen Gesetzes* (Munich: Kaiser, 1992); B. Jacob, *Der Pentateuch* (Leipzig: Veit, 1905), 328; Koch, *Priesterschrift*; and L. Rost, *Studien zum Opfer im Alten Israel* (Stuttgart: Kohlhammer, 1981), 58, 63.

the instructions for the tabernacle or the sacrifice laws do.[52] Attempts to understand Leviticus as a ritual agenda run up against its peculiar literary structure.[53] This goes hand-in-hand with the above mentioned shift of scholarly focus away from the reconstruction of supposed actual rituals and towards the literary unity of the texts[54] and their rhetorical function within the process of compiling the Torah. The evidence that the purity regulations are a compilation is in itself sufficient to show that they were not constructed *a priori* according to a consistent ritual program. Such a program is in any case only hypothetically conceivable. Consequently, we must be aware of the difference between rituals and texts. Recent scholarship focused on ritual studies has argued for such a distinction between text and ritual, noting the difficulties created through the intertwined nature of the written text and the performance of it (with reference to the offering *torot* in Lev. 1–7): 'In other words, *texts are not rituals and rituals are not texts*'.[55] The knowledge of 'practices are gathered into systems that may themselves be driven not by a concern to reproduce practice but a desire to create a legal system commensurate with philosophical or religious principles'.[56]

Another tool that is brought to bear on the connection between the purity regulations and everyday practice is archaeology. However, the vivid discussion within archeological studies seems so far not yet to have featured in the above-mentioned literary-historical discourse. The

---

52. Cf. H. Liss, 'The Imaginary Sanctuary: The Priestly Code as an Example of Fictional Literature in the Hebrew Bible', in *Judah and Judeans in the Persian Period*, ed. O. Lipschits and M. Oeming (Winona Lake, IN: Eisenbrauns, 2006), 663–89, and Erbele-Küster, 'Reading as an Act of Offering'.

53. Cf. Knierim, *Text and Concept*, 17–18, 98–106; L. Grabbe, 'The Priests in Leviticus – Is the Medium the Message?', in *The Book of Leviticus: Composition & Reception*, ed. R. Rendtorff and R. A. Kugler, VTSup 93 (Leiden: Brill, 2003), 207–24 (221), and E. Zenger, 'Das Buch Leviticus als Teiltext der Tora/des Pentateuch: Eine synchrone Lektüre mit diachroner Perspektive', in Fabry and Jüngling, eds., *Leviticus als Buch*, 47–83 (71). Based on the book's systematic message, which centers around a God who is willing to reconcile, Zenger concludes that 'one may exclude the one-sided interpretation that Leviticus is a collection of ritual laws or even a manual for priestly formation'.

54. Cf. Römer, 'De la périphérie au centre', 15, 34, and Watts, *Leviticus 1–10*.

55. Watts, *Ritual and Rhetoric in Leviticus*, 29 (original emphasis). Cf. as well W. Bergen, *Reading Ritual: Leviticus in Postmodern Culture* (London: T&T Clark International, 2010).

56. P. R. Davies, 'Leviticus as a Cultic System in the Second Temple Period: Responses to Hannah K. Harrington', in Sawyer, ed., *Reading Leviticus*, 230–37 (233).

controversies that surround the interpretation of finds identified as *mikvot* (bathing installations for ritual purification) from the late Second Temple period make clear that these baths cannot be seen just as reflections of ritual observance of purity laws.[57] Ronny Reich recently rehearsed his arguments that the installations at Qumran are *mikvot* due to their size, their concentration, their water supply with running water and the steps which hinder drawing water and thus the interpretation as cisterns.[58] Nevertheless, the baths especially found in cities such as Jerusalem or Sepphoris could just as well partly be understood in terms of the hygienic and social practices of a Hellenized urban upper class. Or has the *mikve* emerged as a rival to the Hellenistic bathing culture?[59] Whatever the case may be, even if we are able to identify a pool as a ritual bath, how are we to deduce a practice from it? On the whole, the archaeological findings do not seem to support the idea that observance of the purity regulations was a part of the Israelite's everyday life (in pre-exilic times),[60] as *mikvot* begin to appear in appreciable numbers only around the beginning of the Common Era.[61] The regulations in Leviticus have served as a Mosaic ideal of how one imagined life during the wilderness sojourn.

57. Cf. B. Wright III, 'Jewish Ritual Baths – Interpreting the Digs and the Texts. Some Issues in the Social History of Second Temple Judaism', in *The Archaeology of Israel: Constructing the Past, Interpreting the Present*, ed. Neil Asher Silberman and David Small, JSOTSup 237 (Sheffield: JSOT, 1997), 190–214; and A. Berlin, 'Jewish Life Before the Revolt: The Archeological Evidence', *JSJ* 36 (2005): 417–70. For a differing view, cf. H. Harrington, *The Purity Texts*, Companion to the Qumran Scrolls 5 (London: T&T Clark International, 2004), 31–32.

58. Cf. R. Reich, 'Some Notes on the Miqva'ot and Cisterns at Qumran', in *Viewing Ancient Jewish Art and Archaeology*, ed. Ann E. Killebrew and Gabriele Fassbeck, Supplements to the Journal for the Study of Judaism 172 (Leiden: Brill, 2015), 414–24. Differently H. Eshel, 'The Pools of Sepphoris: Ritual Baths or Bathtubs: They Are Not Ritual Baths', *BAR* 26 (2000): 42–45. (But see the response by Eric M. Meyers, 'The Pools of Sepphoris: Ritual Baths or Bathtubs? Yes, They Are', *BAR* 26 [2000]: 46–49.)

59. This is the view of R. Reich, 'The Hot Bath-House (balneum), the Miqweh and the Jewish Community in the Second Temple Period', *JJS* 39 (1989): 102–7.

60. Cf. M. von Dijkstra, 'Schone Handen. Reinheid in de Culturen van de Levant', *Phoenix* 48, no. 2 (2002): 73–92. He is skeptical that the purity regulations can be used to reconstruct pre-exilic Israelite social or religious history. By contrast, F. Crüsemann, 'Ein israelitisches Ritualbad aus vorexilischer Zeit', *ZDPV* 94 (1978): 68–75, posits a pre-exilic context on the basis of his analysis of a specific archaeological find.

61. Cf. Berlin, 'Jewish Life Before the Revolt', 452: '*mikva'ot* first appear in contexts of early mid-first century BCE; there is no evidence for installations in Jewish settlements before then'.

The multiplicity of interpretations and practices of the purity regulations within Judaism shows that reconstructing such a role is possible only by filling in gaps left open in the texts.[62] The rabbinic writings do this, as when they demand the full immersion not only of the menstruant woman but also of a woman after childbirth (*m. Nid.* 4.3; 10.8; *m. Miq.* 8.1.5). The regulations concerning the size, appearance, water supply, and so on of the ritual bath must be understood against this background.[63]

To conclude: Attempts to portray the legal texts as somehow reflective of reality frequently lead to contradictory statements. By contrast, a rhetorical approach, which will be favored in this study, asks how the rules are transmitted; how they function and what they do and do not explain; and whether their stylized nature might not serve the purpose of a theological and fictional program implying that fictionality is not about conveying fallacious images. Chapter 6 of the present study will highlight the fact that the legal texts have had little impact on narrative parts of the Hebrew Bible. Further questions concern the significance of the texts' narrative frame and whether it is possible that not only might one interpret Leviticus with the help of ritual theories, but that Leviticus itself constitutes a ritual theory,[64] in the sense that it has a reflexive stance towards the ritual. This argument will be taken up at the end of the study.

One way researchers have responded to the organizing structure is by attempting to clarify its underlying notions of purity, an endeavor that has proceeded relatively independently from literary criticism of the same texts or archeological research on purity rules. The former, questions concerning the concept of purity in texts, will be treated now.

c. *Interpretive Models of Purity*[65]

Research on the regulations in Leviticus 11–15 beyond compositional criticism has traditionally focused on analysis of the concepts of purity and impurity. Isolating the concept of purity, researchers have neglected

---

62. Cf. H. Harrington, 'Interpreting Leviticus in the Second Temple Period: Struggling with Ambiguity', in Sawyer, ed., *Reading Leviticus*, 214–29, esp. 215–17, 223, and for the literary concept of gaps see below.

63. For representatives of this argument, cf. E. P. Sanders, *Jewish Law from Jesus to the Mishnah* (London: SCM, 1990), 214–36, and J. Klawans, *Impurity and Sin in Ancient Judaism* (New York: Oxford University Press, 2000).

64. M. Stausberg, 'Ritualtheorien und Religionstheorien. Religionswissenschaftliche Perspektiven', in *Ritualdynamik. Kulturübergreifende Studien zur Theorie und Geschichte rituellen Handelns*, ed. D. Harth, and G. J. Schenk (Heidelberg: Synchron, 2004), 29–48, shows that ritual theories can as well influence ritual practice.

65. See Chapter 7 for a detailed textual discussion on the concept of im/purity.

any concepts of body and gender that the texts use in this context. In the scholarly literature on Leviticus, a distinction is often made between impurities/pollutions that are 'natural' and therefore (at least in part) inevitable, and impurities that result from specific actions and which are therefore forbidden.[66] The two types of impurity have different characteristics. First, impurities that are the result of external causes, such as contact with corpses or the emission of semen, are contagious. For this reason, measures should and can be taken to avoid the threat they pose to the sacred space. These measures include purification rites such as waiting for a certain length of time or washing the body. Impurities that are caused by violating divine ordinances are seen as not contagious on the one hand, but permanent and very hard to remove on the other; as no direct purification ritual is foreseen, the ritual prescribed on the day of *Kippur* in Leviticus 16 includes these transgressions. This classification overlaps with the distinction between ritual and moral impurities as the sources of ritual impurity, according to Klawans, 'are generally natural and more or less unavoidable'.[67] They result often in a contagious defilement, in contrast to moral impurities resulting from transgression which are non-communicable.

A number of competing interpretations of the purity regulations have been proposed,[68] a circumstance that the texts themselves may have encouraged precisely through their silence on their underlying rationale.

---

66. D. Wright, 'Unclean–Clean (OT)', *ABD* 6:729–41, mentions 'permitted impurity', 'natural and necessary conditions' and 'sinful situations' (p. 729); in his later contribution, 'The Spectrum of Priestly Impurity', in *Priesthood and Cult in Ancient Israel*, ed. Gary A. Anderson and Saul M. Olyan, JSOTSup 125 (Sheffield: JSOT, 1991), 157–62, he modifies his designation 'permitted impurities' into 'tolerated impurities'; T. Frymer-Kensky, 'Pollution, Purification and Purgation in Biblical Israel', in *The Word of the Lord Shall Go Forth: Essays in Honor of David Noel Freedman*, ed. C. L. Meyers (Winona Lake, IN: Eisenbrauns, 1983), 399–414, distinguishes between 'ritual pollutions' and 'danger beliefs'.

67. Klawans, *Impurity and Sin*, 23. Klawans has established this classificatory system within scholarly discourse.

68. For overviews, see Milgrom, 'Rationale for Cultic Law: The Case of Impurity', in *Thinking Biblical Law*, ed. Patrick Dale, Semeia 45 (Atlanta: Scholars Press, 1989), 103–9; G. J. Wenham, 'Purity', in *The Biblical World*, ed. John Barton (London: Routledge, 2002), 378–94; J. L'Hour, 'L'impur et le saint dans le Premier Testament à partir du livre du Lévitique. Partie I: L'impur et le pur', *ZAW* 115 (2003): 524–37; Erbele-Küster, 'Körperbestimmungen'; C. Nihan, 'Forms and Functions of Purity in Leviticus', in *Purity and the Forming of Religious Traditions in the Ancient Mediterranean World and Ancient Judaism*, ed. C. Frevel and C. Nihan (Leiden: Brill, 2013), 311–68.

Theorists have attempted to find a coherent system within Leviticus 11–15 and to explain impurity in terms of taboo, magic, ritual, sociology, ethics, aesthetics, medicine or hygiene (the materialistic view), and theology.

Theological-historical approaches interpret the Leviticus impurity scheme as nascent monotheism's way of distinguishing itself from a hostile pagan environment through rejection of pagan objects and practices. This theory could indeed explain such passages from the Holiness Code as Lev. 18.3 and 20.24; the purity regulations would, in this view, amount to a protest against ancestor worship and cults of the dead, just as they forbid the consumption of animals used for sacrifice by neighboring religions. Similarly, the regulations impose restrictions on women's life-generating powers because those powers threaten the sovereignty of the sole (male) God. The driving force behind the regulations would thus be the rejection of fertility cults and foreign religions.[69] This idea that the purity laws serve Israel's sanctification and separation from other ethnic groups might apply for the Holiness code.

By contrast, theories that interpret the purity regulations as apotropaeic magic assume that the regulations derive from a pre-monotheistic worldview.[70] The regulations would imply that evil power can materialize in specific things. Impurity thus relates to demons.[71] Similarly, some argue that during the Persian era, Jerusalem's religious practice was influenced by Zoroastrian purity laws.[72] However, such notions are absent from the texts themselves.

According to ethical models of explanation, Leviticus 11 served to inculcate reverence for animal life.[73] This fits in with a general scheme that understands impurities as a symbol for death. Yet Leviticus 11 is not concerned with whether or not too much meat is eaten. Its focus is on which kind of animals may be eaten and which ones may not. Were protecting animals the concern, one would rather suppose that the animals

---

69. Cf. Noth, *Das dritte Buch Mose*, 77; Elliger, *Leviticus*, 150; and De Troyer, 'Blood', 57. However, the existence of fertility cults is widely challenged today.

70. Cf. Milgrom's criticism of this idea in *Leviticus 1–16*, 260, 766.

71. This is Elliger's surmise in *Leviticus*, 157, in connection with Lev. 12. T. Staubli, *Die Bücher Levitikus, Numeri*, NSKAT 3 (Stuttgart: Katholisches Bibelwerk, 1996), 125, posits that people of the time believed that demons were particularly liable to attack humans engaged in sexual intercourse.

72. For a discussion, cf. A. V. Williams, 'Zoroastrian and Judaic Purity Laws: Reflections on the Viability of a Sociological Interpretation', in *Irano-Judaica III: Studies Relating to Jewish Contacts with Persian Culture throughout the Ages*, ed. S. Shaked and A. Netzer (Jerusalem: Ben-Zvi Institute, 1994), 72–89.

73. Cf. Milgrom, *Leviticus 1–16*, 735.

which are prohibited should be declared 'holy/pure'.[74] Medical-materialist models, which view the purity rules as hygienic, enjoy popularity today outside of exegetical and religious-historical circles. However, the texts do not support these arguments.

The sociological approach sees the regulations as strengthening (priestly) power structures. In current scholarship this explanation has gained popularity due to the general argument that the rhetorical strategies of Leviticus serve to validate the only institution in the Second Temple period: the (Aaronide) priesthood.[75] The priests would have used the regulations to guarantee their grip on ritual practices. The observance of the Torah and the status of the temple are related. This approach explains the social and ideological function of the Purity laws against its presumed context in the Persian period.

The most influential approach to interpreting the biblical purity laws in the twentieth century was Mary Douglas's cultural-anthropological analysis, which she expounded during the 1960s and 70s. Douglas identified transcultural thought patterns that explain the function of impurity within societies. As Douglas emphasized, we can understand other religious and cultural systems only through the filter of our own perceptions. For Douglas, the theme that pervades different cultural understandings of impurity is the violation of order. Purity regulations represent a socio-religious system of order and see to it that the outer world of things corresponds to the inner world of ideas. She thus argues against earlier attempts of understanding pollution beliefs as vague taboos. Rather, '[p]ollution rules…impose order on experience, they support clarification of forms and thus reduce dissonance'.[76] The starting point for Douglas's reflections on this theme was the classification of animals into pure and impure that is found in Leviticus 11.

As a cultural anthropologist, Douglas sees the purity regulations as a symbolic system, according to which the physical body reflects the political body.[77] The regulations draw boundaries on the body (the microcosm) that reflect social boundaries (the macrocosm), thereby enforcing stability. Pollution stands for that which cannot be controlled. This schema is taken over by various current interpretations, either implicitly or explicitly – especially in works taking account of gender issues.[78] Several of the

74. Cf. the argument in Nihan, *From Priestly Torah to Pentateuch*, 305.
75. Watts, 'Ritual Rhetoric in the Pentateuch', and *Leviticus 1–10*, 30, 107–19; Nihan, 'Forms and Functions of Purity in Leviticus'.
76. Douglas, *Pollution*, 51.
77. Cf. Douglas, *Purity and Danger*, 34–37, 114–28.
78. For example: Eilberg-Schwartz, Ellens, Gerstenberger, Milgrom, Rapp, Staubli, Wright and others.

contributors to the anthology *Wholly Woman – Holy Blood* endorse the cultural-anthropological idea that taboos express boundaries between the holy and the impure (i.e., between purity and danger), and they apply this insight productively to the exegesis of Leviticus 12 and 15.[79] The concern for order in Leviticus is effected by means of the gendered body.[80] Hence the body serves as a boundary marker.[81]

Douglas's later monograph, *Leviticus as Literature* (1999), re-evaluates her earlier, cultural-anthropological works from a literary angle. Her focus is now on the structure of Leviticus as a book, on its analogical reasoning and its failure to explain the regulations.[82] According to Douglas, Leviticus is a literary utopia intended to help an exilic readership define itself by means of an idealized sanctuary. The division of animals in Leviticus 11 into pure and impure contains contradictions and gaps that can neither be harmonized nor resolved.

In Douglas's interpretation, the regulations concerning purity and holiness in Leviticus 11–16 can be understood as a development of the Priestly primeval history in Genesis 1–9. This intertextual connection to the larger context further highlights the regulations' programmatic literary character. The regulations are intended to preserve creation and its attendant blessings.[83] 'Leviticus uses the rules to develop the parallel of body with tabernacle. All this emphasis on contamination and uncleanness means that the body and the tabernacle are analogues one of the other.'[84] Douglas envisions the human body as a microcosm of the sanctuary in danger of defilement.

This survey shows that discussions of purity regulations from Leviticus seem likewise often separated along borders such as: gender issues, archaeological issues (see section III.b, below), questions concerning the concept of purity in texts, the literary shape of the text and its historical background. To repeat: the efforts to explain the purity regulations in Leviticus as a coherent system, as Jacob Milgrom did, identifying a

79. Cf. the contributions by Kathleen O'Grady and Kristin De Troyer.

80. Eilberg-Schwartz, *Savage in Judaism*, speaks of a gender symbolism identifying the release of menstrual blood as uncontrollable whereas the ejaculation of semen is a controlled act.

81. Cf. Ellens, *Women in the Sex Texts*, 10, who speaks of a classificatory system in Leviticus as a concern for protection of boundaries.

82. M. Douglas, *Leviticus as Literature* (Oxford: Oxford University Press, 1999), viii: 'General pollution theory still stands, but its application to the Bible is limited'. For a critique of her concept of boundaries and the homology between social and human body, cf. Frevel and Nihan, 'Introduction', 8.

83. Cf. Douglas, *Leviticus as Literature*, 134–37, 244.

84. Cf. ibid., 176, 188.

common denominator for the impurities, have been differentiated or criticized.[85] Rather, the text points in a different direction: Leviticus as a book provides no causal explanation for designating certain things impure regarding the cult. One exception is Lev. 11.44-45, which offers a rationale for the regulations by referring to God's holiness.

As Douglas emphasizes in both her early and her later work, the body is the literary focus. This can be understood against the backdrop of the Persian Period, where priestly authority was established by the concept of purity on domestic matters. The body and its practices form a screen onto which the writers project their worldview, a screen that they themselves create by means of the text. How this is done is one of the main interests of the present study.

d. *Perceptions of the Body and (Its) Gender*
Hans Walter Wolff's classic work on Old Testament anthropology was one of the first to draw attention to the concrete physicality of biblical language about human beings.[86] The Hebrew lexemes for internal organs such as the heart or the uterus designate more than a physical location. For the Hebrew Bible, materiality and experience, body and perception of body, belong together. Granted, Wolff did not extend this insight to the fact that bodies are gendered – he operated with supposedly universal categories. Nevertheless, his view was clearly androcentric. In the aftermath of Wolff's seminal work several anthropological studies in biblical research have emphasized the bodily basis of cultural ideas.[87] The current virulent anthropological quest, especially in German-speaking scholarship, on the construction of personal identity and personhood in the Old Testament tends to incorporate insights from gender studies at the margin.[88]

---

85. Cf. J. Klawans, *Purity, Sacrifice, and the Temple: Symbolism and Supersessionism in the Study of Ancient Judaism* (Oxford: Oxford University Press, 2006), 28–33.

86. Cf. H. W. Wolff, *Anthropologie des Alten Testaments*, 6th ed. (Munich: Kaiser, 1994).

87. Cf. S. Schroer and T. Staubli, *Die Körpersymbolik der Bibel* (Darmstadt: Wissenschaftliche Buchgesellschaft, 1998); and more recently the volume edited by Berlejung, Dietrich and Quack, *Menschenbilder und Körperkonzepte im Alten Israel, in Ägypten und im Alten Orient.*

88. Several volumes have been published in the last decade especially in the German-speaking context: A. Wagner, ed., *Anthropologische Aufbrüche. Alttestamentliche und interdisziplinäre Zugänge zur historischen Anthropologie*, FRLANT 232 (Göttingen: Vandenhoeck & Ruprecht, 2009); C. Frevel, ed., *Biblische Anthropologie. Neue Einsichten aus dem Alten Testament*, QD 237 (Freiburg: Herder, 2010).

Biological and social genders are central themes of the purity regulations, and thus a gender-based perspective on the regulations opens new insights into them. Not counting the Midrash and other rabbinic commentaries that focus with such detail on bodily specifics, and which can thus be understood as gender studies *avant la lettre*,[89] only in recent years have works appeared that address the question of gender in the purity regulations. These works foreground mainly the social and religious position of women, bearing in mind that they do not focus on constructions of the body *per se* but rather on the purity regulations, as did the studies written in the 1980s and 1990s focused on women's social and religious status in the First and Second Testament.[90] In the beginning, commentators paid scant attention to the difference between biological and social gender. When they did so, they assumed that gender was a social construction distinct from sex, which they took to be a biological given.

Filling the gender unawareness gap, different exegetical works by women researchers on body and gender on different topics and books in the Hebrew Bible, or on body images, have been published.[91] The body's vulnerability as reflected in biblical texts, and concrete experiences of violence (then and now), often form the points of departure: 'For feminist theology has an obligation to people, above all women, who experience physical violence or who, because of their sex, skin color, and so on, experience oppression or discrimination or who are pushed to one side because of illness or aging'.[92] Stating that the body is culturally and linguistically constructed, as I do here, does not therefore mean to

---

89. This is one way of understanding the readings given by D. Boyarin, *Carnal Israel: Reading Sex in Talmudic Culture* (Berkeley: University of California Press, 1993), and C. Fonrobert, *Menstrual Purity Rabbinic and Christian Reconstructions of Biblical Gender* (Stanford: Stanford University Press, 2000).

90. For an overview of the history of scholarly discussion, cf. H. Marsman, *Women in Ugarit and Israel: Their Social and Religious Position in the Context of the Ancient Near East* (Leiden: Brill, 2003).

91. To name but a few of the works who have been written by European scholars: M. Grohmann, *Fruchtbarkeit und Geburt in den Psalmen*, FAT 53 (Tübingen: Mohr Siebeck, 2007); Hanne Løland, *Silent or Salient Gender? The Interpretation of Gendered God-language in the Hebrew Bible, Exemplified in Isaiah 42, 46 and 49* (Tübingen: Mohr Siebeck, 2008); C. Maier, 'Körper und Geschlecht im Alten Testament. Überlegungen zur Geschlechterdifferenz', in Berlejung, Dietrich and Quack, eds., *Menschenbilder und Körperkonzepte im Alten Israel*, 183–208.

92. S. Schroer, 'Feministische Anthropologie des Ersten Testaments. Beobachtungen, Fragen, Plädoyers', *lectio difficilior* 1 (2003), online: http://www.lectio.unibe.ch/03_1/schroer.htmn.

negate or downplay bodily experiences: bodies matter.[93] Besides texts, archaeological finds give insight into the specific conditions, both material and social, that shaped human bodies. Representations of women and men on seals and human figurines present us with images showing how human bodies were depicted.[94] Studies in iconography may complement the picture, as art narrates gender, body and sexuality differently than texts. Like historical and cultural-anthropological studies, they highlight that the body is socially and culturally determined, and they indicate the necessity of a cultural anatomy – as well as a discourse history of the body. As in gender studies, it is a commonplace that not only gender identity but also biological gender is culturally constructed. 'Culture, in short, suffused and changed the body that to the modern sensibility seems so closed, autarchic, and outside the realm of meaning'.[95] But this insight has yet to be fully assimilated by biblical exegesis. Conceptual studies on purity, body and gender constructions remain to be done.

IV. *Outline*

In this book I try to investigate the cultural and linguistic construction of all factors such as im/purity, body, gender and sex in Leviticus 12 and 15. To this end I will discuss the gendered language of the body. In contrast to previous analyses, in the center of which stood either the female body or the status of women in general, here, how the body is conceptualized, will be examined with respect to both male and female, so that gender relations will become more evident, and forms of speech, both gender-specific and gender-neutral, become recognizable. The task of this rereading is to trace the discourse history of the gendered body as manifested in the texts and their reception history. The assumption is that the analysis of the discourse deconstructs the discursive power of the text and its interpretation history and may open up new ways of constructing body and gender.[96]

---

93. Cf. Butler, *Bodies That Matter*, 28, in response to the critical objections to such an endeavor: 'One hears warnings like the following: If everything is discourse, what happens to the body? If everything is text, what about violence and bodily injury? Does anything matter in or for poststructuralism?'

94. Cf. the anthology edited by Schroer, *Images and Gender*, and in general the works of the Freiburg School.

95. Laqueur, *Making Sex*, 7.

96. Cf. Fonrobert, *Menstrual Purity*, 9: 'The assumption is that once the constructedness of sexual difference in a text is revealed, alternative readings and alternative

If it is correct that Leviticus can be read as utopian literature, then we need other tools besides source criticism, form criticism, and cultural anthropology to understand it. As Douglas puts it: 'Anthropologists are not trained to interpret utopias'.[97] Instead, the texts require an interpretation of the 'function...this literary quality has for the legislation that is integrated into the priestly texts'.[98] Whereas earlier researchers sought to analyze 'purity' as isolated category, this book builds upon the observation that 'purity' and 'impurity' come into being only as a result of the use of specific (gendered) language. Attention will be given to the way the textuality of body and gender unfolds in the analogical and non-argumentative style of the regulations. I shall make use of recent research in ritual studies taking into account the textuality of the rituals in Leviticus.

The first main part below (Part I) undertakes a detailed analysis of the linguistic and rhetorical form of Leviticus 12 (Chapter 2) and 15 (Chapter 3). The analysis forms the point of departure for determining the relationship between the interrelated concepts of body and gender. An effort will be made to remedy the deficits of previous research, which examined neither the gendered body as part of anthropology, nor the theology of the body, that is, the way that the body is interpreted and constructed within the religious symbol system. In Part II I look more closely at the texts' language of the body as it is manifested in particular themes like circumcision (Chapter 4), genital fluids (Chapter 5) or menstruation (Chapter 6). A central feature is the spatial concept of menstruation and impurity. Common translations of ritual terms such as טמא with 'impure' will be questioned (Chapter 7). I will argue for alternative renderings, namely, non-compliance with respect to the cult or disability in cultic respect. The analysis will thus take the form of a discourse-history of the body, including the history of interpretation, starting with the Greek translation of Leviticus. The study provides a building-block toward the eventual construction of a gender-oriented anthropology of the body. Finally, in the concluding chapter the impact of the findings on the understanding of Leviticus as a whole will be indicated (Chapter 8).

---

cultural choices may open up. Such methods are highly self-conscious or self-critical; they focus on the process of reading as an act of re-inscribing the text, re-appropriating or even re-writing it.'

97. Douglas, *Leviticus as Literature*, 2.
98. Liss, 'Kanon und Fiktion', 13.

Part I

EXEGETICAL ANALYSIS

This first main part of the book will explore Leviticus 12 (Chapter 2) and Leviticus 15 (Chapter 3). The structure of the two chapters is as follows: section I provides an annotated translation of the Masoretic text, while section II offers a presentation of the overall structure of the biblical material. Section III comprises an exegetical analysis, with section IV supplying a translation and interpretation of the Septuagint version. Finally, in section V, the results of the analysis of the Masoretic text will be compared with those of the Greek.

Chapter 2

LEVITICUS 12

I. *Translation (MT)*

¹ YHWH spoke to Moses:
² Speak to Israel's descendants:[1]
A woman, when she produces seed[2] and bears a male child is ritually impure[3] for seven days – according to the days of her destabilized condition[4] of menstruation[5] she is ritually impure.
³ On the eighth day the foreskin of his member[6] shall be circumcised.
⁴ Thirty-three days she shall remain with blood-of-purification. She shall not touch anything holy nor enter the holy place, until the days of her purification[7] are completed.
⁵ If she bears a female child, she is ritually impure fourteen days as during her menstruation. She remains sixty-six days in accordance with[8] the blood-of-purification.

1. Regarding the construct chain בְּנֵי יִשְׂרָאֵל, see section III.a, below.
2. The hiphil form of the verb זרע (see also Gen. 1.11, 12) has a causative sense here: 'to bring forth, develop seed'.
3. Alternative translation: 'not in compliance with the cult'; for a discussion see Chapter 7.
4. In many translations, the infinitive construct דּוֹתָהּ remains untranslated or is simply merged with נִדָּה, the first member of the construct chain (see Chapter 6). The LXX led the way in this regard.
5. Regarding נִדָּה, see Chapter 6.
6. The suffix covers the entire construct chain.
7. The Masoretic vocalization adds the third person feminine singular suffix to the masculine noun טֹהַר, the suffix being recognizable in the *mappiq* in the final ה (as in v. 6a). A different form (without the *mappiq*) is found in vv. 4a, 5b, where the feminine noun טָהֳרָה is used.
8. In contrast to v. 4, the preposition here is עַל. BDB (752) explains the derivation of this preposition's abstract meanings: 'As prep. upon, and hence on the ground of, according to, on account of, on behalf of'.

⁶ When the days of her purification for a son or for a daughter are completed,⁹ she shall bring a yearling sheep¹⁰ as a burnt offering and a dove or turtledove as a purification offering¹¹ to the priest at the entrance to the tent of meeting.
⁷ He brings it into YHWH's presence and completes the purification ritual for her, and she is ritually pure as a result of the source of her blood.
This is the instruction concerning a woman giving birth to a male or a female.
⁸ If she cannot raise the necessary amount for a sheep, let her take two turtledoves or two doves, one as a burnt offering and one as a purification offering, and the priest carries out the purifying act for her and she is ritually pure.

II. *Two Gendered Cases*

Chapter 12 is a clearly defined unit. Like the other chapters in Leviticus 11–15, this chapter opens with the narrative formula, 'YHWH spoke to Moses: Speak to Israel's descendants'. Leviticus 12 is thus cast as a speech by YHWH to Moses. In Lev. 14.1 it is also Moses who alone receives the instructions. By contrast, most of the other introductory formulas to purity teachings also include Aaron (Lev. 11.1; 13.1; 14.33; 15.1; outside of Lev. 11–15, only Exod. 12.1, 43 and Num. 19.1 have this double address).¹² The introductory formula governs the command to transmit the teaching (v. 2a); in the subsequent text, God is not directly quoted.¹³

---

9. The Hebrew can also be parsed such that the phrase 'for a son' or 'for a daughter' modifies 'let her bring' rather than 'the days of her purification'; cf. W. H. Gispen, *Het Boek Leviticus*, COT (Kampen: Kok, 1950), 197.

10. The construct chain meaning 'year-old' contains a pronominal suffix as in Lev. 13.6; 14.10; 23.12.

11. Regarding חַטָּאת as a purification offering, see below. The Hebrew word for sacrifice is etymologically unrelated to the idea of renunciation that informs the German 'Opfer' or even (in popular connotation, not etymology) the English 'sacrifice'. According to the offering-*torot* in Lev. 1, the central idea is gift; cf. Erbele-Küster, 'Reading as an Act of Offering', 36.

12. For Luciani, *Sainteté et Pardon I*, 10 these introductory divine-speech formulas constitute the primary indicators of literary structure ('configuration de base'). Accordingly he divides Leviticus into 36 'discours divins' (pp. 12–13). Zenger, 'Das Buch Leviticus als Teiltext der Tora/des Pentateuch', also bases his structural analysis upon these formulas. He points out that the formulas in Lev. 11–15 differ markedly from those in Lev. 1.7, 8, 10 and therefore indicate a distinct unit (p. 67), since (except for Lev. 12.1) they are directed at Moses and Aaron.

13. Cf. Rendtorff, *Die Gesetze in der Priesterschrift*, 69–70, who accordingly surmises that the regulations were inserted later.

The remaining verses (2ab–7a, 8) report what Moses was supposed to convey. The formula 'this is the instruction about/for NN' (זֹאת תּוֹרַת; cf. Lev. 11.46; 13.59; 14.32, 57; 15.32 and its use as a heading in Lev. 6–7) in v. 7b closes the chapter and serves as an interpretive clue.[14] Verse 8 is an appendix governing the case of a woman of lower social and economic standing.[15]

Chapter 12 envisions two situations: the birth of a male descendant (v. 2), which opens with כִּי, and the birth of a female descendant, which is prefaced with אִם (v. 5). Both cases are phrased conditionally. This structure, which introduces a general case with כִּי and subordinate cases with אִם,[16] occurs in other parts of Leviticus.[17]

The question then arises whether the general case for the chapter consists of v. 2 in its entirety, or whether it comprises only the verb form תַזְרִיעַ (v. 2aα), in which case v. 2aβ (bearing a male child) would itself constitute a subordinate case. In the latter interpretation, both types of birth (male and female) would be on the same logical level.[18] Supporting this is that the description of the purification offering in vv. 6–7 covers both genders of newborn.

The text revolves around the child-bearing woman. The command to circumcise the male newborn (v. 3) interrupts the instructions for the new mother and thus breaks the logical flow.[19] The expression 'to circumcise the foreskin of his member' (v. 3) occurs also on the occasion of the Bible's first circumcision, in Genesis 17. Our understanding of Leviticus 12 is enhanced by a further intertextual link. Specifically, the linking of the postpartum period with the period of menstruation (*niddah*) in vv. 2 and 5 presupposes familiarity with the purity regulations of ch. 15.[20]

---

14. Cf. ibid., 39, 70–74.

15. Cf. Noth, *Das dritte Buch Mose*, 82; Koch, *Priesterschrift*, 103; Elliger, *Leviticus*, 155–57; Gerstenberger, *Leviticus*, 150.

16. Milgrom (*Leviticus 1–16*, 755) implies that the clauses are on the same logical level when he designates them as 'first and second case'. Levine, *Leviticus*, 4–5, sees כִּי and אִם as typical of case-law texts. His statement about Lev. 1–4 (namely, that the אִם-clauses treat the different variations of a particular offering type) accords with the idea of logical subordination. Cf. Rendtorff, *Die Gesetze in der Priesterschrift*, 55; Luciani, *Sainteté et Pardon I*, 60–61.

17. Cf. the main rubric אָדָם כִּי in Lev. 1.2; 13.2 subordinate case with אִם in 1.3; 13.4, 7; and main rubric נֶפֶשׁ כִּי Lev. 4.1; subordinate cases with אִם in vv. 3, 13, 27, 32.

18. Thus Noth, *Das dritte Buch Mose*, 81.

19. Cf. Rendtorff, *Die Gesetze in der Priesterschrift*, 55.

20. Therefore Lev. 12 is seen as a later insertion by Elliger, *Leviticus*, 13, 156.

The italicized transliteration of the Hebrew term נִדָּה as *niddah* reflects the fact that there is no single term in English that adequately renders this distinctive concept (Chapter 6).

III. *Microstructure*

a. *Israel's Descendants*

The construct chain בְּנֵי יִשְׂרָאֵל occurs frequently in introductory formulas for legal passages in Leviticus (Lev. 1.2; 4.2; 7.28; 11.2; 12.2; 15.1; 23.2, 24, 34; 24.2 etc.).[21] It is to this group that Moses and Aaron are supposed to transmit the instructions. What actual audience lies hidden beneath this literary construct? Are the instructions for the new mother in Leviticus 12 intended only for Israel's sons or also for Israel's daughters?[22]

This construct chain is variously rendered in translations and commentaries as 'sons of Israel', 'children of Israel', or 'Israelites'. For many interpreters, this last term includes the nation's female members. In languages in which the male and female form of 'Israelite' differs, some translators use both terms to translate בְּנֵי יִשְׂרָאֵל (e.g. in German by writing 'Israeliten und Israelitinnen'). The linguistic and semantic examination of בְּנֵי יִשְׂרָאֵל that follows should help clarify whom the expression designates and what this implies for the translation.

בֵּן denotes a first-generation male offspring, i.e., a son (cf. Lev. 12.6), and beyond that also a grandson (e.g. in Gen. 29.5; Lev. 10.14). In certain lists the word occurs in parallel with בַּת ('daughter'; cf. Gen. 36.6; Exod. 1.16; 20.10; 32.2 etc.), in both singular and plural. The plural form בָּנִים in particular is often used generically for children or descendants, male and female, as for example in Gen. 3.16; 21.7; 30.1; 31.7; Exod. 21.5; 22.23; Deut. 4.10; Job 1.5. The lexeme's canonically first use in Gen. 3.16 (in the plural) concerns the bearing of children, not just of sons. In 1 Sam. 2.5 and Ps. 113.9 either 'children' or 'sons' could be intended. In addition to the gender-inclusive בָּנִים for the entire people of Israel, the Hebrew Bible employs a second inclusive phrase, namely 'sons and daughters' (בָּנָיו וּבְנֹתָיו; cf. Deut. 32.19; Isa. 43.6; Ezek. 16.20).

---

21. This phrase occurs approximately 630 times in the Hebrew Bible.

22. Ellens, *Women in the Sex Laws*, 48, elucidates the same formula in Lev. 15 as characteristic for the point of view of the text: it 'addresses a male community in the midst of which stand women who are also listening to Moses and Aaron'.

2. *Leviticus 12*

In its construct form, בֶּן designates a member of a class or expresses a common origin, a possession of a particular characteristic.[23] Such a use occurs in the current chapter (Lev. 12.8): the new mother is to offer שְׁנֵי בְנֵי יוֹנָה, which means 'two individuals of the genus dove'[24] and not 'two sons of a dove', also not 'two young doves.'[25] The expression כֶּבֶשׂ בֶּן־שְׁנָתוֹ in Lev. 12.6 accordingly designates a one-year-old male sheep.[26]

In several passages (e.g. Lev. 6.11; Josh. 17.2; Jer. 20.15), the text adds the adjective זָכָר ('male') to בָּנִים to clarify that the intended group of descendants consists entirely of males. Many translations of Lev. 6.11 flow smoothly because they render בְּנֵי generically as descendants: 'All males among Aaron's descendants (כָּל־זָכָר בִּבְנֵי אַהֲרֹן[27]) shall eat it [the sacrificial offering]'.[28] The writers specified 'males' because they knew that the construct plural בְּנֵי has inclusive connotations. This construction makes us aware of how Biblical Hebrew handles what linguists call referential semantic gender. And that gender is conceptualized in Biblical Hebrew differently from the way we do it in English.

On the occasion of the first sacrifice in Leviticus 10, the exclusively male circle that gathers around the sacrificial meal is emphasized and solidified (vv. 12–13) but subsequently opened up, when in vv. 14–15 Aaron's female descendants are also given access:

> [12] Moses spoke to Aaron and to Eleazar and Ithamar, his remaining sons: Take the food offering that is left from the fire offerings to YHWH and eat it unleavened beside the altar, for it is absolutely holy.
> [13] You shall eat it in a holy place, for it is your portion and the portion of your sons from the fire offerings[29] to YHWH, as I have been commanded.

---

23. Cf. P. Joüon and T. Muraoka, *A Grammar of Biblical Hebrew*, Subsidia biblica 279 (Rome: Gregorian & Biblical, 2006), 129j; GesB[17], 103; Ges[18], 157.

24. Cf. GK §128 v; Elliger, *Leviticus*, 27, 156, and C. Houtman, *Exodus*, HCOT, 3 vols. (Leiden: Brill, 2000), 1:13: 'not a young one, but one specimen of a certain sort'.

25. Differently BDB, 121: '*the young* of animals'.

26. GesB[17], 103. An analogous case are the phrases with בַּת in Lev. 14.10 and Num. 6.14, 'a two-year-old she-goat'. In the singular these constructions always have the suffix, except for Exod. 12.5.

27. The preposition בְּ expresses membership of a large group; cf. E. Jenni, *Die hebräischen Präpositionen. Bd. 1, Die Präposition Beth* (Stuttgart: Kohlhammer, 1992), 285.

28. As an exception cf. Elliger, *Leviticus*, 79: '(Nur) alles Männliche unter den Söhnen Aarons'.

29. Regarding the translation of this term, cf. C. Eberhart, *Studien zur Bedeutung der Opfer im Alten Testament. Die Signifikanz von Blut- und Verbrennungsriten im kultischen Rahmen*, WMANT 94 (Neukirchen-Vluyn: Neukirchener, 2002), 40–48.

¹⁴ The breast of the wave offering and the thigh of the elevation offering you shall eat in a pure place, you and your sons and your daughters with you, for they are given to you and to your children as your portion of the well-being offerings made by Israel's descendants.

¹⁵ The thigh of the elevation offering and the breast of the wave offering shall they bring along with the fat portions of the fire offering, in order to offer a wave offering in YHWH's presence. This shall be for you and your descendants with you an eternal ordinance that YHWH has commanded.

Whereas the cereal offering is meant to be consumed in a holy place by the sons only (Lev. 10.12–13; cf. 6.11), a part of the well-being offering is intended for both male and female descendants of the priest (v. 14). The daughters are indeed excluded from the plant-based meal held within the restricted holy area (v. 13), but they receive a portion of the meat that is set aside for Aaron and his descendants, both male and female (cf. Num. 18.11).

In Lev. 10.14 the Hebrew word בָּנִים is used in three different ways in this verse. Next to the sons, it designates Aaron's descendants in general (the first as well as subsequent generations) and those of Israel. Some translators render the second occurrence in v. 15b as 'your sons',³⁰ even though in the preceding commandment both the sons and the daughters of Aaron are given permission to partake of the meat of the sacrificed animal. Rather, the term בֵּן must be understood inclusively in the explanation that is offered for the commandment in the second part of v. 14b and in v. 15b ('for they are given to you and to your children as your portion').³¹ The LXX and the Codex Samaritanus followed this interpretation; in order to emphasize inclusivity, they added 'your daughters' to v. 15, while in v. 14b they replaced 'daughters' with 'house' (בַּיִת, *bayit*), which is similar in both sound and appearance to בַּת (*bat*, 'daughter'), as well as including, metonymically, female as well as male descendants.

The literary sources from which these texts derive have an androcentric structure, and yet occasionally that structure is overcome. Leviticus 6.11–12 and 10.13 clearly exclude female descendants from the enjoyment of certain cultic foods, but should not every occurrence of male in conjunction with בֵּן alert us to the possibility that daughters are elsewhere

---

30. Cf. Elliger, *Leviticus*, 132: 'der dir und deinen Söhnen zustehende Satz'. Noth, *Das dritte Buch Mose*, 73, does not mention daughters at all in his comments on this passage.

31. Cf. Milgrom, *Leviticus 1–16*, 621, who translates 'your children' here and thus emphatically sees the daughters as included.

implicitly included?³² Leviticus 10.14b presents us with a case where בֵּן clearly includes both female and male descendants. Close by (v. 14a), בֵּן occurs in parallel with בַּת, which shows that it can also designate male descendants exclusively. Exclusive and inclusive uses of the term can co-exist in a single verse (cf. Gen. 31.43).

Another passage in which the expression בְּנֵי יִשְׂרָאֵל clearly includes both men and women is in the instructions for the feast of tabernacles, Lev. 23.34, 42–44. This is apparent because it can hardly be meant that only the male population emigrated from Egypt, or that only the men should celebrate the feast.

The term בְּנֵי makes clear that the group is defined genealogically.³³ This is highlighted when the phrase is translated 'children of Israel', which can be taken as infantilizing.³⁴ בְּנֵי יִשְׂרָאֵל also highlights that the group's uniting feature is not primarily political but rather physical, i.e. their status as Israel's (literal) sons and daughters. Since בְּנֵי denotes membership in a group in a gender-neutral way, both women and men are included in the meaning of בְּנֵי יִשְׂרָאֵל. Leviticus intends בְּנֵי יִשְׂרָאֵל inclusively, despite the overall male-centeredness of its conceptual scheme. Accordingly it is translated as 'Israel's descendants' in our study.

These observations can now be applied to the use of בְּנֵי יִשְׂרָאֵל in the introductory formulas to the purity-*torot* in Lev. 12.2a. Although in its specific provisions, the text clearly differentiates the sexes, it also adopts an inclusive introductory formula and thus addresses itself to both male and female Israelites. The following directives are couched in the third person feminine singular.

b. *The Woman Who Produces Seed*³⁵

Verse 2 uses two different images to express the genesis of the child within the woman's body: 'The woman who produces seed (אִשָּׁה כִּי תַזְרִיעַ) in giving birth (ילד) to a male descendant'.³⁶ The birth process itself is ignored; narrative texts elsewhere in the Bible do describe it when something unusual happens (cf. Gen. 25.22-27; 38.27-30). Although the

---

32. Cf. the passages that speak of 'the males among the priests' (Lev. 6.20; 7.6; 2 Chr. 31.19).

33. Levine, *Leviticus*, 4, finds the translation of בְּנֵי יִשְׂרָאֵל as 'children of Israel' to be unsatisfactory, since it fails to convey the structuring principle of peoplehood, even though it emphasizes a genealogical connection.

34. Cf. I. Fischer, 'Über Lust und Last, Kinder zu haben. Soziale, genealogische und theologische Aspekte in der Literatur Alt-Israels', *JBT* 17 (2002): 55-82 (56).

35. See Chapter 5, section II.

36. Cf. Ges¹⁸, 313 'v.d. Frau: Samen austragen, schwanger sein'.

usual verb ילד appears in the qal ('produce', 'give birth to') in the second part of the sentence, the verse as a whole is introduced by זרע in the hiphil, which here carries a causative sense, i.e. 'bring forth (or produce) seed'.[37] This use of the root זרע contrasts with the idea that it is the man who carries the seed (sperm) with which he impregnates the woman (cf. Lev. 18.20), just as the woman is capable of receiving the man's seed (cf. Num. 5.28). In that understanding, the progeny results from the man's seed (זֶרַע), while the woman's role is to gestate and bear.[38] Leviticus 12.2 presents a different view of conception, which also occurs in the letter to the Hebrews (11.11), which attributes to Sarah the power, achieved through her faith, to create seed.

The hiphil form of the verb זרע is also used in Gen. 1.11–12 to describe the power that plants have to produce their own seed. Both Job 1.21 and Ps. 139.15 draw an analogy between the earth and the womb, thereby showing how human reproduction parallels vegetative fertility. Both Lev. 12.2 and Gen. 1.12 associate the child-bearing woman with the fertile earth, in which the seeds of plants germinate and out of which they sprout.

c. *Male and Female Descendants*
As our analysis of the surface structure of Leviticus 12 showed, the chapter's organizing feature is the gender of the newborn child. Gender duality is determinative. The instruction for the child-bearing woman in v. 2 refers to the child not as a 'son' or a 'daughter' – these terms, which imply a social role (gender), come into play only after a specified period in connection with the purification ritual (cf. v. 6) – nor does it speak of a 'boy'or a 'girl', but rather of a 'male' (זָכָר, v. 2) and a 'female' (נְקֵבָה, v. 5) descendant. Both terms designate biological sex in animals as well as humans, and they occur primarily in the literary strata most closely

---

37. Cf. M. Stol, *Birth in Babylonia and the Bible: Its Mediterranean Setting*, with a chapter by F. A. M. Wiggermann (Groningen: STYX, 2000), 7–8, and Milgrom, *Leviticus 1–16*, 743. In his notes, Milgrom gives the literal meaning as 'produces seed', though in his translation he appears to interpret the hiphil as an elative, writing 'at childbirth'. This is in spite of his observation that rabbinic interpreters held that the mother's blood joined with the male seed from the moment of conception. Cf. B. Levine, 'Seed Versus Womb: Expressions of Male Dominance in Biblical Israel', in *Sex and Gender in the Ancient Near East: Proceedings of the 47th Rencontre Assyriologique Internationale*, Part I, ed. S. Parpola and R. M. Whiting (Helsinki: Neo-Assyrian Text Corpus Project, 2002), 337–43. In his Leviticus commentary, Levine interprets the hiphil in a passive rather than a causative sense (Levine, *Leviticus*, 73: 'when a woman is inseminated').

38. Cf. Levine, 'Seed Versus Womb', 342.

related to the purity regulations. According to Gen. 1.27, God created humankind as male (זָכָר) and female (נְקֵבָה). This concerns a biological difference that implies no differentiation of roles.

Nevertheless, the use in Leviticus 12 of נְקֵבָה makes clear that the chapter construes gender in terms of the physical body and that the body depicts those gender differences. The verbal root that underlies נְקֵבָה ('female') is shared by all Semitic languages.[39] In Hebrew, נקב describes a process of 'piercing' (2 Kgs 18.21) or 'drilling a hole' (2 Kgs 12.10).[40] A נְקֵבָה is therefore someone who is 'pierced, drilled through, hollowed out'. The related Akkadian verb *naqābu(m)* has the sense of 'penetrate, deflower'.[41] The virginity of the female demon *ardat lilî* is described by the expression *lā nakpātu*, 'she who has not been penetrated',[42] from the verbal root *nakāpum* 'to push, poke'.[43]

The feminine נְקֵבָה, 'the penetrated one', may thus allude to the infant's outward movement through the vagina during birth as well as to the male's penetration of the vagina from without during copulation. In either case, feminine gender is defined by a potential action upon the woman's body.

By contrast, the etymology of זָכָר ('male') is less clear. In several passages in which זָכָר denotes a sexual difference, the word emphasizes male roles or privileges, as for example when all males are required to appear three times a year before YHWH (see Exod. 12.48). The egalitarian complementarity of נְקֵבָה and זָכָר found in the Priestly creation account does not recur in Leviticus 12. Rather, here the contrast of נְקֵבָה with זָכָר must be read in connection with the cultural and religious construction of gender that is expressed in the different periods of purification based on the newborn's gender. The biological differentiation of the sexes in Leviticus 12 implies a hierarchical relationship.

---

39. Cf. *HAL*, 678–79.

40. In the Siloam inscription, this noun is used to denote a breaking-through or a tunnel; cf. H. Donner and W. Röllig, *Kanaanäische und Aramäische Inschriften Bd. II* (Wiesbaden: Harrassowitz, 1964), Nr.189 1.2.4.

41. Cf. *AHw* II, 743. *CAD* N (1977) 328 reads 'to rape', thus following the sense that the verb has in legal texts (*Laws of Eshnunna* §§26 and 31), in which remedies are stipulated for restoring the injured honor of husbands and fathers (quoted in B. Landsberger, 'Jungfräulichkeit. Ein Beitrag zum Thema "Beilager und Eheschließung"', in *Symbolae Iuridicae et Historicae Martino David dedicatae*, ed. J. A. Ankum et al. [Leiden: Brill, 1968], 41–65 [50, 53]).

42. Cf. Landsberger, 'Jungfräulichkeit', 43–45, although he denies any connection between the verbs, speaking of a confusion with *nakāpu* ('to push').

43. Cf. *AHw* II, 718.

d. *As During the Days of Her Menstruation*

Verse 2 compares the woman's condition after giving birth to that during her menstrual period (כִּימֵי נִדַּת). The reference is to Lev. 15.19–26, which concerns the woman's monthly bleeding. Leviticus 12.2b reads:

> when she produces seed and bears a male child is ritually impure for seven days – according to the days of her destabilized condition of menstruation she is ritually impure.

Using the *waw*-perfect for the first verb and concluding with the imperfect, the verse declares that after childbirth, the mother is ritually impure. It does not, however, explain why childbirth has this effect. After the technical term *niddah* (in the construct state) comes the infinitive construct from the verb דוה (see Chapter 6). Other forms derived from this root connote an destabilzed condition of weakness, and they occur mostly in contexts of lament (cf. Lam. 1.13; 5.17; Ps. 41.4).

According to Lev. 12.2, the woman's ritual impurity after giving birth is like that of her menstrual period, including the duration of seven[44] days in accordance with Lev. 15.19. The wording in the case of a female newborn in Lev. 12.5 is shorter and thereby acquires its own emphasis. In contrast to v. 2, v. 5 does not mention 'the time [lit.: days] of menstruation'. The reasons for this may be more than stylistic. The congruence between the period after bearing a male child in v. 2 and the time of menstruation led many scholars to conclude that this provision is original and that the differentiation between female and male offspring was added secondarily. Accordingly, the woman's ritual impurity after bearing a child is analogous to menstruation only qualitatively and not in terms of time.[45] The text is silent about why the time of impurity is twice as long after the birth of a female child, and as such numerous explanations have been proffered (see below, section f., and Chapter 6).

e. *Foreskin of His Member*

The focus shifts in v. 3 from the mother to her male offspring: 'On the eighth day the foreskin of his member shall be circumcised'. No ceremony is described, nor is the act explained. The circumcision occurs

---

44. The number seven implies totality and completeness (cf. Houtman, *Exodus I*, 66–67 with references).

45. The difference is reflected in the way the prepositions are translated. In v. 2 the translation reads '*according to* the days of her…menstruation' while v. 5 reads '*as* during her menstruation'.

only after the mother's seven-day period of impurity has passed,⁴⁶ so that she can no longer ritually contaminate her son. The verbal root that is used is unique to circumcision. Because the niphal conjugation is used, the subject of the verb is concealed. The object of the circumcision is either the male child or his flesh (בָּשָׂר), which the MT implies but does not expressly designate as the accusative object.

The construct chain בְּשַׂר עָרְלָתוֹ that occurs in Lev. 12.3 (as part of a legal prescription) also occurs in Gen. 17.11, 14, 23–35 (in a narrative context). The translation 'the flesh of his foreskin'⁴⁷ is confusing, since the foreskin contains no flesh. This could be resolved by understanding the expression as an explicative genitive, whereby the governing noun (here בָּשָׂר) is the more comprehensive category.⁴⁸ Likewise בָּשָׂר is understood as a euphemism for the male member.

f. *Remaining in Accordance with the Blood of Purification*

The seven-day period of impurity in the case of a male child is followed by a second, unrelated period of 33 days (v. 4a) or, in the case of a female, 66 days (v. 5b), in which the woman is supposed to remain 'according to' the blood of purification or purity. The translation chosen depends on whether טָהֳרָה is understood as a process or a state.⁴⁹

The text suggests that the woman's postpartum blood flows last shorter or longer depending on the newborn's sex, 7 plus 33 days for a boy and twice that long for a girl. This in turn suggests that the blood is the carrier of the purity or impurity. What theory of gender relations underlies this sex-specific duration of the period of non-compliance with the cult? In rabbinic sources we find a symbolic interpretation arguing that the longer period after the birth of a female child is a consequence of the guilt or

---

46. The pattern of seven days plus the eighth day occupies an important place within the rituals of Leviticus (cf. Lev. 9.1; 14.9–10, 23; 15.13–14, 28–29; 22.27; 23.36, 39; 25.22; Num. 6.9–10).

47. Cf. Noth, *Das dritte Buch Mose*, 81, and J. Scharbert, *Fleisch Geist und Seele im Pentateuch*, 2nd ed., SBS 19 (Stuttgart: Katholisches Bibelwerk, 1967), 50. Elliger, *Leviticus*, 155–56, does concede in a textual note that flesh of the 'foreskin' means 'the member that retains its foreskin'.

48. B. Jacob, *Das Buch Genesis* (Berlin: Schocken, 1934), 424, takes this approach: 'euer Glied, das im Zustand der עָרְלָה'. Milgrom, *Leviticus 1–16*, 748, translates the foreskin of his member'; regarding the *genitivus explicativus*, cf. GK §128 k–o.

49. *DCH* 3:348–49, speculates that this word could denote specific purificatory procedures. Accordingly it suggests the translation '*blood of*, perh. requiring, *purification*'.

impurity that the first woman brought down upon herself.[50] Ramban explains the mother's differing periods of cultic disability by appealing to the cold, moist nature of the feminine: after the birth of a female child, the mother needs more time to divest herself of the surplus of moisture. A different explanation sees the doubling of the purification period for female newborns as an anticipation of the impurity that will arise in the female offspring when she begins to menstruate.[51] It is argued that the discharges are more intense and thicker during the first week (*lochia rubra*) than are the discharges that follow (the more watery, mucus-bearing *lochia alba*, which can persist for up to five weeks). Over against such physiological explanations, which are also clearly culturally and historically conditioned, stands the symbolic meaning of the numbers, which depict a gender hierarchy. In the double length of the woman's cultic disablement after the birth of a daughter, one can see a mirroring of the socio-religious structure of the society.[52] Giving birth to a 'daughter causes a greater impurity because she will have the ability to create life'[53] and therefore in patrilineal society she has an ambiguous role.

In what sense does the woman remain in the blood of purification? Not in the sense that she is confined to the domestic sphere, as some translations would suggest.[54] The text itself, in connection with the birth of the male child, defines the expression as a separation from cultic objects and from the sanctuary (v. 4).

The verb ישׁב occurs with two different prepositions: בְּ in v. 4 and עַל in v. 5b. The preposition בְּ usually designates a physical location.[55] Applied to Lev. 12.4, this would mean literally that the woman sits *in* the blood.

---

50. Cf. the discussion by A. Cooper, 'A Medieval Jewish Version of Original Sin: Ephraim of Luntshits on Leviticus 12', *Harvard Theological Review* 97 (2004): 445–59, especially 456–57.

51. J. Magonet, 'But if it is a Girl, she is unclean for twice seven days... The Riddle of Leviticus 12,5', in Sawyer, ed., *Reading Leviticus*, 144–52, locates the impurity in a physical condition, namely, in the supposed fact that the female offspring already has a discharge of blood (pp. 151–52). As further evidence he cites 'temporary breast development in babies of either sex and even lactation' (p. 152); cf. R. Biale, *Women and Jewish Law: An Exploration of Women's Issues in Halakhic Sources* (New York: Schocken, 1984), 152.

52. Noth, *Das dritte Buch Mose*, 82, interprets the differing lengths of time as cultic inferiority of the female sex.

53. Ruane, *Sacrifice and Gender in Biblical Law*, 187.

54. Cf. GesB[17], 323.

55. Cf. C. Brockelmann, *Hebräische Syntax* (Neukirchen-Vluyn: Neukirchener, 1956), §106a, and Joüon and Muraoka, *A Grammar*, § 113c.

A different interpretation, however, suggests itself in light with the use in v. 5b of עַל. This preposition denotes not only spatial proximity but also an underlying reason.[56] In any case, the use of two different prepositions makes clear that the construction is not to be understood purely spatially, but rather causally or instrumentally.

This regulation inscribes two differently qualified postpartum periods into the female body. While the first period (of 7 or 14 days) can be seen as a static condition of impurity (vv. 2, 5a), the second (of 33 or 66 days) may be understood as a process of purification. The latter period is further characterized by the phrases 'blood of purification' (vv. 4, 5) and 'the time [lit.: days] of her purification' (vv. 5, 6). Both expressions suggest that the postpartum losses of blood are a purifying process. The differentiation into two periods of 7 plus 33 days (or 14 plus 66 days) is based less in the bodily secretions of the woman who has given birth than in the intention to distinguish two phases of a ritual. The 7 or 14 days represent a separation ritual, while the 33 or 66 days of the blood of purification constitute a transformation ritual.[57]

g. *At the Entrance to the Tent of Meeting*[58]

Implied in the prohibition of women's approaching the sanctuary during a limited period after giving birth is their fundamental ability to participate in the cult. Indeed, at the end of this period the woman is required to visit the sanctuary in what amounts to a reintegration ritual by means of a specific offering. That women are qualified to make sacrifice is implied even the basic instructions in Leviticus 1–7, which use the terms אָדָם (Lev. 1.2; cf. 5.3; Num. 19.14) and נֶפֶשׁ (Lev. 2.1; 4.2, 27; 5.1, 1, 4, 15, 17, 21; 7.18, 20, 21, 25, 27; 23.29, 30) inclusively.[59]

---

56. Cf. Joüon and Muraoka, *A Grammar*, §113f.

57. Here I follow Arnold van Gennep's division, *Les rite de passages* (Paris: Picard, 1909), into 'rites de séparation' and 'rites de marge'.

58. For a general discussion on ritual space, cf. G. Klingbeil, *Bridging the Gap: Ritual and Ritual Texts in the Bible*, BBRS 1 (Winona Lake, IN: Eisenbrauns, 2007), 159–68.

59. A similar point is made by M. Gruber, 'Women in the Cult According to the Priestly Code', in *Judaic Perspectives on Ancient Israel*, ed. Jacob Neusner (Philadelphia: Wipf & Stock, 1987), 35–48; cf. also D. Erbele-Küster, 'Der Dienst der Frauen am Eingang des Zeltheiligtums (Exodus 38:8) – Kultisch-religiöse Verortungen von Frauen in Exodus und Leviticus', in *The Interpretation of Exodus: Studies in Honour of Cornelis Houtman*, ed. Riemer Roukema et al., CBET 44 (Leuven: Brill, 2006), 265–81.

In this new instruction, in contrast to vv. 2 and 4, biological terms are not used to refer to the newborn's gender. Instead, the text speaks of a 'son' or a 'daughter', words that express social and family relationships. This shows that as part of the mother's ritual reintegration, the infants too are received into the social group. The sacrificial offering is identical for both son and daughter: a yearling lamb as a burnt offering and a dove or turtle dove as a purification offering (v. 6), or for mothers of more limited means, two doves or two turtledoves (v. 8).

The place to which the woman is to bring the sacrificial animals is specified as 'the entrance to the tent of meeting, to the priest'. Does 'entrance to the tent of meeting' designate the entrance to the courtyard that surrounded the tent of meeting (and in which the altar for fire-offerings stood), or does it mean directly in front of the tent, within the courtyard? And is this location the same as or different from the one designated as 'in YHWH's presence'[60] (לִפְנֵי יְהוָה)? Leviticus uses these terms in various ways in connection with the presentation of offerings, as Table 1 below shows:

Table 1

bring (בוא hiphil) to the entrance to the tent of meeting	Lev. 1.3; 13.11; 17.4
bring (בוא hiphil) to the priest at the entrance to the tent of meeting	Lev. 12.6; 15.29; 17.5
bring (בוא hiphil) in front of the tent of meeting	Lev. 4.14
slaughter it at the entrance to the tent of meeting	Lev. 3.2
bring near (קרב hiphil) into YHWH's presence	Lev. 3.1, 7, 12
bring (בוא hiphil) to the entrance of the tent of meeting into YHWH's presence	Lev. 4.4[61]
slaughter in YHWH's presence	Lev. 4.4

The wording in Lev. 12.6, 'bring to the entrance of the tent of meeting', replicates the standard introductory formula for the offering of an animal that is found at the beginning of the instructions for sacrifice in Lev. 1.3b. Leviticus 1.2b uses a general formulation with the preposition לְ ('for', 'with regard to'), 'when someone among you presents an offering for YHWH'. In this introductory rubric, which mentions no place, the key is

60. According to Haran, *Temples and Temple-Service*, 26, the 58 occurrences of this expression in Leviticus are primarily in cultic passages and designate the area in front of the ark.
61. According to Lev. 15.14, the man who has been cleansed from his discharge shall himself come (בוא qal) into YHWH's presence at the entrance to the tent of meeting.

the transfer of the offering to YHWH. What this suggests is that there is a difference between an instruction that specifies a physical location and one that indicates a theological location that is not determined by human perspective.

In general, 'at the entrance to the tent of meeting' is the location most often specified in Leviticus. The literary frame locates the proceedings at the tent of meeting; it is there that Moses receives YHWH's instructions (Lev. 1.1). At this location, or with reference to it, occur all ritual actions. Put negatively, the action rarely distances itself from this location. The entrance to the tent of meeting is where the worshipper's actions and those of God intersect.[62] The entrance represents a threshold at which one transitions from outside to inside and where sacred and profane meet.

Since the expressions 'in(to) YHWH's presence' and 'at the entrance to the tent of meeting' occur together repeatedly, and the order varies, they can be taken to be synonymous.[63] The expressions describe the same location, yet with different emphases. The specification that an offering is to be brought 'to the entrance to the tent of meeting', occasionally in conjunction with the detail that it is to be delivered 'to the priest' who completes the ritual (Lev. 12.6; 15.29; Num. 6.10), suggests a more ritual-technical sense. The specification 'to the priest' does not occur where לִפְנֵי יְהוָה stands alone. The latter expression, one may assume, envisions more a theological topography than a concrete ritual location.[64] One might object that in Lev. 1.5; 3.7, 14 the expression 'in YHWH's presence' can be understood concretely, since it is there that the animal is to be offered and slaughtered. When this expression does designate a physical location, that location is outside the sanctuary. The phrase expresses God's nearness and serves as a theological term to indicate a location of heightened sanctity that (at least on the literary plane) is reserved for men. As in Leviticus 15, the expression is used in connection only with

---

62. Gorman, *The Ideology of Ritual*, 49, makes a similar point: 'Thus, the tabernacle structure joins together the two ideas of Yahweh's presence in the midst of Israel and Israel's presence before Yahweh in the sacrificial cult'.

63. Cf. 'in YHWH's presence at the entrance to the tent of meeting' (the Hebrew lacks a preposition) in Exod. 29.11; Lev. 14.11; 15.14 (with 16.7 עַל); in reverse order: '(to) the entrance to the tent of meeting in YHWH's presence', Exod. 29.42; Lev. 4.4a.

64. Cf. J. Wegner, 'Coming Before the Lord: The Exclusion of Women from the Public Domain of the Israelite Priestly Cult', in Rendtorff and Kugler, eds., *The Book of Leviticus*, 451–65 (453) 'in/into the presence of YHWH'; a different understanding is presented by A. S. van der Woude, 'פָּנִים *pānīm*', *THAT* 2:432–60 (434). Van der Woude sees the prepositional phrase לִפְנֵי יְהוָה as a technical cultic term. Accordingly he expresses reservations about seeking a theological meaning.

the man (v. 14) and not with the woman (v. 29), and here in Leviticus 12 it does not occur at all. Consequently, Wegner argues that women were excluded from direct access to that presence.[65] Nevertheless, in terms of topography, the same place is meant. By speaking of women's occasional exclusion from the ritual realm, the texts not only imply women's usual inclusion, but they even require that women go 'to the entrance to the tent of meeting' to be reintegrated into the cultic community.

h. *She Shall Present a Yearling Sheep as a Burnt Offering*
After her period of cultic ineligibility has passed, the woman is to bring a sheep and a dove (v. 6) or, as the equivalent, two doves or turtledoves (v. 8),[66] to the priest for a burnt offering (עֹלָה) and a purification offering (חַטָּאת). Both types of offering presuppose the basic instructions found in Leviticus 1–7, and are summarized below.

The first offering type discussed by Leviticus is the עֹלָה[67] (Lev. 1). This is the most common type of sacrifice in the Hebrew Bible. From a canonical standpoint it also has pride of place: the first to offer the עֹלָה is Noah (Gen. 8.20). Leviticus 1.2 characterizes the עֹלָה as קָרְבָּן (from the root קרב qal 'approach', hiphil 'offer'), i.e., as an offering that is presented before God or at the altar. The way that Leviticus describes ritual offerings makes it clear that the Hebrew Bible has no concept of sacrifice in the sense of something willingly surrendered or foregone. Rather, the key principle of sacrifice is קָרְבָּן meaning rapprochement, whereby both the offerer and the object offered are brought closer to the divine.[68] The specific types of presentation emphasize functional aspects such as the slaughter offering.

The instructions in Leviticus 1 specify what types of gift from a person's herd or flock are acceptable. The animal can be a bull (vv. 2, 3) or a ram or goat (vv. 3, 10); all must be male and unblemished.[69] Doves (v. 14) are a possible substitute. Laying one's hand on the animal,

65. Wegner, 'Coming Before the Lord', 457.
66. These substitute offerings for hardship cases are the same as those to be brought after an unusual genital discharge in a man (Lev. 15.8) and an unusual discharge of blood in a woman (Lev. 15.19–20). In Luke 2.24 Mary takes advantage of this provision.
67. Cf. Eberhart, *Studien zur Bedeutung der Opfer*, 16–76.
68. Cf. A. Marx, *Les systèmes sacrificiels. Formes et fonctions du culte sacrificiel Yhwh*, VTSup 108 (Leiden: Brill, 2005), 109.
69. N. S. Meshel, *The 'Grammar' of Sacrifice: A Generativist Study of the Israelite Sacrificial System in the Priestly Writings* (Oxford: Oxford University Press, 2014), 33–35. Ruane, *Sacrifice and Gender in Biblical Law*, 40–76, discusses the question of the gender of sacrificial animals and the preponderance of male animals.

slaughtering it, draining its blood, and burning it are listed as elements of the ritual, whereby the full combustion is the distinguishing feature of the עֹלָה. It is this feature that gave rise to the LXX's neologism ὁλοκαύτωσις ('something fully burned'). The usual translation of the Hebrew term into English emphasizes this aspect (cf. 'burnt offering').

In distinction to the voluntary עֹלָה, the חַטָּאת is introduced in Leviticus 4 as an obligatory way of expiating for unintentional violations of the commandments. The term חַטָּאת is equivocal, capable of designating either the trespass incurred or the ritual means of removing it.[70] It derives from the privative piel stem ('absolve', 'purify') of a root whose qal stem means 'to sin'. As opposed to the common translation of חַטָּאת as 'sin offering',[71] a more adequate rendering for the term as it is used in Leviticus 12 and similar passages is 'purification offering'[72] or 'reintegration rite'.[73]

The חַטָּאת offering for the anointed priest requires a bull (Lev. 4.3, 14). A leading personage is to offer a he-goat (v. 23), while an ordinary person offers a she-goat (v. 28) or a sheep (v. 32). Leviticus 5.1–13 describes additional situations which call for a חַטָּאת, and in doing so reveals that persons suffering financial hardship may make their purification offerings (חַטָּאת) using doves or, failing that, flour (vv. 11–13). Except for the plant-based חַטָּאת, all forms of this rite go beyond the specifications for the עֹלָה by adding ritual manipulations of the victim's blood: the blood

---

70. Cf. Rendtorff, *Leviticus*, 148.

71. This translation emphasizes the qal meaning of the root חטא ('to sin'). Rendtorff, *Leviticus*, 221, argues for retaining this translation, although he emphasizes that the word's double meaning (i.e., both the trespass and its removal) must always be kept in mind.

72. Cf. J. Milgrom, 'Sin-Offering or Purification-Offering', *VT* 21 (1970): 237–39, and *Leviticus 1–16*, 253–54. In addition to semantic considerations, Milgrom adduces morphological and etymological arguments. חַטָּאת 'appears as a *pi'el* derivative...which carries no other meaning than "to cleanse, expurgate, decontaminate"' (*Leviticus 1–16*, 237). Hieke, *Leviticus*, 2:88–92 proposes a translation in the line of the piel privative sense of the verb: 'Entsündigungsopfer'. Cf. also N. Kiuchi, *The Purification Offering in the Priestly Literature: Its Meaning and Function*, JSOTSup 56 (Sheffield: JSOT, 1987), and R. Gane, *Cult and Character: Purification Offerings, Day of Atonement, and Theodicy* (Winona Lake, IN: Eisenbrauns, 2005), 50–51, 119. For criticisms of Milgrom's position, cf. Rendtorff, *Leviticus*, 221, and A. Schenker, 'Interprétations récentes et dimensions spécifiques du sacrifice hattat', *Biblica* 75 (1994): 59–70.

73. Marx argues for this idea (cf. *Les systèmes sacrificiels*, 181, 'rituel de réintégration'). He emphasizes that חַטָּאת can have different meanings depending on the context (pp. 183–88).

is applied to the horns of the altar and, in case of a sin on the part of the entire community, to the curtain that conceals the inner sanctum of the tent (vv. 5–7, 18, 25, 30, 34). The remaining blood is then poured out at the base of the altar. As the sacrificial regulations in Leviticus 1–7 show, the blood manipulation lies in the hand of the priest which brings them near to the altar.[74] The significance of the entire ritual is given in the recurring formula, 'and he [the priest] performs the purification ritual for her [him] and it is forgiven her [him]' (vv. 26, 31, 35). Leviticus 5 thus characterizes the offering's purpose as cleansing and forgiveness. Similarly, the חַטָּאת in Leviticus 12 is offered as part of a rite of cleansing and reintegration into the cultic community.[75] There is no connection to sin, just as there is none in the passages where the חַטָּאת is connected to the Nazirite vow (Num. 6) or the inauguration of the altar (Lev. 8.15).[76] If the blood ritual is the decisive part of the procedure,[77] then in the special case of Leviticus 12, the woman's blood can be set over against the blood of the offering. On the other hand, the poverty exception, which permits a plant-based offering for the חַטָּאת (Lev. 5.11–13), calls the centrality of blood into question, for in hardship cases the purification and reintegration are not dependent on blood. Besides this, one must consider the dual structure of the ritual in Leviticus 12 and 15: in the purification rituals of these chapters, in addition to a חַטָּאת an עֹלָה is required, which contradicts the characterization of the latter in Leviticus 1 as a purely voluntary offering.

---

74. Cf. William K. Gilders, *Blood Ritual in the Hebrew Bible: Meaning and Power* (Baltimore: The Johns Hopkins University Press, 2004), 78–81.

75. A. Marx, 'Sacrifice pour les Péchés ou Rite de Passage? Quelques Réflexions sur la Fonction du *Hattat*', *RB* 96 (1984): 27–48, interprets חַטָּאת for this reason not as sacrificial offering but as *rite de passage*. Willi-Plein, *Opfer und Kult*, 96–98, also classifies חַטָּאת not as a sacrifice but as a ritual.

76. This causes B. A. Levine, *In the Presence of the Lord: A Study of Cult and Some Cultic Terms in Ancient Israel* (Leiden: Brill, 1974), 103, to differentiate between two forms of חַטָּאת: one for ritual cleansing and the other to atone for transgression. Ina Willi-Plein's definition, *Opfer und Kult im alttestamentlichen Israel: Textbefragungen und Zwischenergebnisse*, SBS 153 (Stuttgart: Kohlhammer, 1993), 96, according to which חַטָּאת is a means to restore a state of order, combines both senses.

77. Cf. Rendtorff, *Leviticus*, 163; Milgrom, *Leviticus 1–16*, 254–58, 1031–34, and Gerstenberger, *Leviticus*, 59–60. According to B. Janowski, *Sühne als Heilsgeschehen. Studien zur Sühnetheologie der Priesterschrift und zur Wurzel KPR im Alten Orient und im Alten Testament*, WMANT 55/2 (Neukirchen-Vluyn: Neukirchener, 2002), 233, 241–43, who cites Lev. 17.11, the blood ritual's more specific effect is to atone.

The declaratory formula 'and she is pure' suggests that the חַטָּאת in Leviticus 12 and 15 should be interpreted as a purification offering whose effect is anticipated by the woman's loss of blood during the birth and by the passage of the required amount of time.

In general, 'the purpose of these offerings, as for men [in Lev. 15.29-30], is to reintegrate the impure person into the community. Fundamentally, they give social power back to the person who has been excluded'[78] from participating in the cult. The purification offering of Leviticus 12 marks the transition from the old condition of cultic impurity which is a time of separation from the sanctuary, to the condition of purity and hence of reintegration into the ritual community. These instructions for women presuppose that they are ordinarily cultically active, despite their lack of the sign of circumcision. They themselves are responsible for the offerings that the priest presents on their behalf.

i. *He Completes the Purification Ritual*
The priest's activity is summarized by two actions in v. 7a: he brings it into YHWH's presence and completes the purification ritual for her (כפר). The first verb (קרב hiphil) can denote the entire offering procedure, or it can simply mean the physical presentation prior to slaughter (cf. Lev. 1.3). The second verb (כפר piel in v. 8) appears in two other instances in connection with the affirmation 'and he/she/it is pure': in the case of someone undergoing the purification ritual after an episode of skin disease (Lev. 14.20) and that of an infected house (Lev. 14.53). In Lev. 16.30 the goal of the action (piel כפר) is purity (cf. Lev. 16.18–19). In these cases, the ritual act aims for cultic purity, which restores access to the sanctuary, since impurity threatens the sanctuary and with it the holiness and presence of God.[79]

Accordingly, in such contexts the piel form of כפר has the technical meaning 'to remove cultic impurity' or 'to restore to cultic eligibility'.[80] In its brevity, the formula, 'the priest completes the purification procedure for her, and she is pure' in Lev. 12.7, 8 alludes to other passages within

---

78. Ruane, *Sacrifice and Gender in Biblical Law*, 29.
79. Milgrom, *Leviticus 1–16*, 440–42, 486–88, 1079–81, conceives of impurity as a dynamic potential that accumulates in the sanctuary. Accordingly, purification rituals are directed solely toward the sanctuary itself.
80. By contrast Milgrom, *Leviticus 1–16*, 1079–84, supposes that in ritual texts like Leviticus, the verb has the sense primarily of 'rub off, wipe' (p. 1081), although he admits that the so-called abstract meaning of 'expiate' is also connoted (pp. 1081, 1083).

Leviticus. Nevertheless, Leviticus 12 uses the piel form of כפר differently than do Lev. 4.20, 26, 31; 5.6, 10, 18. In the latter passages, the verb denotes the removal or forgiveness of individual guilt and is frequently connected with the expression 'and her/his sin is forgiven'. The fact that the כפר-formula can occur in the absence of a prior blood ritual (in Lev. 5.16 in connection with flour; in Lev. 14.18 with oil) shows that the blood connection is not essential to it.[81]

In Leviticus 12 the woman is 'purified from the source of her blood' (v. 7b), i.e., from her postpartum bleeding, after a specified time. There is no connotation of guilt; rather, as in Lev. 15.15, 30 and Num. 6.11, the person finds herself in an unintentional, often unavoidable but in any case remediable condition of cultic ineligibility, in the first case because of genital secretions and in the second due to contact with a corpse.

The piel form of the verb כפר occurs in various constructions.[82] In Lev. 12.7.8 it occurs with the preposition עַל and the third person feminine singular suffix. The preposition עַל frequently denotes the person or group[83] on whose behalf the ritual is performed.[84] Leviticus 12 gives no further indication of the means of the purification or of the condition from which the person is purified, either of which can also be appended using עַל. This preposition is used with reference to the sanctuary (Lev. 8.15; 14.53; 16.18) in passages that suggest the purely local meanings 'over' or 'upon'. The idea may also carry an implicit nuance of a physical cleansing or contact. Nevertheless, the key idea involves neither a concrete location nor a specific physical act, but rather the nexus to the person or object that undergoes the ritual (see, e.g., Lev. 8.34 and Num. 15.25). Even the basic instructions in Leviticus 1–7 give no such concrete details. The preposition עַל instead signals a process that involves or benefits a person or thing and alters his or its (conceptual) position relative to the sanctuary.

---

81. Cf. Rendtorff, *Die Gesetze der Priesterschrift*, 76. This observation, as well as the lack of the characteristic rite of laying-on of the hands (esp. in Lev. 14 – where the piel form of כפר is applied to houses) led to his critique of the concept of vicarious atonement (cf. Eberhart, *Studien zur Bedeutung der Opfer*, 220).

82. Cf. the survey in Janowski, *Sühne*, 186–87.

83. The preposition בְּעַד can perform the same function. In very few passages does עַל combine with an impersonal object such as the altar or the sanctuary (for the differences between the prepositions, cf. Kiuchi, *Purification Offering*, 88–89).

84. Cf. Lev. 1.4; 4.20, 26, 31, 35; 5.6, 10, 13, 16, 18, 26; 8.34; 10.7; 14.18, 19, 20, 21, 29, 31; 15.25, 30; 16.30, 33b, 34; 17.11a; 19.22; 23.28.

The piel form of the verb כפר denotes a priestly activity without specifying details.⁸⁵ The כפר-formula serves both to mark the conclusion of the ritual and to interpret it by highlighting the priestly activity.⁸⁶

j. *She Is Pure as a Result of the Source of Her Blood*

In contrast to the ritual procedure, whose agent is named (the priest), the closing comment 'and she is pure' (vv. 7, 8) qualifies its subject but describes no action on her part. The direction of communication changes over the course of the passage; the priest does not figure in the final declaration.

The summary formula following the sacrificial ritual, 'and she is pure as a result the source of her blood' (וְטָהֲרָה מִמְּקֹר דָּמֶיהָ, v. 7) cannot be taken to mean that what the woman has been purified of is her (impure) issue of blood, since earlier there was mention of blood of purification. The phrase 'source of her blood' occurs also in Lev. 20.18 in the context of sexual taboos involving menstruating women. It denotes the region of the woman's body that is the subject of the taboo: under no circumstance is the woman to bare the 'source of her blood' to a man. In the first part of that verse, the word מָקוֹר is used alone for the female pudenda, in parallel with 'nakedness'.

The basic meaning of the noun מָקוֹר is 'wellspring'.⁸⁷ Springs make life possible, as biblical poetry recognizes in such phrases as 'wellspring of life' (Ps. 36.10; Prov. 10.11; 13.14; 14.27; 16.22) and 'wellspring of living water' (Jer. 2.13; 17.13). Zechariah 13.1 speaks of a purifying spring opening up for Jerusalem's residents. The word connotes water, fertility, and life. Accordingly, Leviticus 12 equates the womb with a wellspring.⁸⁸

---

85. Rendtorff, *Leviticus*, 176–78 speaks of a ritual and technical use and translates it as 'to complete the act of atonement'.

86. Cf. Elliger, *Leviticus*, 36, and E. Jenni, *Das hebräische Piel. Syntaktisch-semasiologische Untersuchung einer Verbalform im Alten Testament* (Zurich: EVZ-Verlag, 1968), 241. Janowski, *Sühne*, 253, understands the piel form of כפר as an interpretation of the meaning of the ritual acts performed by the priest. Watts, *Ritual and Rhetoric*, 130–41, discusses the suggestion that this word may serve as an explanation of the ritual given by the text itself. He stresses that it is a priestly activity and hence the interpretive leitmotif serves to reinforce the priests legitimacy (134).

87. In the occurrences of this term in the Hebrew Bible, the geological meaning is not prominent but is always connoted; the boundary with metaphor is thus always ill-defined (cf. GesB¹⁷, 456, which does not distinguish between literal and metaphorical senses).

88. R. Whitekettle, 'Levitical Thought and the Female Reproductive Cycle: Wombs, Wellsprings and the Primeval World', *VT* 47 (1996): 376–91 (382–84), posits

In Prov. 5.18a מָקוֹר is a metaphor for the wife and parallels the phrase 'wife of one's youth' in v. 18b. The same passage (v. 16) describes the wife as a 'wellspring of life', applying metaphors of the natural world to woman.[89]

Ritual and mythological texts from Ugarit also use 'wellspring' metaphorically for the female genitalia. However, these texts do not use the term in connection with menstruation, but rather with male sexual desire. In a hymn to the goddess Nikkalu, (male) worshippers ask that woman's wellspring not be shut (*KTU* 1.13) and that it might exude water (*KTU* 1.11.24);[90] the hymn's general theme is the exaltation of sexual desire,[91] which in turn expresses the moon god's wish for female fertility. Thus a shared meaning for the image of wellspring for female genitalia emerges from Ugaritic texts and the Hebrew Bible, one that is primarily positive, Lev. 20.18 being an exception.

The term מָקוֹר in Leviticus 12 should therefore be understood as the anatomical locus of the flow of blood – the genital region or vulva.[92] The Mishnah develops the general image of wellspring for the internal female genitalia into a complicated system,[93] interpreting מָקוֹר spatially: depending on where the blood originates from.

How are we to translate the preposition מִן in the phrase 'the woman is pure *from* (מִן) the flow of her blood'? The preposition מִן indicates a direction: '(away) from/(out) from within'.[94] These meanings indicate a separating movement. The frequent causative use of the preposition

---

homology between 'womb' and 'wellspring'. He cites parallels from the ancient Near Eastern environment in which the female body corresponds to the natural world. This in turn leads him to see parallels between the primeval occurrences in Gen. 1–9 and the rituals of our chapters.

89. S. Schorch, *Euphemismen in der Hebräischen Bibel*, OBC 12, Wiesbaden: Harrassowitz, 2000), 154, classifies this term as 'specialized erotic vocabulary'.

90. Cf. J. de Moor, *An Anthology of Religious Texts from Ugarit* (Leiden: Brill, 1987), 137–43.

91. A secondary aim is the impregnation of the goddess; cf. U. Winter, *Frau und Göttin. Exegetische und ikonographische Studien zum weiblichen Gottesbild im alten Israel und in dessen Umwelt*, OBO 53 (Freiburg: Universitäts Verlag, 1983), 320, who emphasizes the fertility aspect.

92. Milgrom, *Leviticus 1–16*, 761: '*māqôr* here stands for the female pudenda'. Cf. Whitekettle, 'Levitical Thought', 382–83, who interprets it to mean 'womb'.

93. The Mishnah divides it into room, anteroom, and upper room (cf. *m. Nid.* 2.5 and Fonrobert, *Menstrual Purity*, 50–52).

94. Cf. GesB[17], 435; GK §119v; and Brockelmann, *Hebräische Syntax*, §111f.

('because', 'as a result of') rests on this meaning of 'going out, emerging from'.[95] The text says not only that the woman was cult-disabled because of her flow of blood, but also, and more importantly, that she is pure 'from out of' the flow, that is, as a result of it. In Leviticus 12 the period of impurity is accompanied by the blood of purification. The formulation is decisive: the woman is not purified 'of her blood flow',[96] but rather by means of or as a result of it (see my translation). After the specified time has passed, the woman is pure thanks to her 'spring', from deep within, or in medical terms, as a result of the residual bleeding of her womb.[97]

IV. *The LXX Rendering*

a. *Translation*

> [1] And the Lord spoke to Moses:
> [2] Speak to Israel's descendants and say to them: a woman who is inseminated and bears a male shall be impure for seven days, according to the separation of her menstruation is she unclean.
> [3] On the eighth day she shall circumcise the flesh of his foreskin.
> [4] Thirty-three days shall she remain sitting in her impure[98] blood. She shall touch nothing holy and shall not enter the holy place until the days of her purification are completed.
> [5] If however she bears a female, she shall be impure twice[99] seven days according to the menstruation. And sixty-six days shall she remain in her impure blood.
> [6] When the days of her purification for a son or for a daughter are fulfilled, then she shall bring an unblemished[100] yearling sheep for a whole burnt offering and a young dove or a turtle dove for sin[101] to the door of the tent of witness to the priest.

---

95. Cf. Gesenius/Kautzsch §119z.
96. Cf. Gane, *Cult and Character*, 112–20, who translates מִן here in a privative sense.
97. Cf. Rapp, 'The Heritage of Old Testament Impurity Laws', 32, who proposes an overarching meaning of מָקוֹר as postpartum bleeding (*lochia*).
98. A few manuscripts read 'holy' or 'pure' (see below).
99. The Greek text here refers back to the seven-day period of impurity for a male issue (v. 2) and draws attention to that the period for a female issue is twice as long.
100. Added by the LXX.
101. Cf. *Septuaginta Deutsch*, ed. W. Kraus (Stuttgart: Deutsche Bibelgesellschaft, 2009), 111, 'ein Für-(die)-Sünde', and *La Bible d'Alexandrie: Le Lévitique*, ed. P. Harlé and D. Pralon (Paris: Éditions du Cerf, 1988), 134, 'pour la faute'.

⁷ And he shall offer¹⁰² before the Lord and the priest shall perform the atonement ritual¹⁰³ for her and shall purify her from the source of her blood. This is the law for a woman who bears a male or female.

⁸ If however her hand should not find the necessary amount for a sheep, she shall take two turtledoves or two young doves, one for the whole burnt offering and one for sin, and the priest shall complete the atonement ritual for her, and she shall be made pure.¹⁰⁴

b. *Coining New Words*
The unusual verb form that the Hebrew text of v. 2 uses for conception, which pictures fertilization as self-reflexive, caused the LXX to coin a new word,¹⁰⁵ one that is used in connection with human reproduction in only one other place (Num. 5.28). Here the verb is in the aorist passive (σπερματισθῇ, third person feminine singular passive), implying that fertilization is a passive act for the woman: i.e., she receives the male seed. This formulation accords with that of the Samaritan, which renders the verb as a niphal.

c. *Remaining in Her Impure Blood*
The Hebrew text of Leviticus uses two different lexical roots to express purity and impurity. In contrast, the Greek uses the same root to express both concepts, impurity being derived from purity through the addition of a privative prefix.¹⁰⁶ The LXX uses the same terminology in Genesis (Gen. 7.2; 8.20) to designate pure (καθαρός) and impure (ἀκάθαρτος) animals. The translation into Greek of the roots טמא and טהר followed this pattern and thus laid the groundwork for the reception of the lexemes as a pair of opposites based on the same lexical stem. This occurred even though Greek possesses a distinct word meaning 'to declare impure' (μιαίνω)¹⁰⁷ and both ἀκάθαρτος and καθαρός connoted differing states of (physical) cleanliness. Most strikingly, in contrast to the MT, the LXX

---

102. The Greek lacks the personal pronoun.
103. Cf. K. Huber, *Untersuchungen über den Sprachcharakter des griechischen Leviticus* (Giessen: Töpelmann, 1916), 62: 'die Sühnegebräuche für jem. vollziehen', whereby in addition to the first περὶ (with genitive object for the person) the preposition may also be used a second time for the matter (cf. Lev. 4.35).
104. In contrast to the MT, the LXX here uses a passive verb form.
105. Cf. Liddell/Scott, 434: 'to conceive'.
106. In Hebrew, the privative sense can be expressed by the piel stem, so that the contrary meaning can seem to be inherent in the root.
107. This word is used, for example, to translate the impurity declaration in Lev. 13.3, 14.

speaks in vv. 4 and 5 of the woman's remaining in 'her impure blood' and not 'the blood of purification'. The LXX text thus obscures the Hebrew's ambiguity.[108] Interestingly, a few manuscripts that belong to the relatively late C-recension, which corrects the LXX according to the MT, as well as the Armenian translation, speak of the blood as being pure rather than impure.

Verses 5 and 6 establish a relation between the postpartum blood flow and purity through the phrase 'the days of her purification'. For טָהֹר the Greek chooses a term that alludes to the previously drawn analogy with menstruation, κάθαρσις being a *terminus technicus* for the latter.[109] Soranus speaks of menstruation as a catharsis: 'since, as some people say excreting blood from bodily excessive matter, it effects a purgation of the body. In most women the menstrual flux is pure blood',[110] i.e., not mixed with other substances. Classical antiquity did not associate menstruation with impurity as opposed to purification.[111]

In contrast to this stands the evidence of vv. 4, 5, which in the so-called primary textual witnesses speaks of impure blood. Nevertheless, among the uncial MSS, G (fourth or fifth century) as well as numerous minuscules speak of pure blood. Possibly the majuscule MSS that Wevers follows in his edition of the LXX understood the blood in terms of an impure secretion whose expulsion was necessary for purification and healing.

d. *According to the Days of Her Menstrual Separation*
The LXX applies a clearly cultic interpretation to the woman's condition during the second period of 33 or 66 days. Using the verb 'to sit'[112] this translation defines the condition as the impermissibility of touching holy things or entering into the holy place (v. 4b). The verb is one reason for understanding the woman's state as social and ritual separation. Her state is compared to 'the days of her menstrual separation'. דוה remains untranslated, and instead נִדָּה is rendered doubly with χωρισμός

---

108. I differ here from Wevers, *Notes on the Greek Text of Leviticus*, 166–67, who essentially denies this shift. Regarding the few Greek MSS that deviate from the LXX by using a form of καθαρός (in the pure blood), Wevers posits a misunderstanding (167), because for him, impurity is a key characteristic of menstruation (for further criticism of Wevers' position, cf. de Troyer, 'Blood', 58).

109. Cf. W. Pape, *Griechisch-Deutsches Handwörterbuch* (Braunschweig: Vieweg, 1880), 310: 'monatlicher Reinigung'.

110. Soranus Ephesius, *Soranus Gynecology* 16f IV.

111. Cf. Marsman, *Women in Ugarit*, 488: 'Already in Ancient Egypt menstruation was called a time of purification'.

112. In contrast to Heb. ישב, κάθημαι connotes inactivity and staying in one place.

and ἄφεδρος. χωρισμός means 'separation, secretion',[113] a semantic field that encompasses physiological secretion or exudation of blood as well as the woman's social isolation.[114] ἄφεδρος alludes to Lev. 15.19, which concerns the menstruating woman. This term was current in ancient medical treatises[115] and is derived from the verb ἑδράζω ('to sit'). It could be that language here mirrors women's social reality, as one (typical) comment on this term suggests: 'The term focuses on the isolation which the menstruant must undergo; it is a "sitting away from", an isolation'.[116] On the other hand, it is equally possible that writers and translators are attempting here to institute such a separation through their use of language.

e. *The Priest Shall Complete the Atonement Ritual*

In addition to its differing interpretation of the concept of impurity, the Greek text also introduces peculiarities into the purification ritual itself: in connection with the ritual procedure in v. 7 we read 'and the priest completes the atonement ritual for her and purifies her'. In other words, the LXX explicitly identifies the subject of the ritual action: the priest.[117] Besides this, in contrast to the MT's result-oriented approach ('and she is pure'), the LXX treats the declaration of purity as a discrete act on the priest's part. In v. 8, the future passive καθαρισθήσεται ('she shall be purified') has, in contrast to the MT, not such a strong declarative and confirmatory character.

---

113. Cf. Liddell/Scott, 2016. Elsewhere in the LXX the term appears in Lev. 18.19; Zech. 13.1; 3 Macc. 3.4; Matt. 3.4.

114. De Troyer, 'Blood', 60–62, sees a double meaning in this term. She therefore proposes to include both meanings in the translation: 'the days of the secretion of her menstruation', which denotes the discharge of blood, and 'he days of the isolation of her menstruation', which denotes her own (temporary) 'discharge' from the ritual community, whereby the Greek text leans toward the latter sense.

115. Cf. Dioscorides 2.75; Liddell/Scott, 287; A. Bailly, ed., *Dictionnaire grec – français* (Paris: Hachette, 1961), 16950; W. Bauer, *Griechisch-deutsches Wörterbuch*, 6th ed. (Berlin: de Gruyter, 1988), 250. *La Bible d'Alexandrie*, 134, differs, claiming that the term does not occur in Classical Greek.

116. Wevers, *Notes on the Greek Text of Leviticus*, 233. See also Bauer-Aland, *Wörterbuch*, 250, and Bailly, *Dictionnaire grec-français*, 323, '1. période menstruelle, pendant laquelle les femmes juives vivaient dans la retraite'.

117. The LXX clarifies the MT's ambiguity regarding the ritual agent in other passages as well in favor of the priestly agents, e.g., Lev. 1.5; 3.13; cf. Erbele-Küster, 'Reading as an Act of Offering'.

Whereas the emphasis in the LXX purification ritual lies on the priest, for the circumcision the woman who has given birth is responsible. Whereas the MT formulates passively, the LXX invites us to take the woman as the subject of the third person singular active verb,[118] suggesting that she performs a ritual procedure without the aid of a licensed expert.

The LXX also eliminates the parallelism that exists between the two types of sacrifice in the Hebrew. A lamb is offered as a whole burnt offering (εἰς ὁλοκαύτωμα), while a young dove or a turtle dove is brought for sin (περὶ ἁμαρτίας). Not only are different prepositions used for each offering, but also the Greek counterpart to עֹלָה (ὁλοκαύτωμα) is a distinctive technical term, whereas for חַטָּאת the LXX did not create its own term. The LXX frequently uses the genitive construction τὸ περὶ ἁμαρτίας ('that which pertains to trespass or guilt'[119]). The verb ἁμαρτάνω in Classical Greek means to 'miss the mark', 'commit an error'. As such it is similar in meaning to the Hebrew root חטא.[120] In contrast to the Hebrew חַטָּאת, the Greek term cannot designate both the trespass and the means by which the trespass is removed. The Greek may have employed the expression elliptically: 'disant "faute" au lieu de "sacrifice de faute"'.[121] Further, the animal itself is never called ἁμαρτία, but instead usually gift or animal.[122] In Lev. 12.6 the LXX renders 'a yearling sheep for a whole burnt offering and a young dove or turtledove for sin', which may be an abbreviation for a longer expression. In sum: while the Hebrew חַטָּאת can mean both the offense and the ritual for its removal, the Greek appears to connote only the former.

V. *The Origin of Cultic (Dis)ability and of the Gendered Body*

Our analysis of Leviticus 12 in the MT and the LXX highlighted how the body arises with the construction of gender. Since the rules distinguish two sexes from the very beginning of human existence along with two distinctive periods of cultic disability, gender is constructed with birth. This occurs independently of the child's body, but through the medium of the mother's body. It is the mother, after all, who experiences in her own

---

118. The verb form could also be translated impersonally.
119. Cf. Huber, *Untersuchungen über den Sprachcharakter*, 52, who sees the genitive as possessive.
120. Cf. S. Daniel, *Recherches sur le Vocabulaire du Culte dans la Septante* (Paris: Klincksieck, 1996), 308, 310.
121. Ibid., 305.
122. Cf. ibid., 302.

body whether she has borne a boy or a girl: the newborn's sex can be read in the differing durations of the mother's cultic disability, such that cultic disability becomes a sexual category, a form of gender pollution. Female corporeality is developed in three different ways: dichotomously to the other sex, in relation to the body of the child, and self-reflexively.

The human body's relationship with the holy differs according to sex: the male body has its God-relatedness inscribed upon it through circumcision. Over against that stands the dynamic that proceeds from the female body during menstruation, which creates temporary incompatibility with the realm of the holy. By using a metaphor from the realm of nature (a spring of water) for the female body in v. 3, the MT stresses the female body's innate activity and sets it in a positive light. Subsequent reception history often applied a reductive understanding to this dynamic, such that women became ontologically and not just metaphorically identified with nature and sexuality.

The LXX's reference to impure blood in Leviticus 12 became significant within the reception history in two ways: first, in contrast to the MT, the LXX divests the woman's blood of any cleansing role, and second, through its (body-)language it reduces impurity to a non-entity, to something privative, a negative condition. Likewise it minimizes the dynamics of the purification ritual wherein the woman has her share.

The wording in Lev. 12.3 LXX suggests that the woman is the one who performs the circumcision on her infant son. In such ritual acts as sacrifice and circumcision, as well as in its distinctive cultic terms, the LXX signals as well a distinctive ritual theology. With its translation of the Hebrew roots טמא and טהר as a pair of opposites based on the same lexical stem, the LXX created its own conception of purity, which subsequently wielded a powerful influence even over the understanding of the Hebrew text.

At the same time, not least through its peculiarities and its neologisms, the Greek version refers back to the Hebrew text. The Hebrew technical term נִדָּה, which analogizes the period after birth to menstruation, is rendered in the LXX as ἄφεδρος, a term that derives from classical medical literature. This analogy between the postpartum period and the period of monthly blood flow refers to the rules for the menstruating woman in Leviticus 15, which will be examined more closely in the next chapter. By specifying how the holy is to be protected from contact with impurity, the text sketches the sanctuary's topography. The category טָמֵא (ritually impure; endangering the cult; cultic disability) requires further inquiry (see Chapter 7).

Chapter 3

LEVITICUS 15

I. *Translation (Masoretic Text)*

¹ YHWH spoke to Moses and Aaron:
² Speak to Israel's descendants and say to them:
Every man[1] who has a discharge, his discharge being from his body,[2] he (it)[3] is ritually impure[4].
³ This is his ritual impurity in[5] his discharge, [whether] his member runs[6] with it or his member is obstructed because of[7] his discharge; his ritual impurity is this:
⁴ Every[8] bed upon which the one with the discharge lies is ritually impure. And every object on which he sits is ritually impure.

1. The expression אִישׁ אִישׁ can also be used gender-inclusively, as for exemple in Lev. 17.3, 10 and 24.5. A. B. Ehrlich, *Randglossen zur Hebräischen Bibel. Textkritisches, Sprachliches und Sachliches* (Hildesheim: Olms, 1968), 52, supposes that this is a case of dittography.

2. בָּשָׂר means primarily flesh or body in its entirety (v. 7), but it can also mean the male member, as in v. 3 (see Chapter 4).

3. Grammatically, the pronoun can refer either to the man or to the discharge.

4. Alternative translations are: 'not in compliance with the cult' and 'cult-disabled'; regarding the problem of translation of טמא, see Chapter 7.

5. Elliger, *Leviticus*, 191, translates the preposition בְּ as 'durch' ('through, on account of'); other possibilities are 'along with' or 'during'.

6. The *hapax* רִיר has a direct object. Accordingly the verb is understood as transitive or reflexive, in the sense of 'allow to flow' (cf. *HAL* 4:1147).

7. The preposition מִן here designates the cause or source (cf. Joüon and Muraoka, *A Grammar of Biblical Hebrew*, § 133e).

8. Cf. C. den Hertog, 'The Treatment of Relative Clauses in the Greek Leviticus', in *Helsinki Perspectives on the Translation Technique of the Septuagint: Proceedings of the IOSCS Congress in Helsinki 1999* (Helsinki: Finnish Exegetical Society; Göttingen: Vandenhoeck & Ruprecht, 2001), 65–97 (91–93), regarding the construction of כֹּל with a noun and a definite article in the singular; see also GK §127 b.c.

⁵ Every person who touches his bed shall wash his clothes and bathe in water, and he shall be ritually impure until evening.

⁶ And whoever sits upon the object upon which the one with the discharge has sat, that person shall wash his clothes and bathe in water, and he shall be ritually impure until evening.

⁷ Whoever touches the body of the one who has the discharge shall wash his clothes and bathe in water, and he shall be ritually impure until evening.

⁸ If the one who has the discharge spits upon someone who is ritually pure, then the latter shall wash his clothes and bathe in water, and he shall be ritually impure until evening.

⁹ Every saddle upon which the one with the discharge rides becomes ritually impure.

¹⁰ Whoever touches anything that is under him becomes[9] ritually impure until evening. Whoever picks them[10] up shall wash his clothes and bathe in water, and he shall be ritually impure until evening.

¹¹ Everyone whom the man with the discharge touches – unless he has rinsed[11] his hands with water – shall wash his clothes and bathe in water, and he shall be ritually impure until evening.

¹² Every clay pot that the man with the discharge touches shall be broken in pieces, and all wooden vessels shall be rinsed with water.

¹³ And when the man who has the discharge is pure from his discharge, he shall count seven days for himself for his cleansing, wash his clothes, bathe his body in living water, and he is ritually pure.

¹⁴ On the eighth day he shall bring two turtle doves or two doves and come into YHWH's presence, at the entrance of the tent of meeting and give them to the priest.

¹⁵ The priest shall prepare one as a purification offering and one as a burnt offering. The priest completes the purification ritual for him before YHWH because of[12] his discharge.

---

9. Usually the formula 'and he/she/it is impure until the evening' (vv. 5, 6, 7, 8, 10b, 11, 16, 18, 22, 27) is constructed with the *waw*-perfect, thereby expressing a consequence of what precedes. Here, by contrast, the imperfect is used, as also in vv. 19b and 23. This raises the question whether the different tenses point to different meanings. In vv. 4, 9, 20 the imperfect also appears, which, according to Milgrom, *Leviticus 1–16*, 910, 937, expresses the temporary nature of the impurity.

10. The grammatical reference of the plural pronominal suffix is ambiguous.

11. שָׁטַף also appears in v. 12 and Lev. 6.21. In contrast, the verbs רחץ ('to bathe') and כבס ('to wash') are used for the body in its entirety, or for a complete set of clothes.

12. The preposition מִן is understood here, as in v. 30, causatively (cf. Milgrom, *Leviticus 1–16*, 902–3; but see also Gane, *Cult and Character*, 116–19).

[16] A man out of whom an emission of semen comes shall bathe his entire body in water and shall be ritually impure until evening.

[17] Every garment or piece of leather which has the emitted semen upon it shall be washed in water,[13] and it shall be ritually impure until evening.

[18] A woman who lies[14] with a man[15] who has an emission of semen: both shall bathe in water, and they are ritually impure until evening.

[19] And a woman, when she has a discharge, her discharge being blood in[16] her body, seven days she is in her menstrual state.[17] Whoever touches her is ritually impure until evening.

[20] Everything upon which she lies in her menstrual state becomes ritually impure, and everything upon which she sits becomes ritually impure.

[21] Everyone who touches her bed shall wash his clothes and bathe in water, and he shall be ritually impure until evening.

[22] Everyone who touches any object upon which she sat shall wash his clothes and bathe in water, and he shall be ritually impure until evening.[18]

[23] If[19] something[20] is on the bed or the object upon which she sits, the person who touches it shall be ritually impure until evening.

[24] If however[21] a man lies with her, her menstrual state is communicated to him, and he shall be ritually impure for seven days. Every bed upon which he lies shall be ritually impure.

13. Den Hertog, 'Relative Clauses', 91, points out that the second half of the sentence is joined synthetically with the first (compare v. 32). He therefore translates: 'then it shall be washed'.

14. Regarding the construction of שכב with אֵת, see Chapter 5, section II.b.

15. The Samaritan reads 'her husband' and thereby suggests that the intercourse in question is a legitimate one.

16. In connection with the woman, the preposition בְּ is used; in v. 3b, by contrast, מִן is used for the man.

17. For an explanation of this translation, see Chapter 6, section I.c.

18. Cf. den Hertog, 'Relative Clauses', 90: 'And whosoever touches upon any vessel qualified by the fact that she...sat upon it, shall wash his clothes'.

19. The conditional construction of the sentence (וְאִם) is unique within the chapter.

20. The pronoun הוא (masculine singular) probably refers back to the objects; cf. D. P. Wright, *The Disposal of Impurity: Elimination Rites in the Bible and in Hittite and Mesopotamian Literature*, SBLDS 101 (Atlanta: Scholars Press, 1987), 192; and Milgrom, *Leviticus 1–16*, 936, 939. The Samaritan and the LXX read a feminine pronoun here and refer it to the woman; cf. Philip, *Menstruation and Childbirth*, 53–54.

21. An infinitive absolute in first position, in connection with a finite verb of the same root, can be understood adversatively within a conditional sentence; cf. Joüon and Muraoka, *A Grammar of Biblical Hebrew*, §123g.

²⁵ A woman, if her flow of blood²² flows many days outside the time of her menstrual state,
or if she continues to have a flow beyond the time of her menstrual state, during the entire time of her discharge of impurity she shall be as during her menstrual period; she is ritually impure.

²⁶ Every bed upon which she lies during the entire period of her discharge shall be for her as the bed of her menstrual state. Every object upon which she sits shall be ritually impure like the impurity of her menstrual state.

²⁷ Whoever touches these [things]²³ becomes ritually impure; he shall wash his clothes and bathe in water, and he shall be ritually impure until evening.

²⁸ And when she is pure from her discharge, then she shall count seven days for herself, and after that she is pure.

²⁹ On the eighth day she shall take two turtledoves or two doves and bring them to the priest at the entrance to the tent of meeting.

³⁰ The priest shall prepare one as a purification offering and the other as a burnt offering. The priest carries out the purification ritual for her before YHWH because of her ritually impure discharge.

³¹ You [pl.] shall separate²⁴ Israel's descendants from their ritual impurity, so that they do not die in their impurity, when they contaminate my dwelling that is in their midst.

³² This is the instruction concerning the one who has a discharge, and for him who has a seminal emission, such that he becomes ritually impure,

³³ and concerning her in the unstable condition²⁵ of her menstrual state, and concerning the one who has a discharge, whether male or female; and concerning a man who lies with²⁶ a ritually impure woman.

II. *Structural Symmetry as Gender Symmetry?*

Leviticus 15 defines how genital discharges make one ritually impure. It also stipulates a series of actions designed to limit, to the extent possible, the deleterious effects of these bodily secretions on the sanctuary. The

---

22. Here, instead of using a participle (as in v. 3 or v. 19) to describe the person, the Hebrew uses a construct chain to denote the discharge as something that the woman has or experiences.

23. The MT has a plural suffix here; some Hebrew MSS and the LXX read a singular.

24. The verb is unlikely to be a scribal error for a verb from the stem זהר (hiphil), 'to warn' (*pace* GesB¹⁷, 194; Elliger, *Leviticus*, 192, 199); rather, it derives from נזר (hiphil), 'to consecrate'. Cf. Levine, *Leviticus*, 98, 'you shall cause to avoid, to be separate from', and Milgrom, *Leviticus 1–16*, 945.

25. In many translations the adjective דָּוֶה is understood in terms of pathology (see Chapter 6, section II.a).

26. In contrast to the preceding verses, the verb here is used not with a direct object but with the preposition עִם.

instructions are to be passed on to Israel's descendants (v. 3a). The text describes various types of people who can be made impure by various bodily secretions and how such people should respond. The text seems to be addressed to laypeople, which makes one wonder if the instructions were in fact followed in everyday life.

The preeminent Hebrew term for the gendered body is בָּשָׂר, which can refer to flesh, the body as a whole, or more particularly, either the male member (cf. Exod. 28.42; Lev. 6.3; 12.3; 16.4) or the female genitalia (Lev. 15.19). Our discussion below will take into account this term's ambiguity.[27]

a. *Is the Introduction Gender-inclusive or Gender-specific?*[28]
The first case opens with the phrase אִישׁ אִישׁ כִּי, which may be understood either inclusively (everyone who) or gender-specifically (every man who). The word אִישׁ can refer to a man, male, husband, someone, or human being.[29] It is used inclusively in Gen. 9.5; 13.16; Exod. 16.29; Ps. 1.1.[30] In 1 Chr. 16.3, an inclusive and an exclusive use occur in the same verse. The phrase אִישׁ אִישׁ is distributive, generally meaning 'each man [everybody]' (cf. Lev. 17.3, 8, 10; 22.18; 24.15; Num. 9.10 passim).[31] In certain contexts the idiom can be gender-exclusive, as in Lev. 22.4 and Num. 5.12.[32]

Leviticus 15.3 is the only occurrence of this phrase within chs. 11–15. The meaning of specific instances of אִישׁ is usually inferred from context. However, in the case of one idiom, a purely formal deduction of the meaning 'man' is possible, namely, when אִישׁ is paired with אִשָּׁה ('woman'), as in Gen. 2.23; Exod. 21.28, 29; 36.6; Lev. 13.9, 38; 19.20; 20.13, 18, 27; Num. 5.6, 30, 31. Every occurrence in Leviticus 15 (vv. 2, 5, 16, 18, 24, 33) must be examined separately to determine whether אִישׁ

---

27. Regarding בָּשָׂר, see Chapter 4.
28. Regarding the gender-inclusive reading of the introductory formula, see Chapter 2, section III.a.
29. Cf. *HALOT* 1:41–42.
30. Cf. GesB[17], 32–33; Joüon and Muraoka, *A Grammar of Biblical Hebrew*, §147b, and C. Houtman, *Exodus*, HCOT (Kampen: Kok, 1993), 1:6–7 §3.2.2.
31. Cf. GK §123c, and E. König, *Syntax der Hebräischen Sprache, in Historisch-kritisches Lehrgebäude der hebräischen Sprache* (Leipzig: Hinrichs, 1897), §75, 76 and 88. Joüon and Muraoka, *A Grammar of Biblical Hebrew*, §135d, understand the repetition of the noun to express the plural; in Exod. 36.4, they translate אִישׁ אִישׁ as 'each man, everybody'.
32. See below Chapter 5; however in v. 2 in the construction כָּל־אִישׁ it could be understood gender neutrally.

is used generically or specifically. In v. 5, אִישׁ is clearly meant generically: 'every person who touches his bed' (i.e., the bed of the man with the discharge) shall perform the indicated procedures, not just 'every man'. By contrast, the context in v. 16 makes clear that אִישׁ means 'man', as is also the case in v. 18 and v. 24, where אִישׁ is paired with אִשָּׁה. In the closing formulation of v. 33, אִישׁ is again used inclusively, as the ensuing comment makes clear ('whether male or female'). But what about v. 2b?

The phrase אִישׁ אִישׁ כִּי in v. 2b is conditional, and it introduces a subordinate clause. This syntax occurs in three other places within the legal texts: in Lev. 24.15 it is used gender-inclusively; in Num. 5.12 it stands in contrast to אִשָּׁה (woman) and thus designates men only; and in Num. 9.10, as in Lev. 24.15, it is used inclusively.[33] The formula occurs without כִּי in 16 additional passages throughout the Hebrew Bible (Lev. 17.3, 8, 10, 13; 18.6; 20.2, 9; 22.4, 18; Num. 1.4, 44; 4.19, 49; 1 Kgs 20.20; Ezek. 14.4, 7). Analogous formulas that encompass both genders occur in the introductory notices to the various types of sacrifice: נֶפֶשׁ כִּי (Lev. 4.2; 5.1, 4, 15, 21; 7.21) and אָדָם כִּי (Lev. 1.2).

Some have speculated that the introductory formula in Lev. 15.2 originally encompassed both genders, thus lending support to a one-body model.[34] This gender-neutral preface would then lead into a brief section on seminal emissions followed by a treatment of gender-specific discharges of women, such that the female body would constitute a special case of the model. However, in the Masoretic version, אִישׁ אִישׁ clearly covers men only, as is evident not least from the chapter's structure, in which a section devoted to men (vv. 3–17) is offset by one (v. 19 and following) devoted to women.

Women are mentioned for the first time in v. 18, in connection with sexual intercourse with men. This verse thus serves as a bridge[35] between the two gender-distinct sections. The instruction is binding on both sexes, even though it is addressed only to the male partner. The section on women displays a similarly peculiar rhetorical structure: the precepts are not addressed directly to women, but rather focus on third parties who can be rendered impure by her.

---

33. M. Fishbane, *Biblical Interpretation in Ancient Israel* (Oxford: Clarendon, 1985), 103, sees this construction as typical for the holiness texts.

34. Cf. Elliger's surmise in *Leviticus*, 193.

35. Cf. Milgrom, *Leviticus 1–16*, 904–5, and R. Whitekettle, 'Leviticus 15.18 Reconsidered: Chiasm, Spatial Structure and the Body', *JSOT* 48 (1991): 31–45. Noth, *Das dritte Buch Mose*, 97, and Elliger, *Leviticus*, 196, see the verse as a later addition.

Many commentators have detected a concentric and chiastic structure in the chapter (see Table 2).[36] On this theory, the middle is made up of section B (seminal emissions, v. 16–17) together with section B' on menstruation (vv. 19–24). Surrounding these are the so-called pathological forms of the same conditions (A/A'), although it must be noted that the text itself recognizes no such distinction. First come the abnormal genital discharges of the man (A, vv. 2b–15), balanced by the abnormal blood flows of the woman (A', vv. 25–30). Two instructions for men are thus counterposed to two for women. The introductory verses (vv. 1–2a) portray the chapter as a speech by YHWH to Moses and Aaron. The coda (vv. 31–33a) explains why it is important to draw lines of separation. Finally, the categories of person for whom the chapter is relevant are listed (v. 33b).

Table 2

O		vv. 1–2a: Introduction
	A	vv. 2b–15: Male genital discharges
	B	vv. 16–17: Seminal emissions
	C	v. 18: Sexual intercourse
	B'	vv. 19–24: Menstruation
	A'	vv. 25–30: Abnormally prolonged uterine bleeding
O		vv. 31–33: Conclusion

b. *Does the Chapter's Structure Imply Equality of the Sexes?*
If this theory of the chapter's structure is accepted, then structural symmetry could be taken to imply ontological symmetry. Accordingly, some have construed the chapter as a gender-political declaration of equality.[37] However, although the terminology for men's and women's bodies is roughly analogous, the analogy is not perfect. Further, men appear in v. 24 in the instructions concerning women's menstrual flows, in connection with sexual intercourse.

---

36. Cf. Milgrom, *Leviticus 1–16*, 931; Levine, *Leviticus*, 93; D. Klee, 'Menstruation in the Hebrew Bible' (Ph.D. thesis, Boston University, 1998), 66–69; K. O'Grady, 'The Semantics of Taboo', in de Troyer et al., eds., *Wholly Woman*, 1–28, 4; D. Ellens, 'Menstrual Impurity and Innovation in Leviticus 15', in de Troyer et al., eds., *Wholly Woman*, 29–44 (32–35), and *Women in the Sex Texts*, 47–72; Rapp, 'Old Testament Impurity Laws', 34–35; Luciani, *Sainteté et Pardon I*, 74–76; R. Péter-Contesse, *Lévitique 1–16*, CAT 3a (Geneva: Labor et Fides, 1993), and *Lévitique*, 237, speaks of 'presque symétrique'.

37. Klee, 'Menstruation', 69, speaks of a 'gender-balanced way'. Ellens, 'Menstrual Impurity', 32, states pointedly: 'The structure pictures the woman equal to the man'. See also Ellens, *Women in the Sex Texts*, 51: 'Thus, structural symmetry constitutes gender symmetry'.

In fact, the chapter's organization is less obvious than the interpreters would have us believe. The text contains no category for illness. The chapter itself does not classify in this way, which has not stopped exegetes from positing the distinction between 'normal' and 'abnormal', which denigrates the latter and sets up a (hygienic) standard.[38] Indeed, the use of the same technical term (זוֹב) for differently composed discharges from both male and female genitalia makes clear that the Hebrew text operates with physiological categories that are incompatible with modern medical concepts. The term is differentiated by grammatical gender in its application to men (זָב, v. 3) versus women (זָבָה, v. 19), with the latter term receiving further elaboration. The rough gender parallelism between v. 3 and v. 19 conceals important differences in detail that the text establishes.

The terms for an unusual penile discharge (A) and for ejaculation (B) do not overlap, whereas the woman's irregular blood flow (A′) is expressly related to and compared with menstruation (B′). This link between B′ and A′ is obscured by a simple chiastic model that connects A′ only to A. In fact, the model depicted in Figure 2 fails in several respects: on the one hand, the term for discharge (זב) is supposed to be the unifying concept, yet the male genital discharge that this term designates represents precisely the not usual case (A), while the male's ordinary seminal discharge (B) is described using an entirely different term. The sole point that all the chapter's secretions seem to have in common is that they issue from the male or female flesh (בָּשָׂר), that is, the genitalia. The woman's regular discharge of blood in v. 19 (B′) would seem to represent a species of the genus epitomized by the man's irregular genital discharge (A), in that it is a discharge of blood in the woman's body, as the verse states.

The text also introduces a specific term for the woman's condition: נִדָּה (*niddah*). Verses 25–27 speak of 'a discharge of her blood' (זוֹב דָּמָהּ) that extends past the period of the *niddah*. The text correlates the woman's irregular discharge of blood (A′) not only with the man's irregular discharge (A) but also with the *niddah* (B′). These analogies and connections run through the entire chapter (see Table 3). Only ejaculation (C) in vv. 16–17 is not set in connection with other parts. The usual male genital discharge, semen, is not described by the term זוֹב. The question whether the chapter promotes gender symmetry should be judged from the chapter's own perspective. In the section on women's genital discharges,

---

38. Fonrobert, *Menstrual Purity*, 44, suggests that we think in terms of 'common' versus 'uncommon'. The only normative point of reference that the text suggests is the regular or normal duration of menstrual bleeding, in comparison with which the woman's extraordinary discharge of blood is defined.

the gaze turns quickly away from women and toward their surroundings, which become impure through contact with her.[39]

In what follows I will examine the differences between the ways the various discharges are described, in order to ascertain the extent to which gender symmetry does or does not prevail in the exposition. The connections that Leviticus 15 establishes are more multi-layered than a simple ABB′A′ relationship would suggest (see Table 3).

Table 3

O		Introduction: Persons with a discharge (זָב)
	A	Instructions for a male with a discharge (זָב)
	B	Instructions concerning ejaculation
	A′	Instructions for a female with a discharge (זָבָה): *niddah*
	A″	Instructions for a discharge that lasts longer than *niddah*

III. *Microstructure*

a. *YHWH Spoke to Moses and to Aaron*

In v. 1, YHWH addresses not just Moses but also Aaron, i.e., the priestly family.[40] By contrast, the decrees in ch. 12 are directed solely to Moses. This introduction (vv. 1–2a), together with the closing exhortation (v. 31), represents a literary framework. However, its narrative structure is eclipsed by the chapter's non-narrative style. Nevertheless, the writer or editor makes a clear attempt to set the decrees in a narrative framework.

b. *A Man Who Has a Discharge*

In literal translation, Lev. 15.2 reads: 'if he is a discharger, his member is discharging, impure is he'. With the help of the masculine participle of the verb 'to flow' (זוּב) and the imperfect of the verb 'to be', the passage addresses a condition that will obtain in the future.[41] The discharge's nature is not further specified, but the preposition מִן ('out from') makes clear that the secretion oversteps the body's boundaries. The contrast of this with the phrase 'in her body' (v. 19) makes the image of the gendered body clear in each case.

---

39. Rapp, 'Old Testament Impurity Laws', 34–35, stresses that we see the woman from the masculine perspective (i.e., from the perspective of the text), and that the woman therefore is perceived only as the one who contaminates.

40. See Chapter 2, section II.a.

41. Cf. Joüon and Muraoka, *A Grammar of Biblical Hebrew*, §121d and GK §107a.

The pronoun in the sentence 'he [it] is ritually impure' can refer either to the discharge or to the man. This expression, used frequently in Leviticus 13 in connection with skin eruptions, serves as a declaratory formula, in contrast to imperfect forms of the cognate verb טמא ('to be impure'), which characterize a temporary, often precisely delimited period of impurity (cf. Lev. 12.2; 15.4).[42] Using this formula, a priest declares a person whom he has examined to be impure (cf. Lev. 13.15, 36). In ch. 15, however, the context is different.

The question whether the person or the discharge is being declared unclean gives rise to the more general question: Does the text differentiate between the two? After all, the Hebrew speaks of the person as being discharging. The text should probably be understood in this double sense.

Verse 3 opens with the peculiar idiom 'this is his impurity (טֻמְאָתוֹ) in his discharge', an assertion that is expanded upon in vv. 4–6. In between (v. 3b) comes a more detailed, physiological description of the types of discharge that are meant. Leviticus 5.3 and 7.21 use the same noun (טֻמְאָתוֹ) as a general term for impurity caused by contact with impure humans or animals. The noun as used at the beginning and end of Lev. 15.3 seems similarly abstract. Quite possibly, the verse starts over with a kind of resumptive repetition stressing the cultic state of impurity.

c. *A Woman, When She Has a Discharge*

Verse 19 signals a clear break: it inaugurates a series of instructions about flows of blood from women. The phrase 'her discharge being blood in her body' (v. 19) makes use of the general term for (male) genital discharges from vv. 2–3. The opening of each set of instructions is formulated similarly, using the word for 'man (person)' or 'woman' followed by כִּי. However, the doubling in the phrase אִישׁ אִישׁ כִּי ('a man [person] who') stands out, since by analogy with 'a woman who' (אִשָּׁה כִּי), a simple 'a man who' (אִישׁ כִּי) would have sufficed. Does the phrase אִישׁ אִישׁ therefore have an inclusive ring after all, even though its position in the chapter conduces to an exclusively masculine interpretation? The feminine grammatical forms in v. 19 underscore the sex. The text finds it necessary to specify that the woman's discharge consists of blood. The substance of the secretion having been named, its materiality enters the field of view.

---

42. Cf. Milgrom, *Leviticus 1–16*, 907: 'The adjective is used for indefinite periods of impurity'. Cf. ibid., 648.

The linguistic symmetry between male and female bodies is further disrupted by the following detail: the woman's discharge is '*in* her body' while the man's comes 'from (out of) his body' (v. 3b). The prepositions conjure up different body images:[43] for the woman, the preposition בְּ connotes an interior space,[44] while for the man, the preposition מִן stresses separation and externalization, the establishment of distance from the body.

The text characterizes the female body more precisely than the male, describing the woman's condition during her discharge of blood with a technical term: 'she is in her *niddah*'. This term has been coined to describe the condition of a menstruating woman. Further, it probably has been transferred to describe the woman's condition after birth.

d. *A Man Who Has a Seminal Emission*

The Hebrew text describes in v. 16 a man's seminal emission with the phrase 'to issue from' (יָצָא מִן) and with the construct chain שִׁכְבַת־זֶרַע, a technical term associated with the literary layer to which the chapter belongs.[45] The substance of the emission is called 'seed'. Commentators often render the expression שִׁכְבַת־זֶרַע as 'outpouring of semen'[46] or 'flowing of semen',[47] thereby implicitly accepting the derivation of the noun שִׁכְבָה from a verbal root meaning 'to pour out'. Does the verb יצא imply that only involuntary emissions are meant?[48] The case opens as follows: 'A man out of whom comes an emission of semen' (v. 16a). Compared to the opening of the chapter, which focused on an unspecified genital discharge (vv. 2–3), this passage describes the seminal emission in completely different terms. The words for (male) flesh (בשר, i.e., 'member') and for the physiological process of secretion (זוב, 'to flow')

---

43. This difference is obscured in most translations and commentaries: Elliger, *Leviticus*, 191, renders both prepositions identically. Milgrom, *Leviticus 1–16*, 934, likewise translates both prepositions the same ('from'). Fonrobert, *Menstrual Purity*, 47–49, traces the way in which rabbinic interpretation, reflecting on this preposition, developed a specific understanding of the female body.

44. KBL³, 101, notes that in geographical descriptions, בְּ can mean 'from... away', but that technical sense does not apply to this passage. בְּ here has a local meaning and designates the area or condition in which someone or something finds itself (cf. *HALOT*, 104, 'basic meaning local and instrumental, in at').

45. The term occurs only in Lev. 15.16, 17, 18, 32; 19.20; 22.4; and Num. 5.13 (cf. Chapter 5, section II.b).

46. Milgrom, *Leviticus 1–16*, 927.

47. Levine, *Leviticus*, 96.

48. Cf. Milgrom, *Leviticus 1–16*, 926–27.

are absent. In the subsequent purification instructions, the man is told that he must wash all his flesh. It appears that the word 'all' (כֹּל) was inserted to contrast with v. 3, where 'flesh' denotes only the male member, and thereby to make clear that in v. 16 the entire body is meant.

Curiously, the woman's monthly loss of blood is described in the same terms as the male genital discharge that opens the chapter, but the man's seminal emission is not. Commentaries that characterize the unspecified זוֹב of vv. 2b–15 as pathological further heighten its distinctness from the seminal emission. The lack of connection is sometimes explained in literary-critical terms, such as by positing that the passage on seminal emissions was a later insertion.[49]

e. *Bleeding Beyond the Period of* Niddah

The MT indicates a break between v. 24 and v. 25 with the insertion of פ, known as *parashah*, a scribal section divider. The text resumes in v. 25 with two new cases, each of which is introduced with כִּי:

a. A woman, *if* her flow of blood flows many days outside the time of her menstruation,
b. or *if* she continues to have a flow beyond the time of her menstrual state.

Most commentaries take these two formulations to be descriptions of the same medical condition. Repeated reference is made to the *niddah* (נִדָּה) of v. 19. The text does not diagnose the cause of the prolonged flow of blood (v. 25); rather, the sole criterion is that the bleeding lasts longer than the *niddah* or occurs outside of it.

The intensity of the discharge is expressed through the use of a finite verb, 'her discharge of blood flows' (v. 25a), rather than through a participle, as was done in v. 3 and v. 19 (he/she is discharging). Note that the word denoting the discharge is the subject of this sentence, since the finite verb agrees with it in gender. In the next sentence, by contrast, the woman is the subject of the finite verb, 'she discharges' (v. 25b), which is either intransitive or has 'blood' or 'discharge' as its understood object. The subtle differences from v. 19 (the bleeding of the *niddah*) are instructive. While in v. 19 the material of the discharge is identified simply as blood, v. 25a uses the expression 'her bloody discharge' (זוֹב דָּמָהּ). Parallel to this is the expression 'the discharge of her impurity' (זוֹב טֻמְאָתָהּ, v. 25b), a formulation that suggests that טֻמְאָה ('impurity') is understood in a

---

49. Cf. Elliger, *Leviticus*, 194–96.

material sense.⁵⁰ In contrast to the man's unspecified 'discharge', which necessitates the purification ritual in v. 15, for the woman the necessitating condition is 'her impure discharge'.

The construct chain in v. 26, 'the impurity of her menstrual state', is the only place in Leviticus where the terms נִדָּה and טֻמְאָה are combined in this way. Together with later (post-biblical) uses of the term נִדָּה, this combination favored the identification of menstruation with impurity.

The phrase 'outside the time of her menstrual state' seems to imply a physiological connection between menstruation and the prolonged issue of blood. The text constructs female physiology in such a way that *niddah* is the reference point for various types of bleeding.

f. *Whoever Touches Something...Shall Be Ritually Impure*

The text explains in detail how impure bodies and objects communicate their impurity, and it offers corresponding countermeasures. In contrast to those afflicted with skin disease in Leviticus 13, those with the described genital discharges are not required to separate themselves from the community. They are allowed to remain within the inhabited area.⁵¹

For the man with a discharge (vv. 4a, 4b, 5c, 9, 11, 12) and the woman with uterine bleeding (v. 20), the regulations are cast in the form of subordinate clauses or introduced by participles (vv. 6, 7, 10, 19b, 21). The formulations about the woman in her *niddah* presuppose those about the (male) discharging person.⁵² The objects that can be contaminated are, in the case of the woman, listed in a generalized way. The regulation for the unusually long flow of blood also uses the particle כֹּל (v. 26) and mentions, as in the case of the discharging person, the bed and generally all objects that can be sat upon. In this way, what is said about the man with a discharge is repeated. The objects are set in relation to the period of the *niddah* and cast in terms of the preceding instructions: every bed is 'as the bed of *niddah*' and every object is 'impure as in the impurity of her *niddah*'. And although purification procedures have already been described, v. 27 re-states them, though with the addition of the summary formulation, 'whoever touches these [things]'. This is in contrast to the sections on genital discharges and the *niddah* itself, which contain

---

50. The equation of טֻמְאָה ('impurity') with a substance that induces impurity is misleading, since it reduces impurity to material tarnishment (cf. Chapter 7, section I).
51. By contrast, Num. 5.2–3 prescribes that those having a discharge be removed from the camp.
52. Cf. Fishbane, *Biblical Interpretation*, 170–72, who shows how a detailed list within a law can be generalized through the addition of כֹּל.

separate purification instructions for each object that can be contaminated through lying, sitting, or touching. The masculine plural suffix in v. 27 refers back to the named things – the bed and other objects. Within the earlier instructions, the point of view changes back and forth between that of the contaminator, i.e. the man with a discharge (זָב, vv. 8, 9, 11, 12) and that of his surroundings (vv. 6, 7, 10).

From the text we can distinguish three categories of cultic contamination:[53]

1. The ritual impurity of the male (v. 3) or female (v. 25)[54] dischargers.
2. The impurity that the discharger communicates to other persons or objects.
3. The impurity that such objects can communicate to third parties who touch them.

The types of contact through which the discharging male and the menstruating female contaminate other persons or things are expressed through the verbs lie (vv. 4, 20, 26), sit (vv. 4, 6, 22, 23), touch (vv. 10, 12), and spit (v. 8), the last being used only for the male. Through sitting (vv. 6, 20, 23) or touching (vv. 7, 10, 11, 12, 19b, 21, 22, 23, 27) as well as picking up (v. 10) another person can draw the impurity onto himself. This is the so-called mediated (or secondary) impurity.

The regulations challenge readers, both male and female, to an intertextual interpretation, since in order to apply the instructions, it appears necessary to read individual verses in connection with the entire chapter. The purity rules do not merely command physical actions; they also open up a space for interpretive activity that is framed by the following questions:

Are the regulations pertaining to the man with a genital discharge applicable to all cases in the chapter, since they are the longest and most detailed? They alone, for example, specify what should be done with contaminated objects. Pottery that has been touched by the man with the

---

53. Cf. Wright, *The Disposal of Impurity*, 181–195. Milgrom, *Leviticus 1–16*, 910 speaks of three degrees of contamination. Levine, *Leviticus*, 94–95, cites the two rabbinic distinctions: the originator (Av ha-tuma'ah, 'a primary category of impurity') and the mediator (ri'shon le tuma'ah, 'impurity of the first order'). J. E. Hartley, *Leviticus*, WBC 2 (Dallas: Word, 1992), 206, subsumes the contamination of third parties under 'secondary kinds of uncleanness'.

54. Note that the text does not explicitly state that the menstruating woman is ritually impure. Rather, this is deduced from the statement about the man and his discharge in v. 3.

discharge is to be shattered, and wooden vessels are to be rinsed out.[55] Why must a person who has touched the bed of the man with the discharge wash his clothes (v. 5) when the person who sits upon a contaminated object is not required to do the same (v. 6)? Clothes-washing is also not explicitly commanded in connection with the touching of contaminated riding gear (v. 9). Is washing implicitly commanded, being derivable from other instructions?[56] Why are saddles specifically mentioned, when v. 5 has already stated that every object upon which the impure discharger sits is ritually impure? The subsequent statement that 'whoever touches anything that is under him becomes ritually impure' (v. 10a) also seems redundant in this context. Why is it emphasized that whoever picks such an object up must wash his clothes (v. 10b)? Why is clothes-washing required after touching an object contaminated by a menstruating woman (v. 22), when the same is not commanded for a person who sits upon an object on which the man with a genital discharge has sat?

These questions demonstrate the difficulty of deciding how much weight to give to individual instructions. To the extent that our analysis shows the ordinances in vv. 4–12 to be fundamental, the impression grows that the male with a discharge represents the norm of which the menstruating woman is a special case. In recent scholarship it has been observed widely that the text on a structural level leaves questions open. This phenomena has been called by literary theorists 'gap' or 'blank'.[57] Jonathan Klawans speaks of 'gap-ridden biblical rituals'.[58]

One may suggest this reflects a gender asymmetry, i.e., the impurity communicated by a menstruating woman is more serious than that communicated by a man with a genital discharge. Similarly, the lack of a mention of saddles in the section on women would express a gender asymmetry in the everyday life of men and women.[59] However, the Hebrew Bible mentions women who ride: in Gen. 24.61, Rebekah and her maids ride

---

55. Cf. the handling of textiles affected in Lev. 13.47–59, where washing and burning are prescribed.

56. This is Wright's contention in *The Disposal of Impurity*, which he illustrates with diagrams of chains of contamination and removal of contamination.

57. On the concept and function of informational gaps, cf. Erbele-Küster, 'Reading as an Act of Offering'.

58. Klawans, *Purity, Sacrifice, and the Temple*, 52.

59. Horses were not widely used as mounts or as beasts of burden or draft in the ancient Near East (cf. Bienkowski, 'Horse', in Bienkowslki, ed., *Dictionary of the Ancient Near East*, 147). Even camels were domesticated only toward the end of the first millennium BCE.

upon camels behind Abraham's servant; in 1 Sam. 25.20, 42 and 2 Kgs 4.24 we read about wealthy women who act on their own initiative and who ride (רכב) animals.[60] A seminal emission causes the man having it, as well as any textiles or leather articles that come in contact with it, to be impure until evening (vv. 16–17). Rather pragmatically, the text directs that the man should wash his entire body, but only those articles upon which the seminal fluid has directly fallen must also be washed. Why is nothing said about the spread of ritual contamination from such a man, apart from sexual intercourse, which ritually disqualifies both man and woman (v. 18) and requires a bath?

In the regulations for a woman with a discharge, the provisions that apply to a man are not simply repeated. If the text had wanted to express gender symmetry, it could have used the expression כַּאֲשֶׁר,[61] which can be found in other ritual texts (e.g. Lev. 4.10; cf. Deut. 22.26) as shorthand for 'as was explained above, so too should be done here'. Hence interpretation is necessary to determine the relevance of the regulations for the discharging male to the woman. The text does not require a menstruating woman to bathe in water after her *niddah*. Nor is there any mention in Leviticus 15 of a *mikveh* as a place for post-menstrual purification. That is part of the post-biblical exegesis of the chapter.[62]

Our observations make clear that the structural details of Leviticus 15 do not suggest any coherent system. For example, the perspective changes from verse to verse with no discernible pattern. Touching a man who has a discharge makes one impure and requires that one wash one's body and clothes (v. 7). Then the perspective changes: in v. 8, the man who has the discharge actively contaminates another person by spitting upon him or her. In v. 11, the man with the discharge is once again the active party:

---

60. Recent interpreters of Lev. 12 and 15 have attempted to deduce gender norms for daily activities, construing the absence of riding gear in the discussion of women's discharges to mean that women either did not ride or did so only seldom, a fact that would have made it unnecessary to mention of this item in connection with women. But everyday life was not so segregated: according to biblical texts women were riding camels or sitting on them. The purity regulations discussed here heighten the comedy of Gen. 31.34–36, in which Rebekah, sitting on a camel saddle, explains her failure to rise with reference to her menstrual period (cf. Chapter 6, section III.b).

61. Regarding the use of this formula, cf. Fishbane, *Biblical Interpretation*, 216–17.

62. Philip, *Menstruation and Childbirth*, 51. A different view is taken by H. K. Harrington, *The Impurity Systems of Qumran and the Rabbis: Biblical Foundations*, SBL Dissertation Series 143 (Atlanta: Scholars Press, 1993). She argues that these matters are implicit in the biblical text and can reliably be deduced from it.

he can transmit the condition of cultic impurity to another person through touch, 'if he has not washed his hands'. Immediately following the introduction to the section on the menstruating woman (v. 19a), the text directs our attention to the effect that such a woman has on others: 'Whoever touches her becomes ritually impure' (v. 19b). The subsequent verses (20–22) express in concise and general fashion how ritual disablement can be communicated by contact with a menstruating woman or with objects upon which she has sat. Verses 23 and 24 both constitute special cases of general rules laid out in vv. 20–22.

Alongside the gaps, which evoke a multiplicity of questions, there are also attempts of systematic elaboration. The instruction, 'Every saddle upon which the one with the discharge rides becomes ritually impure' (v. 9) elaborates something already stated,[63] namely in v. 4b, which already states that everything upon which the man with a discharge sits becomes impure. Even more emphasis is placed on this detail: v. 10 summarizes by repeating the same idea in different words: 'Whoever touches anything that is under [the man with a discharge] becomes ritually impure'.

The way that v. 23 describes the communication of impurity is peculiar: the condition of impurity can be transmitted to others not just through their touching the menstruating woman's bed (v. 21), but also through contact with an object that is lying on the bed. Nevertheless, as the participial construction makes clear, the menstruating woman must be sitting on the bed at the same time. The chain of transmission thus has two intermediate links: the bed and the object that lies upon it. The direct contact between the bed and the source of the impurity, the menstruating woman, effects a union between her and the bed for as long as she stays on it, so that the object on the bed can itself communicate impurity. Although this is a case of tertiary contamination, both (the bed and the object) constitute a field of impurity in that moment.

The case of v. 24 introduces a further elaboration:[64] sexual intercourse with a menstruating woman causes a man to be impure not just until the evening – that is a given for intercourse outside the woman's period. Rather, like the woman in *niddah*, the man becomes impure for seven days, since, as the peculiar formulation states, 'her *niddah* shall come upon him'.[65] The logic of v. 23, among other considerations, suggests

---

63. Cf. Elliger's literary-critical analysis in *Leviticus*, 191–92.

64. I interpret אם as opening a subordinate case in line with Joüon and Muraoka, *A Grammar of Biblical Hebrew*, §167e.

65. The man's impurity lasts seven days, irrespective of how much or how little of the woman's own seven-day *niddah* has transpired at the time of intercourse. In other words, the ritual condition of *niddah* is transferred to him in its entirety.

that the man himself can then also communicate impurity. He becomes a primary source of impurity, and we can assume that the same rules apply to him as to the menstruating woman.[66] As an example of this phenomenon, v. 24b stipulates that 'every bed upon which he lies shall be ritually impure'. A man upon whom the condition of נִדָּה has come can himself cause contamination (v. 24), although the text leaves open how far the chain of contamination can extend.

The treatment of the rules governing a woman with an unusually prolonged flow of blood shows that they are formulated against the backdrop of the preceding instructions.[67] The indeterminate length of the bleeding is expressed in a highly formal manner. The text states laboriously and in two different ways that the bleeding in question goes beyond the usual period of the woman's *niddah*. The statement that every bed and every object shall be as it is during the *niddah* could imply that all of the preceding regulations about secondary contamination and its removal (such as in v. 23) apply. Accordingly, some Hebrew manuscripts as well as the LXX read the pronominal suffix at the beginning of v. 27 as feminine singular rather than masculine plural (i.e., as בָּהּ rather than בָּם), interpreting the verse as a new case in which the matter is direct contact with the woman herself, not as a further development of the theme of contact with contaminated beds or objects.

The apparent elaborations in vv. 9, 10, 23 and 24 seem like a first effort at halakhic exegesis. They indicate a direction that was taken by later interpreters, who derived ever more detailed systems out of the seemingly incomplete regulations. The internal development of the text itself draws inferences from the existing rules for purification and extends them into the gaps. At first sight it might serve the practicability of the regulations. However, upon closer scrutiny it becomes visible that it serves the logic of the impurity system. If one takes the gaps seriously, they imply a certain understanding of the text's genre. According to Gorman, 'The informational gaps in the texts might be an indication that the texts were written for writing and hearing, not for enactment'.[68] Hence, rather than being a ritual agenda, they have a programmatic utopian character, as will be explored in the final chapter.

---

66. Milgrom, *Leviticus 1–16*, 941, maintains that 'all of the regulations concerning the menstruant' apply to him. For a different opinion, cf. Klee, *Menstruation*, 54–55.

67. Cf. Elliger's analysis of redactional layers, *Leviticus*, 191–92, 195.

68. F. Gorman, 'Pagans and Priests: Critical Reflections on Method', in *Perspectives in Purity and Purification in the Bible*, ed. N. Meshel et al., LHBOTS 474 (New York: T&T Clark International, 2008), 96–110 (108) (see Chapter 8).

g. *Every Person, Who…, Shall Wash His or Her Clothes*
The clothes that must be washed are not only those that have come into direct contact with the impurity, but all of them. The clothes of a person who has touched the man with a genital discharge must be washed whether the contact occurred through the clothes or directly to the skin. These and similar observations make it clear that the impurity's material aspect is only superficially decisive. For example, the person who sits upon an impure object (v. 6) must bathe, but it is not mentioned (as in vv. 5. 7 *passim*) that the clothes must also be washed. In ch. 15 the concern is clearly not about the danger of infection from a man with a genital discharge. The passage of a day, the washing of one's body and clothes, fulfill within the purity regulations a different function than a medical or hygienic one, since in this chapter, pathological discharges rank next to seminal ones. Danger of infection is conceivable only through the male's genital discharge, whose nature is not further specified. At no point does it appear to be assumed that some hypothetical cause of the discharge can be transmitted; only the ritual impurity can be communicated. The man with the discharge is not viewed as a sick person, but rather as a (temporarily disabled) participant in the cult. On the other hand, the regulations are formulated relatively independently of the sanctuary and the priests. Only in the case of the man with the discharge (vv. 13–15) and of the woman with the prolonged flow of blood (vv. 28–30) is a purificatory rite involving sacrifice demanded. The menstruant is required neither to bathe nor to bring an offering.

The washing of clothes and of wooden vessels, the shattering of clay vessels – probably because of the porosity of the material – and the bathing of one's body therefore cannot be ascribed to hygienic materialism. Leviticus 15.13 (cf. Lev. 14.5, 6, 50, 51, 52 and Num. 19.17) demands water of a particular sort: namely, living (i.e., flowing) water, which possesses a heightened effectiveness.

The symbolic character of the time that must pass before a person can be declared ritually pure is reflected in the number of days: either one or seven. The purity regulations think in spatial and temporal categories: a person or object is impure if it must be kept at a distance from the cult for a specified length of time, because it threatens the sacred.[69] In those cases where a sacrificial offering is required, the priest's declaration seals the worshiper's reintegration into the cult.

---

69. Cf. Wright, *The Disposal of Impurity*, 164, 273, and Douglas, *Leviticus as Literature*, 150.

h. *A Woman Who Lies with a Man*

Verse 18 deals with the simultaneous impurity of a man and a woman due to sexual intercourse. The verse constitutes the imaginative center of the chapter.[70] Only at this place in the chapter do we find a plural verb form and a statement that encompasses both sexes:

> Both shall bathe in water, and they are ritually impure until evening. (v. 18b)

The verse is strangely constructed. The topic of the preceding verses (vv. 16–17) is the man with an emission of semen. Verse 18 begins, however, as if the woman were the main focus: 'a woman who' (וְאִשָּׁה אֲשֶׁר). It appears that the verse introduces a new case, even though new cases are usually introduced with כִּי, as in the following v. 19. Possibly v. 18 starts with 'a woman' in order to anticipate the transition to the subsequent verse.[71] The scribal editors understood it this way in any case, and marked a division before v. 18 with the Hebrew letter פ, so that v. 18 is reckoned part of the regulations concerning women.[72] The answer to the verse's classification depends upon whether אֲשֶׁר is understood as a relative pronoun, as in the above translation, or as conditional.[73]

The sentence's first Hebrew word ('and a woman') is the nominative absolute of a *casus pendens* construction and thus acquires emphasis. The relative pronoun אֲשֶׁר follows immediately. Since the Hebrew relative pronoun is indeclinable (in contrast to Greek),[74] the antecedent is often clarified by a pronoun within the relative clause[75] – here by אֹתָה, which

---

70. In the context of the instructions for women, sexual intercourse is treated again, but with a different point: the menstruating woman transfers her specific condition, the *niddah*, to the man in intercourse, such that the man also becomes ritually impure for seven days (v. 24).

71. Milgrom, *Leviticus 1–16*, 930, speaks of 'an inverted hinge as a transitional unit' between the section concerning men (vv. 3–17) and the one concerning women (vv. 19–30).

72. Philip, *Menstruation and Childbirth*, 45–47, instead reckons v. 18 as part of the instructions concerning men in vv. 16–17.

73. Whitekettle, 'Lev 15.8 Reconsidered', 35–36, argues in favor of seeing it as a relative pronoun; for a critique of this position, cf. Ellens, *Women in the Sex Texts*, 51–52.

74. Cf. den Hertog, 'Relative Clauses', 69.

75. E. Hostetter, *An Elementary Grammar of Biblical Hebrew* (Sheffield: Sheffield Academic, 2000), 61, speaks of a 'resumptive or retrospective pronoun'. Cf. B. Waltke and M. O'Connor, *An Introduction to Biblical Hebrew Syntax* (Winona Lake, IN: Eisenbrauns, 1990), 4.7b and c; Joüon and Muraoka, *A Grammar of Biblical*

refers back to woman at the beginning of the sentence. The dependent clause introduced by אֲשֶׁר is therefore to be understood as relative rather than conditional. The LXX understood it that way, taking the relative pronoun אֲשֶׁר to have a distributive character and translating with καὶ γυνή ἐάν.[76]

The root שׁכב, which is used here with the basic meaning of 'lie (down)',[77] occurs in the Hebrew Bible 52 times[78] in the qal with the meaning of sexual intercourse. It is used primarily with the preposition עִם (27 times) or the accusative particle (20 times),[79] whereby the latter, when free of a suffix, can also be read as the preposition אֵת, which is synonymous with עִם.[80] In the literary layers related to this text (Leviticus, Numbers and Ezekiel), the accusative particle אֵת is always used, with the exception of Lev. 15.32. In Deuteronomy, by contrast, the prevailing usage is שׁכב with עִם.[81] שׁכב is a neutral expression for sexual intercourse. In all cases, the main connotations are of the sexual act itself (Exod. 22.15, 18; Lev. 20.11, 12, 18, 20) or of sexual gratification (Gen. 39.7, 10, 12, 14; 2 Sam. 11) rather than the desire for progeny (Gen. 19, where a woman is the subject, is an exception). The verb can connote an illegitimate, forcible claim depending on the context. For example, in 1 Sam. 2.22 the sons of Eli the priest engage in sexual contact with the women who serve at the entrance to the tent of meeting, and Eli's comments make clear that their behavior is reprehensible.

The sentence under examination continues with verbs in the plural: both shall bathe themselves, and both are impure. The opening note struck by אִשָּׁה is therefore not continued. The apparent subject and the predicates of the sentence do not agree in number. Both the man and the woman are supposed to bathe and are ritually impure.

Hebrew, §156a: 'A noun or a pronoun is often placed at the head of a clause in such a way as to stand aloof from what follows, and then resumed by means of a retrospective pronoun'.

76. Cf. den Hertog, 'Relative Clauses', 84.

77. Cf. GesB[17], 825.

78. Following Schorch, *Euphemismen*, 202, and H. M. Orlinsky, 'The Hebrew Root ŠKB', *JBL* 63 (1944): 19. Cf. W. Beuken, 'שָׁכַב *šākab*', *ThWAT* 6:1311–13.

79. Besides these constructions, the verb is used with an unmarked accusative in a handful of places and once (Gen. 39.10) with the preposition אֵצֶל ('beside').

80. Orlinsky, 'The Hebrew Root ŠKB', and Schorch, *Euphemismen*, demonstrate the untenability of the view, occasionally put forward, that שׁכב עִם connotes intercourse that is morally unobjectionable and consensual whereas שׁכב with the accusative marker implies rape.

81. Cf. Orlinsky, 'The Hebrew Root ŠKB', 20–21.

The underlying argument seems to be that sexual contact that leads to ejaculation renders the participants impure (Lev. 15.18). Not the sexual act as such, but the emission of semen is what causes the condition of cultic disability.[82] In the coda to this chapter (vv. 32–33), sexual intercourse is not mentioned as a separate category; rather, the focus is on emission of semen. And in v. 6 we already learned that a man who has a seminal emission is impure until evening. This underlines that the decisive factor is the loss of sperm and that the sexual act in itself does not put one in a condition of ritual impurity. From this it is not clear, however, what v. 18 adds to v. 16. The woman becomes impure on a second level by getting in touch with the primary source of impurity: the semen. Apparently the combination of two factors – seminal emission and intercourse – is decisive: 'the impurity stems from some aspects of the whole event, the emission of semen in sexual intercourse'.[83]

i. *You [pl.] Shall Separate Israel's Descendants*

In the verse from which the above quote is taken (Lev. 15.31), both the tone and the direction of communication change.[84] The earlier instructions, stated in the third person, give way here to direct address in the second person plural. Those addressed are not named, but based on the chapter's introduction, we may assume that they are Moses and Aaron, who are here commanded to separate Israel's descendants from their impurity. The use of the root נזר ('separate out', 'practice abstinence', 'consecrate') invites a comparative reading of this passage with the instructions for the Nazirite in Numbers 6, in which נזר also plays a central role. The introductory formula in v. 2 makes clear that what follows are regulations incumbent upon a person who is consecrating him- or herself to God by a vow. With one and the same verb (נזר hiphil) the text expresses a double separation: in the protasis (v. 2), a positive separation for YHWH, and in the apodosis (v. 3) a negative separation, i.e. abstinence from wine and other alcoholic beverages. The hiphil form of נזר should be understood to mean 'separate, hold oneself apart, practice abstinence'.[85] It describes

---

82. Wenham, 'Why Does Sexual Intercourse Defile?', 434 proposes that semen represents a life liquid whose loss contaminates the man (cf. Milgrom, *Leviticus 1–16*, 934, 1001–2, in agreement with Ramban; for a critique, see Whitekettle, 'Leviticus 15.18 Reconsidered').

83. Whitekettle, 'Leviticus 15.18 Reconsidered', 36.

84. This, as well as the diction, points to a redactional insertion (for one reconstruction, cf. Elliger, *Leviticus*, 191–92).

85. Cf. BDB, 634: 'separate, in relig. and ceremonial sense'. It is therefore not necessary, *pace* KBL, 684, to attribute the meaning 'to hold oneself back from'

a transfer of ownership that entails abstinence on the part of the person transferred. The man or the woman (v. 2) therefore lives in a space that is set apart in two senses: in relation to God and in relation to everyday life.

As in Lev. 15.31, so too in Num. 6.3 is the preposition מִן ('from', 'away') is used. What is demanded is a separation from all ritual impurity, not from life in society. The admonition also contains a rationale for the rules: it is a matter of protecting human life. The people would die if they were to approach the sacred precinct in a state of cultic incompatibility. This verse contains the chapter's theological program in a nutshell: the preservation of the inviolability of God's dwelling.

j. *This Is the Instruction*

The phrase in v. 32a, 'This is the instruction concerning the one who has a discharge', can be understood as a summarizing notice for the chapter of genital discharges. זוֹב thus functions here as a bigendered expression. Then comes the division into gender-specific cases: in v. 32b the focus is on every man who has a discharge of semen – regardless of whether it occurs during intercourse – and then in v. 33aα on the menstruant. In the next section of the verse, reference is made to both sexes: a person, whether male or female, who has a discharge (v. 33aβ). Probably this comprises the abnormally long-lasting flow of blood from the woman. Finally, both sexes are comprehended in a single case: that of the man who lies with an 'impure one' (v. 33b). To whom does it refer to? Deborah Ellens has identified it as a woman with anomalous flow as in v. 25 her flow is identified there as impure.[86] Technically, it could also mean a menstruating woman. Note, however, that *niddah* is not used here. Reference would then be made back to the special case within the regulations concerning the menstruating woman (v. 24a), which emphasizes its importance.[87] In both cases it would mean intercourse including a double flow and encompass blood which is a strong impurity marker (see below). Sexual intercourse in general (v. 18) is not referred to in the summary.

---

only to Lev. 15.31 and then to see the occurrences in Num. 6 as derivative from that ('3. [denom.] to live as a Nazirate...with מִן to abstain from'). *DCH* 5:651 distinguishes no fewer than three different meanings within Num. 6: '1. to consecrate, be a Nazirate' (Num. 6.2, 5, 6), '2. separate oneself from, abstain from' (Num. 6.3), and finally '3. consecrate, separate' (Num. 6.12).

86. Ellens, *Women in the Sex Texts*, 54–55.

87. Elliger, *Leviticus*, 197, explains this with reference to redaction history, inferring from the apparent expansion of the closing summary (v. 33b) that v. 24 was the last provision to be inserted into the chapter.

After the gender-encompassing opening in v. 32a, each sex is treated separately, so that unity and difference between the sexes are expressed. In the chapter's final statement the woman is identified with impurity breaking up the gender symmetry. These verses therefore reflect a classification that differs from that of the chapter as a whole.

We turn now to the analysis of the Greek text of Leviticus 15.

IV. *The LXX Rendering*

a. *Translation*

> ¹ And the Lord spoke to Moses and Aaron, saying:
> ² Speak[88] to Israel's descendants and say to them: With respect to any man,[89] if he experiences a discharge from his body, his discharge is impure.
> ³ And this is the law of his impurity: If he has a genital discharge from his body on account of his discharge, or his body is obstructed because of the discharge, then this is his impurity: all the days of the discharge from his body or while his body is obstructed because of the discharge, this constitutes his impurity.
> ⁴ Every bed upon which the man with the genital discharge[90] lies shall be unclean, and every object upon which the man with the genital discharge sits shall be unclean. ⁵ And the person[91] who touches his bed shall wash his clothes and bathe in water, and he shall be unclean until evening. ⁶ And the one who sits upon the object upon which the man with the genital discharge has sat shall wash his clothes and bathe in water, and he shall be unclean until evening. ⁷ And he who touches the skin[92] of the man with the genital discharge shall wash his clothes and bathe in water, and he shall be unclean until evening. ⁸ If the man with a genital discharge spits on someone who is clean, the clean person shall wash his clothes and bathe in water, and he shall be unclean until evening. ⁹ And every donkey saddle upon which the one with a discharge in his member mounts shall be unclean until evening. ¹⁰ And everyone who touches anything that is underneath him shall be unclean

---

88. The imperative is singular, even though v. 1 portrays Moses and Aaron as being addressed.

89. Cf. *La Bible d'Alexandrie*, 146, 'pour un homme, pour toute homme'.

90. ὁ γονορρυής is a neologism. *La Bible d'Alexandrie*, 147, takes the term to signify the medical condition of gonorrhoea, a word derived from the Greek. However, that concept probably represents a later development. *Septuaginta Deutsch* translates as 'der Samenflüssige' (the one with a discharge of semen).

91. The LXX interprets אִישׁ in the Hebrew as gender-neutral, rendering ἄνθρωπος and not ἀνήρ.

92. Here LXX specifies the point of contact.

until evening. And if someone picks it up, he shall wash his clothes and bathe in water, and he shall be unclean until evening. [11] And whomever the one with a genital discharge shall touch, not having rinsed his hands, that person shall wash his clothes and bathe in water, and he shall be unclean until evening.

[12] And a clay vessel that has been touched by the man with a discharge in his member shall be broken in pieces. A wooden vessel shall be rinsed with water, and it shall be clean. [13] But when the man who has a genital discharge is purified of his discharge, he shall count off seven days for himself with respect to his cleansing, and he shall wash his clothes and bathe his body in water, and he shall be clean. [14] And on the eighth day he shall take two turtledoves for himself or two young doves, and he shall bring them[93] before the Lord to the door of the tent of witness, and he shall give them to the priest. [15] And the priest shall prepare them: One for sin and one as a whole burnt offering, and the priest shall perform the atonement ritual on his behalf before the Lord because of[94] his discharge.

[16] And a person who has a seminal emission shall wash his entire body with water, and he shall be unclean until evening. [17] And every garment and every animal skin upon which there is any semen shall be washed with water, and it shall be unclean until the evening.

[18] And a woman,[95] if a man sleeps with her and there is an emission of semen, they shall wash themselves with water, and they shall be unclean until the evening.

[19] And a woman, when she has a discharge of blood, the discharge shall be in her body, seven days shall she be in her menstruation. Everyone who touches her shall be unclean until evening. [20] And everything upon which she lies during her menstruation shall be unclean. And everything upon which she sits shall be unclean. [21] And everyone who touches her bed shall wash his clothes and bathe his body with water, and he shall be unclean until evening. [22] And everyone who touches any object upon which she sat shall wash his clothes and bathe with water, and he shall be unclean until evening. [23] And if she is on her bed or upon an object upon which she is sitting, whoever touches this[96] shall be unclean until evening. [24] But if someone sleeps with her, then her uncleanness comes upon him, and he shall be unclean for seven days. And every bed upon which he has lain shall be unclean.

---

93. The MT, differently from the LXX and Targum Jonathan, reads the verb as a qal without a suffix.

94. Cf. Wevers, *Notes on the Greek Text of Leviticus*, 231, who translates the preposition ἀπο likewise.

95. The Greek attempts to imitate the Hebrew's *casus pendens* construction.

96. The feminine pronoun αὐτῆς refers here not to the woman with the discharge but rather to her bed.

²⁵ And a woman, when she has a discharge of blood[97] many days outside the period of her menstruation, and if she continues to discharge blood beyond her menstrual period, all the days of her unclean discharge are like the days of her menstruation; she shall be unclean. ²⁶ And[98] every bed upon which she lies during all the days of her discharge shall be like the bed of her menstruation. And every object upon which she sits shall be unclean according to the uncleanness of menstruation. ²⁷ Everyone who touches her[99] shall be unclean and wash his clothes, and he shall be unclean until evening. ²⁸ But when she has become clean from her discharge, she shall count seven days for herself, and thereafter she shall be clean. ²⁹ And on the eighth day she shall take two turtledoves for herself or two young doves and bring them to the priest at the door of the tent of witness. ³⁰ And the priest shall offer one for sin[100] and one as a whole burnt offering. And the priest shall perform the atonement ritual before the Lord on her behalf because of her unclean discharge.

³¹ You shall make Israel's descendants reverent in relation to their uncleannesses, so that they do not die because of their uncleanness, by defiling my tent that is among them.[101]

³² This is the law for the man with a genital discharge, and for anyone who has an emission of semen, such that he is made unclean by it.

³³ And for the woman with a bloody discharge in her menstruation, and for a person with a genital discharge,[102] male or female, and for the man who sleeps with a set-apart woman.

Overall, the Greek version displays a tendency toward greater elaboration. In v. 12 an extra clause is added to announce that the wooden vessel that was rinsed out is clean. And by speaking in v. 7 of touching the skin (χρωτός) of the man with a discharge rather than his flesh as in the MT (בָּשָׂר), the LXX explicitly rules out the possibility that it is the (male) member that is touched. Verse 9 specifies the type of saddle that can be ritually contaminated: a donkey saddle. This verse also adds the chronological note 'until evening'.

---

97. The Greek employs the verb ῥέω ('to flow') and uses a *figura etymologica*.

98. The LXX begins with καί, while the MT lacks a copula.

99. The MT has a third person plural suffix here and thus refers to the objects mentioned in v. 26, while the Greek αὐτῆς refers to the woman herself.

100. Cf. Wevers, *Notes on the Greek Text of Leviticus*, 231, who translates the preposition ἀπό similarly: 'because of his discharge'.

101. The Greek uses the verb μιαίνω ('to soil') as opposed to the more common formulation with the adjective ἀκάθαρτος (so also in v. 32).

102. The Greek elaborates here with ἐν τῇ ῥύσει αὐτοῦ ('in his discharge'), which parallels the preceding phrase about the woman, ἐν τῇ ἀφέδρῳ αὐτῆς.

b. *Hebraisms in the Greek Text*

In many places the Greek text imitates the style of the Hebrew, as in its frequent use of καί (vv. 16, 18, 19). Even the neologisms seem to be Hebraizing; for example, the verb 'spit upon' in v. 8 (προσσιελίζω) is a *hapax legomenon*. The use of κοίτη ('bed') and the phrase κοίτη σπέρματος in vv. 16, 32 represents a Hebraism for שִׁכְבַת־זָרַע.[103] The linguistic peculiarities of Leviticus 15 LXX become more comprehensible in the light of the Hebrew text.

The construction ἀνδρὶ ἀνδρὶ attempts to imitate the Hebrew אִישׁ אִישׁ.[104] The translation thereby leaves open the gap we found in the MT. Verse 3 is longer than in the MT, containing a doublet[105] that emphasizes the impurity of the man with a discharge.

c. *Genital Discharges*

Moving on, we next examine the Greek technical terms for genital secretions. The table presents an overview of the Hebrew terms and their corresponding translations in Leviticus 15 LXX (and 12 LXX).

Table 4

σῶμα	15.2, 3, 19	בָּשָׂר
σάρξ	12.3	בָּשָׂר
ῥύσις	15.2	זוֹב
ῥέων γόνον	15.3	זוֹב
γονορρυής	15.4, 6, 7, 8, 11, 12, 13, 32, 33[106]	הַזָּב
ἢ ῥέουσα αἵματι	15.19	זָבָה דָם
ῥύσις αἵματος	15.25	זוֹב דָּמָהּ
ἄφεδρος	15.9, 20, 25, 26, 33; 12.2	נִדָּה
ἀκαθαρσία	15.24	נִדָּה
αἱμορροούσῃ	15.33	דָּוָה
ἀτοκαθημένης	15.33	טְמֵאָה

---

103. Cf. Huber, *Untersuchungen über den Sprachcharakter*, 102–3.

104. T. Muraoka, *A Greek–English Lexicon of the Septuagint: Chiefly of the Pentateuch and the Twelve Prophets* (Leuven: Peeters, 2002), 36, characterizes the construction as a Semitism and apparently takes it to be inclusive ('anyone'). Wevers, *Notes on the Greek Text of Leviticus*, 224, stresses that this phrase would not have made sense to a monolingual Greek audience. The sense is in fact distributive (cf. den Hertog, 'Relative Clauses', 83).

105. Wevers, *Notes on the Greek Text of Leviticus*, 225, posits that the LXX depends here on the Samaritan.

106. In this verse the Hebrew word הַזָּב ('one with a discharge') covers both genders.

The Greek σῶμα, which is the usual translation for בָּשָׂר (in Lev. 12 LXX it is however σάρξ), is gender-neutral and designates the body in its entirety. The Greek text introduces gender-specificity in its designations of the various secretions:

In contrast to the Hebrew, in the LXX the nature of the discharges is specified more and more from v. 3 on. Verse 3 speaks of ῥέων γόνον, while v. 19 speaks of ἣ ῥέουσα αἵματι; in v. 25 as well, the substance (blood) is named. One's interpretation of the expression ῥέων γόνον in v. 3 determines one's view of how the chapter is structured: Does v. 3 already refer to seminal emissions? Or should we understand ῥέων γόνον as a generic term for a genital discharge other than semen, since otherwise why would a sacrifice and a specified period of purification be necessary? To sort this out we must make reference to both words in the phrase. The verb ῥέω is used in the sense of flow for the Hebrew זוב. This root describes secretions of both the man and the woman. Nevertheless, the Greek cannot completely mirror the Hebrew structures; for example, in the Hebrew, the participle in v. 3 designates the man with the discharge, whereas the Greek is forced to render in such a way that the participle designates the discharge.[107] In addition, the noun ῥύσις in vv. 3, 13, 19, 25, 26, 28, 33 represents a general, gender-neutral term (analogous to זוב) that designates outflowings. This is obscured in gender-specifying translations.[108]

Lexica give three meanings for the masculine noun γόνος: (1) 'that which is begotten', (2) 'semen',[109] and (3) 'the male member'.[110] When the second meaning is applied, the phrase ῥέων γόνον designates an emission of semen (cf. Num. 5.2).[111] Accordingly, the German translation of the LXX supplies the title 'the semen emitter' to vv. 3–14.[112] But γόνος in v. 3 appears to have had a more general meaning related to sex

---

107. Péter-Contesse, *Lévitique 1–16*, 234: 'Le participe de זוב désignant une personne était probablement impossible à rendre de manière littérale en grec...; LXX a donc traduit *ad sensum*'.

108. Cf. J. Lust, *Greek–English Lexicon of the Septuagint*, 2nd ed. (Stuttgart: Deutsche Bibelgesellschaft, 2015), 418: '*issue of blood, flow* Lev 15,19; *discharge or issue of seed* Lev 15,2'.

109. Muraoka, *Greek–English Lexicon*, 102.

110. Cf. F. Rehkopf, *Septuaginta-Vokabular* (Göttingen: Vandenhoeck & Ruprecht, 1989), 63.

111. Muraoka, *Greek–English Lexicon*, 102 and 503: 'having a discharge of semen'.

112. Cf. Wevers, *Notes on the Greek Text of Leviticus*, 226, who understands γονορρυής as 'Spermatorrhea', i.e. 'involuntary discharge of semen' and thereby distinguishes it from infectious discharges such as those of gonorrhea.

or the male genitalia, for if it meant semen, then vv. 16–17, which deal specifically with seminal emissions, would have been redundant. Further, the neologism γονορρυής in vv. 4, 6, 7, 8, 11, 12, 13, 32, 33, which is translated as genital discharge,[113] makes apparent that genital secretions of a particular nature are under consideration and not ordinary emissions of semen. This coinage captures the specific nature of male genital secretions other than semen, which, by contrast, is designated in v. 16 by the phrase κοίτη σπέρματος. As in the MT, these verses make no use of the roots denoting '(out)flowing' (ῥέω = זוב).

In Classical Greek, the primary meaning of the feminine noun κοίτη is 'bed' (Lev. 15.4, 5, 21, 23, 24, 26).[114] To conclude from this that v. 16 has to do exclusively with nocturnal emissions[115] is not persuasive. The noun σπέρμα designates semen.[116] The phrase κοίτη σπέρματος therefore is translated as seminal emission both in the context of intercourse (Lev. 15.18) and independently therefrom (Lev. 15.16).[117]

Turning now to the woman, we find that the LXX uses the simple noun ῥύσις in various combinations to specify the secretion: αἱμορροούσῃ ('[woman] with a discharge of blood') in v. 33, ἣ ῥέουσα αἵματι in v. 19, ῥύσις αἵματος in v. 25. The discharge is in each case specified through the indication of its substance, blood. The various constructions differ in their details, but no basic terminological distinction is made between regular and irregular blood flows.

The LXX's use of these specific terms for female genital secretions is based on ancient Greek medical texts, above all on the *Corpus Hippocraticum*. The ῥύσις αἵματος ('flow of blood') is a widely discussed phenomenon in ancient medical literature.[118] In the Hippocratic writings, balance in the bodily fluids is part of the overall balance of health. This balance can be achieved by inducing outflows, such as blood from the nose. For example, if menstruation stops, then induced bleeding from

---

113. Cf. Lust, *Greek–English Lexicon*, 92: 'discharge of seed or blood, suffering from gonorrhea'.

114. Cf. Muraoka, *Greek–English Lexicon*, 323: '1. bed; 2. pen; 3. sexual intercourse'.

115. Cf. Wevers, *Notes on the Greek Text of Leviticus*, 231–32.

116. Cf. Rehkopf, *Septuagintavokabular*, 263: 'Same'; Muraoka, *Greek–English Lexicon*, 518: '1. seed. 2. offspring 3. sowing'.

117. Cf. Muraoka, *Greek–English Lexicon*, 323: '*emitted semen*' in Lev. 15.16 and '*sexual intercourse*' in Lev. 15.18 and 18.20.

118. Cf. the compilation in A. Weissenrieder, *Images of Illness in the Gospel of Luke: Insights of Ancient Medical Texts*, WUNT 2/164 (Tübingen: Mohr Siebeck, 2003), 241–48.

the nose can compensate (*Aph.* 5.32–33). The menstrual period, like pregnancy, was seen as essential to women's health.¹¹⁹ Menstruation is described as 'the woman's secretion' (ῥόω γυναικέως, *Aph.* 5.56). If a woman loses too much blood through menstruation, balance is disturbed and illnesses occur. In the Hippocratic theory, the regular loss of blood in the menses is a prerequisite of the woman's health.¹²⁰

In contrast to the Hebrew text, the LXX coined no special term for the woman's cultic status resulting from menstruation. In most places where Leviticus 12 and 15 have נִדָּה, the LXX uses ἄφεδρος. In choosing this word, the LXX opts for a term that was common in ancient medical literature.¹²¹ The various dictionaries and translations accordingly render ἄφεδρος with technical terms.¹²² This is difficult in cases where נִדָּה does not designate menstruation per se but rather the condition of cultic endangerment that menstruation causes, as for example in v. 24. What is transferred to the man who has intercourse with a menstruant is clearly not menstruation itself but rather this cultic condition. Here the LXX glosses with ἀκαθαρσία ('impurity'), since the Greek has no term like *niddah* that designates the cultic status caused by menstruation. In the closing formula in Lev. 15.33 the menstruating woman is called 'one who sits apart' (ἀποκαθημένης, Lev. 15.33; cf. Lev. 20.18).

V. *Gender Neutral and Gender Specific Language of the Body*

The structure of Leviticus 15 oscillates between gender symmetry and asymmetry. Depending on how the formula אִישׁ אִישׁ in Lev. 15.2 (MT) is interpreted, the chapter begins either on a gender-neutral note or gender-specifically with an eye toward the man. 'The chapter's rigid symmetry conceals the unequal relationship of its themes. The symmetry seems to

---

119. A. E. Hanson, 'The Medical Writers' Woman', in *Women's History and Ancient History*, ed. S. B. Pomeroy (Chapel Hill: University of North Carolina Press, 1991), 309–37 (317), and, in the same volume, L. Dean-Jones, 'The Cultural Construct of the Female Body in Classical Greek Science', 111–37 (125, 127, 130).

120. Hippocrates, *Aph.* 5.57; cf. Dean-Jones, 'The Construct of the Female Body', 119.

121. As, e.g., in Diocorides Medicus (Dsc 2.75), a physician active around 50 CE, or in writings by Galenus (Gal 14.208); cf. Liddell/Scott, 287; Bailly, *Dictionnaire grec-français*, 16950. According to Bauer/Leander, 259, it is a medical *terminus technicus* in the LXX.

122. Cf. *Septuaginta Deutsch* translates with 'Menstruation'; Liddell/Scott, 287, 'menses muliebres'; Muraoka, *Greek–English Lexicon*, 78, 'menstruation'. Differently: *La Bible d'Alexandrie* renders it with 'indisposition'.

present a subtle logic where in fact none exists.'[123] The substance of the secretion is named only in the woman's case. Only the woman's cultic status is designated by a special term. The language that is conditioned by its use for the male body is applied to women as well, such that the male body becomes the norm.[124] Hence, the chapter's symmetrical construction, which suggests an equality of the sexes, nevertheless contains a (sexual) asymmetry.

The Greek version describes the chapter's overall theme in v. 3 with the phrase 'genital secretion from the body', ῥέων γόνον ἐκ σώματος. With this neutral formulation, the chapter seems to contemplate a different outline from the MT. In the course of the chapter, the secretions are specified. Verse 3 also gives another hint that characterizes the subsequent text as an instruction, specifically concerning a man's impurity. Where the MT has the verb form תִּהְיֶה in v. 3, the Greek translators probably read תּוֹרַת ('law'). What follows in vv. 3 through 15 relates only to the man's specific discharge. As against this, v. 32 closes the chapter by calling it ὁ νόμος τοῦ γονορρυοῦς, and the subsequent dative forms in vv. 32–33 make it clear that the chapter's expositions concern both sexes.

The LXX's coinages and Hebraisms allow us to recognize that the Greek in this chapter strives to imitate the style of the Hebrew. At the same time, in its description of genital secretions, the Greek text makes use of terms and ideas from ancient Greek medical literature. The LXX, unlike the Hebrew text, did not coin a technical term for the menstruating woman's cultic status. Instead, it used a variety of terms. In the case of the expression דָּוָה ('destabilized'), used by the MT to characterize the menstruating woman in Lev. 15.33a, the LXX renders interpretatively as '[woman] with a discharge of blood' (αἱμορροούσῃ), which is an analogous construction to γονορρυής, the masculine term in v. 32. The menstruating woman in v. 33b is characterized, not as ritually impure as in the MT, but rather as someone who sits apart.

Because the Greek translates the Hebrew בָּשָׂר with σῶμα, the Hebrew's ambiguity and sexual connotations are removed, since σῶμα is not used for the male genitalia (the passage concerning circumcision in Lev. 12.3 uses σάρξ).[125] The Greek translation thus attempts to employ gender-neutral language effecting the body while imparting a medical-physiological character to the discussion. This tendency is also evident in the fact that

123. Staubli, *Die Bücher Levitikus*, 129.
124. Cf. Philip, *Menstruation*, 47. Ellens, *Women in the Sex Texts*, 72, underlines the gender asymmetry of language referencing females and argues for gender symmetry concerning the structure.
125. As noted by Wevers, *Notes on the Greek Text of Leviticus*, 224.

for the man as well as for the woman, the substance of the secretion is specified (as ῥέων γόνον). By contrast, the Hebrew text emphasizes more the cultic dimension of bodily secretions. The Greek translation, through its linguistic *Gestalt*, shaped its own conceptions of the body and genital impurity that deviated from those of the Hebrew text; those of the Hebrew text will be thoroughly investigated in Part II.

Part II

BIBLICAL ANTHROPOLOGY AS DISCOURSE OF THE BODY

Understanding literature as discourse by which communities organize the production of meanings, Part II will subject the multiple discourses of the body in the texts from Leviticus discussed in Part I to a thorough analysis focusing on the semantics. In the hope of avoiding certain fallacies, the analysis of semantics will be embedded in the discourse analysis. In the following chapters I will outline biblical literary anthropology as discourse of the body, incorporating issues of cultural anthropology. By looking at the different ways that bodies are semantically and syntactically represented, it will become apparent how language helps to construct and maintain human and bodily gendering.

The purpose of Part II is to investigate the use of the terms designating the gendered body and bodily processes from Leviticus 12 and 15 in other biblical texts. The scope of the history of discourse shall be limited mainly again to Greek translations and modern dictionaries, which play a large part in shaping conceptions. The spectrum of meanings of terms and phrases that compose the body and the connections between their different semantic fields will be highlighted. Through this, clarity regarding the discursive praxis of language establishing body, gender and purity will be gained.

Our analysis will gather building blocks needed for a history of discursive processes and cultural practices related to the discourse of the body in Leviticus. We shall focus mainly on two periods: (1) the redaction of biblical writings up to rabbinic times and, (2) the last century of historical-critical exegesis and Bible translations.

In the first two chapters of Part II – Chapter 4, 'Flesh', and Chapter 5, 'Bodily Fluids' – I clarify certain terms that can be used both in gender-specific and gender-neutral ways. In Chapter 6, 'Menstruation', the focus is on lexemes that are used gender-specifically for the female body. Through the designation of a person or a bodily phenomenon as 'impure', language shapes bodies and defines their norms. As such, in Chapter 7 I examine this cultic characterization of bodies and how physical phenomena affecting the human gendered body define the cultic concept of impurity. Again, the final section of each chapter offers a concise summary of the discussion.

Our discourse analytical approach and the outline of the chapters makes clear the term 'body' is used as an overall category for the various Hebrew terms and phrases. It serves as a heuristic category to highlight the diverse bodily practices described in Leviticus 11–15 that establish and mark binary differences, including, most notably, male/female and pure/impure. The analysis of specific bodily organs and physiological processes opens up new interpretive possibilities for a historical-cultural and biblical-theological conception of the body, even beyond the specific corpus of the purity regulations in Leviticus. The presumption is that discourse analysis of each term and concept separately unfolds at the same time the interrelatedness of the three concepts body, gender and purity in the regulations of Leviticus 12 and 15.

Chapter 4

FLESH

I. *The One-Gender Model*[1]

Both the male and the female body are designated in Leviticus 15 by בָּשָׂר.[2] The term denotes the flesh of humans and animals, whether living (Gen. 2.21 *et passim*) or dead (1 Sam. 17.44; Deut. 14.8; in the sense of food in Lev 7.15; 1 Sam. 2.13, 15 *et passim*). Biblical Hebrew has no general term for body. בָּשָׂר corresponds most closely with our concept of body or embodiment[3] in its creatureliness, and it is therefore a central as well as gender-neutral (or non-gendered) anthropological concept. It encompasses both humankind and animals (Gen. 6.17; 9.15; Isa. 40.5, 6). The term is not, however, used for God, despite other anthropomorphisms that are so used.[4] In some passages (as Pss. 63.2; 84.3; Job 13.14; 14.22), the term occurs in *parallellismus membrorum* with נֶפֶשׁ ('throat', 'life-force', 'desire'), where it expresses the relation of human existence to God. In this sense, בָּשָׂר denotes something dynamic rather than substantial.

No other book of the Hebrew Bible comes close to Leviticus in its number of uses of בָּשָׂר. Leviticus uses it 61 times, mostly to refer to sacrificial offerings or to the human body, although in some cases it specifically denotes the male genitalia and even, in one case (Lev 15.19), the female genitalia.[5] In what follows, we will examine this diversity of usage, at times gender-neutral and at others gender-specific, which emphasizes the sameness and difference of bodies.

---

1. In reference to Laqueur, whose theory of the 'one gender model' recognizes that up until the eighteenth century the female body was understood in terms of the male body (cf. Laqueur, *Making Sex*).
2. Cf. N. P. Bratsiotis, 'בָּשָׂר *bāśār*', *ThWAT*, 1:850–67, and *DCH* 3:227.
3. Cf. בָּשָׂר KBL³, 156–57, and Gerlemann, 'בָּשָׂר *bāśār* Fleisch', *THAT* 1:377.
4. According to Marjo Korpel, *A Rift in the Clouds: Ugaritic and Hebrew Descriptions of the Divine* (Münster: Ugarit-Verlag, 1990), 117–18, in contrast to Ugarit.
5. Cf. the table in Gerlemann, בָּשָׂר, 1:377.

In the story of God's creation of man and woman in Genesis 2, the term בָּשָׂר helps to highlight the unity and correspondence of the בָּשָׂר of the man with the בָּשָׂר of the woman. When the first earthly creature faces his vis-à-vis he exclaims: 'Bone of my bone and flesh of my flesh' (v. 23). This expression occurs elsewhere in the Hebrew Bible to denote biological kinship (cf. Gen. 29.14; Judg. 9.2) as well as a bond of loyalty (2 Sam. 5.1; 19.13).[6] The concluding formula in Gen. 2.24 ('they shall be one flesh') expresses the close relationship that the first two human creatures bear to each other. Differences such as gender have not yet entered the picture.

Along with its focus on gender-specific secretions, Leviticus 15 sketches a unified, gender-neutral picture of the human body with the help of the gender-encompassing term בָּשָׂר. The chapter uses בָּשָׂר in different ways: gender-neutrally for the body in its generic sense, and gender-specifically for the male member on the one hand and the female genitalia on the other. In passages whose main concern is the purity of the sanctuary, the term denotes the male sexual organ (cf. Exod. 28.42; Lev 6.3; 12.3; 16.4). In the sole instance in Leviticus 15 (i.e., v. 19) where the term denotes the female pudenda (vulva), by that very use the text analogizes the female-gendered body to the male-gendered body. In other words, sexual difference is neutralized within a 'non-gendered body model'.[7] Verse 16 illustrates how בָּשָׂר can be both gender-specific and gender-neutral: after a seminal emission, the man must wash his entire body (כָּל־בְּשָׂרוֹ).[8] The particle כָּל is inserted in order to emphasize that the object of the washing is not just the male member, which is what בָּשָׂר means in v. 3, but rather the entire body (cf. Lev. 15.7).

Since בָּשָׂר highlights the unity of the sexes, Leviticus 15 resorts to different prepositions in order to inscribe gender difference into bodies. For example, a woman is said to have 'a discharge *in* her body' (v. 19) while a man's discharge is 'from (out of) his body' (v. 2).[9] The prepositions

---

6. In Gen. 37.27; Lev. 18.6; 25.49, בָּשָׂר has a juridical meaning, in contrast to the more physiological term שְׁאֵר, which denotes flesh infused with blood.

7. In contrast to Philip, *Menstruation and Childbirth*, 105, I take the use of בָּשָׂר in Lev. 15.19 to be gender-neutral or gender-encompassing (with the male body being understood as normative) rather than as indicative of a bi-gendered noun.

8. This expression can also mean 'all living creatures' (Ps. 136.25) or 'everyone' (Isa. 66.16, 23, 24).

9. Cf. Fonrobert, *Menstrual Purity*, 44: 'It is the difference between these two letters, or prepositions...which to the rabbinic sages establishes the male body in terms of surface, as exteriority, and the female body in terms of space, as interiority'.

sketch differing conceptions of the gendered body (see above, Chapter 3). The text discloses a view not only *of* the female body, but also *into* it: by its use of 'in her body', it characterizes that body as a hollow space, which recalls the application of the term מָקוֹר ('spring') to the vulva in Lev. 12.7 and 20.8.

Hence Leviticus 15 characterizes men's and women's bodies as analogous, in that בָּשָׂר denotes both male and female genitalia, but also as differing: though the two bodies are distinct, they are conceptualized within a single model. It is with this in mind that the following section examines the difference created by the circumcision of the male body.[10]

II. *Circumcision of the Flesh*[11]

Circumcision has become a central feature of Jewish identity. When in history this happened, or even more important, whether it is binding, are matters of controversy. Both 1 Macc. 1.48 and 2 Macc. 6.10 report that in 165 BCE, Antiochus Epiphanes prohibited circumcision in an attempt to suppress Jewish identity. Among other effects of the practice of circumcision was that for Judaism, physicality (embodiment) became constitutive.[12] Although in Jewish self-understanding, circumcision is a central rite (at least for the male sex), in the legislative traditions of the Hebrew Bible its position is marginal. In Leviticus 12, for example, the circumcision commandment is simply inserted into the purity regulations for the parturient. The circumcision commandment also occurs in a narrative context in the Hebrew Bible, namely in the Abraham story of Genesis 17. This late literary layer seeks to anchor circumcision at the beginning in the times of the patriarchs and matriarchs. Analysis of

---

10. Here we discuss only male circumcision. The Hebrew Bible shows no awareness of a corresponding operation for women's bodies. Excision (removal of all or part of the clitoris) and infibulation (removal of the clitoris along with parts of the labia) are both forms of female genital mutilation.

11. Cf. D. Erbele-Küster and E. Toenges, 'Beschneidung', in *Sozialgeschichtliches Wörterbuch*, ed. Frank Crüsemann et al. (Gütersloh: Gütersloher Verlagshaus, 2009), 47–49.

12. This point is highlighted by the title of Boyarin's monograph, *Carnal Israel*, as well as by that of the essay collection edited by H. Eilberg-Schwartz, *The People of the Body: Jews and Judaism from an Embodied Perspective* (Albany, NY: State University of New York Press, 1992). The authors infer the central importance of physicality not just from circumcision but also from Jewish discussions of the female body.

these and other texts makes clear that circumcision appears only in some literary layers and that it did not exist from the beginning as a continuous, ongoing practice.[13]

a. *Circumcision as a Surgical Procedure*
Circumcision, whether it be the full removal of the foreskin or merely an incision into it, represents a surgical intervention into the body[14] that results in a flow of blood. It is the only bodily incision that the Hebrew Bible permits. Otherwise, it insists absolutely on the body's integrity (cf. Lev. 19.28). No medical rationale is given for the procedure, and not until Hellenistic times does one encounter, in a treatise on comparative religion by Philo, any medical or hygienic justifications for it.[15]

Only one passage of the Hebrew Bible (Exod. 4.24–26) mentions the bleeding caused by circumcision. As Jewish interpretations of circumcision developed, the bleeding acquired significance.[16] Thus Targum Neofiti Exod. 4.26 speaks of circumcision blood's healing power.[17] Another text equates circumcision blood with the blood of the Passover offering (*Shem. R.* 19.6).

The account in Genesis 34 of the circumcision of the Shechemites portrays the seriousness of the intervention by describing its side effects

---

13. Cf. A. Blaschke, *Beschneidung: Zeugnisse der Bibel und verwandter Texte*, TANZ (Tübingen: Francke, 1999), 107–8, regarding the silence about circumcision of some biblical books.

14. Cf. ibid., 2–3 (with bibliography).

15. Cf. ibid., 193–223, and M. A. Tolbert, 'Philo and Paul: The Circumcision Debates in Early Judaism', in *Dem Tod nicht glauben. Sozialgeschichte der Bibel*, ed., F. Crüsemann et al. (Gütersloh: Gütersloher Verlagshaus, 2004), 394–407. Tolbert concludes that as a result of Philo's arguments, circumcision loses its character as a mark of distinctiveness: 'In Philo's eagerness to present circumcision as a reasonable practice, he downplays its distinctiveness as a Jewish custom' (ibid., 400). Herodotus reports the belief, held by some, that circumcision is performed for reasons of purity (Herodotus 2.37).

16. According to S. Cohen, 'A Brief History of Jewish Circumcision Blood', in *The Covenant of Circumcision: New Perspectives on an Ancient Jewish Rite*, ed. E. Wyner Mark (Hanover, NH: Brandeis University Press, 2003), 30–42, this occurred in post-Talmudic times, approximately in the eighth century, after *Pirque de Rabbi Eliezer*.

17. Cf. *The Aramaic Bible*, 2:25 for Targum Neofiti Exod. 4.26: 'Then Zipporah gave praise and said: How beloved is the blood that has delivered this bridegroom from the hand of the angel of death'. A similar paraphrase is found in Targum Pseudo-Jonathan Exod. 4.25–26; in both Targumim, circumcision has an atoning function analogous to that of animal sacrifice (cf. Exod. 4.24–26 LXX).

in adult men, namely pain and disablement. In Josh. 5.8, the Israelites themselves remain in camp until their post-circumcision wounds have healed.

The act of circumcision is denoted by the verb מול,[18] a technical term whose use is limited to these contexts and that reveals nothing about the type or extent of the incision. In the qal, מול usually occurs with an accusative of person (Gen. 21.4; Exod. 12.44; Josh. 5.3–5, 7).[19] Only in Exod. 4.25 is a different word used for the action: כרת, 'cut (off or out)'. In Gen. 17.23 the object is 'the foreskins of their members'; in Jer. 9.24 the foreskin; in Deut. 10.16 the 'foreskin of the heart'; and in Deut. 30.6 the heart itself. More often the verb is in the niphal (Gen. 17.10, 11, 12, 13, 14, 24, 25; 34.15, 22, 24; Exod. 12.48; Lev. 12.3; Josh. 5.8) in the sense of 'allow oneself to be circumcised' or 'be circumcised', making passive and reflexive senses difficult to distinguish.[20]

In Jer. 4.4, 'circumcision of the heart' is described in terms of the heart's foreskin being 'removed' (סור hiphil). Compared to the technical term מול, 'to remove' sheds more light on how the process is carried out. As a further detail of the ritual practice, Exodus 4 and Josh. 5.2, 3 specify the instrument with which circumcision is performed: a sharpened, pointed stone.

All told, the Hebrew Bible contains only sparse indications of how circumcision is to be performed: in the two main accounts, Genesis 17 and Leviticus 12, the procedure is described without the male body's physicality or vulnerability becoming visible. Although the foreskin (עָרְלָה) is mentioned, this term's abstract and figurative use – mainly as a category of ethnic difference, as we shall see in what follows – seems to push its physical meaning into the background.

b. *Circumcision as Rite*
The earliest textual evidence for a detailed rite of circumcision date from post-biblical times,[21] but even in the Hebrew Bible, the ritual character

---

18. G. Mayer, 'מול *mûl*', *ThWAT*, 4:734–38.

19. In most cases, the accusative object is marked with the particle אֶת (Gen. 17.11, 14, 25), but not in Gen. 17.24 or Lev. 12.3.

20. Cf. Jacob, *Genesis*, 424, where he ascribes a theological meaning to the grammatical form: 'The Torah consistently speaks of circumcision in the passive voice. Rather than describe an act, it requires a condition.'

21. The ritual itself underwent continuous change. For the development of ritual forms, cf. S. Cohen, *The Beginnings of Jewishness: Boundaries, Varieties, Uncertainties* (Berkeley: University of California Press, 1999).

of the practice is obvious. The timing that both Genesis 17 and Leviticus 12 prescribe for the rite, namely a few days after birth, pushes the sexual aspect into the background. Instead, Genesis 17 interprets the rite theologically as the sealing of the covenant.

Passages like Genesis 17, 34 and Exodus 4 contain elements suggestive of both nuptial and fertility rites.[22] After his circumcision, Abraham is able to produce a fully legitimate heir. The notice of Ishmael's circumcision at the age of 13 years (Gen. 17.25) evokes associations with puberty rites. In Genesis 34, the men of Shechem may marry Israelite women only after allowing themselves to be circumcised.

Whereas generally spoken circumcision has been originally a life-cycle rite that marked the transition from boyhood to manhood (Gen. 17.25), in post-exilic discourse it became a rite that sealed one's membership in an ethnic or a religious group. Both elements, however, are retained in the story of Abram's name-change to Abraham in Genesis 17, which is given the folk-etymological meaning 'father of many peoples'.

Exodus 4 connects circumcision with marriage, while ascribing implicitly to it both apotropaic and purifying functions.[23] After Zipporah removes her son's foreskin (Exod. 4.25), YHWH relents from his attempt to kill Moses. In the Targum *Pseudo-Jonathan* on Exod. 4.24 we read:

> My husband wanted to perform the circumcision, but his father-in-law prevented him. Now may the blood of this circumcision make atonement for my husband. How precious is the blood of this circumcision, which has saved my husband from the hand of the destroying angel.

---

22. Hall, 'Circumcision', 1026, speaks of 'a marriage or fertility rite'. L. A. Hoffman, *Covenant of Blood: Circumcision and Gender in Rabbinic Judaism* (Chicago: University of Chicago Press, 1996), 39, emphasizes the connection with fertility rites. The metaphor is used in the context of agriculture in Lev. 25. Joseph Fleishman, 'On the Significance of a Name Change and Circumcision in Genesis 17', *JANES* 28 (2002): 19–32, interprets circumcision ultimately as a sign of sexual purity. Israel's holiness is portrayed on the body over against the 'corrupt sexual practices of the Canaanites' (27–28). The traditional interpretation of circumcision in Islam is similar, in that it is partly described in terms of purity (cf. F. M. Denny, 'Circumcision', in *Encyclopedia of the Qur'an*, 1:336).

23. A. Brenner, *The Israelite Woman: Social Role and Literary Type in Biblical Narrative*, The Biblical Seminar 2 (Sheffield: JSOT, 1985), 71, interprets Zipporah's act as an 'apotropaic act of expiation [that offers] to the god-demon a part of Moses' manhood'. Douglas, *Leviticus as Literature*, 181, sees circumcision in Lev. 12 as apotropaic. This explains, in her view, why the period of impurity for a male child is only half as long as that for a female child.

By ascribing saving power to the blood of circumcision, this early Aramaic paraphrase attempts to explain an episode that is as unclear in its details as the nocturnal darkness in which it occurs. The MT's semantic ambiguities permit varying interpretations. Exodus 4.24 does not specify whom YHWH is attacking, and the third person masculine singular suffix in v. 25 leaves open whose 'feet' Zipporah touches with the severed foreskin.[24] What is clear is that Zipporah's action alters the course of events by causing God to abandon his murderous intention.

Zipporah's concluding explanation of her action remains enigmatic: 'a bridegroom of blood with respect to the circumcisions' (v. 26b).[25] Twice we hear about this 'bridegroom of blood' from Zipporah's mouth (vv. 25, 26), although it is unclear to whom the term refers. חתן bears the general meaning of 'relative' and the more specific meanings of 'son-in-law' and 'bridegroom'. The cognate Arabic term denotes both circumcision and son-in-law or bridegroom.[26] In this light, Zipporah's circumcision of her son and the symbolic touching of Moses' feet with the foreskin could represent her establishment of a blood-relationship with Moses and his tribal group (over and above the marriage bond). However, if true, this use of the metaphor of blood would be unique in the Hebrew Bible, which otherwise does not use that metaphor to symbolize family relationships (cf. Lev. 18 and 20).

Zipporah is the sole agent in this scene. In contrast to other passages, in this one a woman performs the circumcision. This does not justify the ascription to her of a priestly function, since in the Hebrew Bible circumcision is not a priestly task.[27] Because of corresponding verb's predominantly passive formulation, in many places it remains uncertain who performs the rite, as is the case with other ritual-technical details of the procedure.

---

24. Targum Neofiti Exod. 4.25 resolves the ambiguity by having Zipporah touch her son's foreskin to *the attacking angel's* feet.

25. Cf. concerning the possible significance of the *hapax legomenon* and *plurale tantum*; see Houtman, *Exodus*, 1:438.

26. Cf. 'K̲H̲ITĀN', in *The Encyclopaedia of Islam* 5:20–22 (20): 'Some words connected with the root k̲h̲-t-n denote the father-in-law, the son-in-law, the daughter-in-law (k̲h̲atan, k̲h̲atana), or marrying (k̲h̲utūna)'. See also Ehrlich, *Randglossen zur Hebräischen Bibel*, 276.

27. In Josh. 5, Joshua (who is not a priest) is commanded to circumcise the wilderness generation. Marsman, *Women in Ugarit and Israel*, 558, 617, leaves open whether Zipporah's role in Exod. 4 is priestly or magical. In 2 Macc. 6.10, women are responsible for performing circumcision on their sons (cf. 1 Macc. 1.60–61 and Josephus, *Ant.* 12.56).

c. *Circumcision as Covenant Sign*

Whereas in Leviticus 12 the commandment to circumcise stands isolated and unexplained among the regulations for the parturient, in Genesis 17 it receives a theological interpretation: the covenant between God and Abraham and his offspring is interpreted as a covenant sign:

> [10] This is my covenant between me and you and your offspring after you which you shall observe: Every male among you shall be circumcised.
> [11] You shall be circumcised in the flesh of your foreskin; let it be as the sign of the covenant between me and you.

The text stresses the irrevocability of this covenant; three times we hear that it is eternal (vv. 7, 13, 19). It is God who takes the initiative in establishing it (v. 2, 7), and thus he speaks of my covenant (vv. 2, 4, 7, 9, 13–14). Promise and commandment are thus artfully woven together. Highlighting the reciprocity, the text has God say, 'You shall keep my covenant' (v. 9). Whoever avoids circumcision will bear no divine sign and thus will be excluded from the community (v. 14).

In the words of Gen. 17.11b, the circumcised male flesh (or, as the Samaritan has it, the 'foreskin') is a covenant sign, a designation that puts it in the same class as the rainbow, which encompasses likewise 'all flesh', i.e., human beings (כָּל בָּשָׂר in Gen. 9.11, 15–17) and the Sabbath (Exod. 31.13, 17). This sign is a physical reminder[28] that is inscribed exclusively into male bodies (בָּשָׂר).[29] In other words, male bodies transmit the covenant. The sign also bears upon eligibility to participate in the cult, since only circumcised men are permitted to enter the sanctuary or to celebrate the Passover (Exod. 12.48). Because circumcision marks only the man's flesh (בָּשָׂר), it also brings only the man's fertility and sexuality into connection with God,[30] leaving the female sex outside.

---

28. Cf. F. Stolz, 'אות *ʾōt* Zeichen', *THAT* 1:91. 1 Macc. 1.15 denounces the surgical restoration of foreskin, which was practiced by some Hellenizing Jews, as apostasy from the holy covenant.

29. Cf. Hoffman, *Covenant of Blood*. As the title of his book suggests, Hoffmann traces the ways in which circumcision has served the religious and sexual identity-formation of Jewish men through history, thereby making apparent Judaism's 'male-dominated culture' (ibid., 22–26). Scharbert argues differently; in *Fleisch*, 50, he writes that 'the important thing is not that the covenant sign is made specifically on the male member, but rather that it is applied to "flesh" at all, that is, to the human body'.

30. Cf. Eilberg-Schwartz, *The Savage*, 167–72, and Hall, 'Circumcision', 1026.

d. *Circumcision as Identity Marker*

In the Dinah story in Genesis 34 circumcision serves to distinguish Jacob's clan from the Shechemites. The language used ('you will be like us') suggests that circumcision removes otherness. It is the *sine qua non* for sexual contact and family relations with the Israelites. The term that the story uses for the Shechemites (v. 14), 'foreskinned ones' (i.e., uncircumcised men), is used elsewhere *par excellence* of the Philistines to convey contempt for them (Judg. 14.3–4; 15.18; 1 Sam. 14.6; 17.36; 18.27; 31.4; 2 Sam. 1.20; 3.14; 1 Chr. 10.4). Among ancient Israel's neighbors, circumcision was practiced by Edomites, Ammonites, Moabites, and Egyptians (Jer. 9.25),[31] although it later declined under the influence of the Greeks, as Herodotus records. Only in a context where circumcision was not common could circumcision become a distinguishing characteristic. Specifically, it became central for the constitution of the identity of the Israelites for the first time in exilic or post-exilic times, since Babylonians did not practice it. The books of Maccabees, whether their polemics reflect an internal Jewish dispute[32] or the reaction to an external prohibition, testify to the importance of circumcision for the Jews. In 1 Macc. 1.41–64 circumcision is a physical sign of cultural-religious identity. Circumcision was also practiced beyond the tribal society and the cult, i.e., in the Diaspora, as a way to signal identity and separation[33] by ritually regulating membership in the Jewish community.[34] The male body thus became a contested sign of religious and ethnic identity.[35] In a

---

31. Cf. J. Sasson, 'Circumcision in the Ancient Near East', *JBL* 85 (1966): 473–77.

32. M. Hengel, *Judentum und Hellenismus. Studien zu ihrer Begegnung unter besonderer Berücksichtigung Palästinas bis zur Mitte des 2. Jh.s v. Chr.*, WUNT 10, 3. durchges. Aufl. (Tübingen: Mohr Siebeck, 1988), 515–34, thinks that the Maccabaean edicts betray a thoroughly Palestinian perspective. He finds it highly probable that the debate arose from internal Jewish conflicts.

33. Concerning the role of circumcision in the perception of the other, cf. Cohen, *The Beginnings of Jewishness*, 39–49: 'Did Circumcision Make Jews Distinctive?'

34. This distinctiveness was exploited by various anti-Jewish policies through the ages: 'Thus, the *fiscus Judaicus* ("Jewish tax") was levied after 70 BCE upon every circumcised Jew' (Hengel, *Judentum und Hellenismus*, 561).

35. Boyarin, *Carnal Israel*, 7, describes it thus: 'For the Jews of late antiquity, I claim, the rite of circumcision became the most contested site of this contention, precisely because of the way that it concentrates in one moment representations of the significance of sexuality, genealogy, and ethnic specificity in bodily practice' (cf. D. Boyarin, *A Radical Jew: Paul and the Politics of Identity* [Berkeley: University of California Press, 1993], 36).

paraphrase of Genesis 17 that is found in Josephus, *Ant.* 1,191–93, 214, circumcision is portrayed as a badge of Jewish identity whose purpose was to prevent mixing with non-Jews. The physical procedure mirrors affiliation, particularly religious affiliation – it becomes 'circonfession'. Accordingly, circumcision is part of the initiation rite for converts.[36]

The account of the first Passover in Exodus 12 stipulates that 'no one with foreskin may eat of it' (v. 48; cf. Josh. 5.2–10). This is directed, not at all non-Israelites, but only at the נֵכָר (cultural and religious aliens, v. 43),[37] as well as at the resident alien and day-laborer[38] (v. 45). If foreigners residing in the land (גֵּר)[39] wish to participate in the Passover celebration (v. 48ab), they may do so if all males in their community are circumcised. According to Exod. 12.44 and Gen. 17.12, domestic slaves acquired by purchase have an outright duty to observe the Passover if they are circumcised. These distinctions appear to be redundant in the light of the statement in Exod. 12.49 that one *torah* shall apply to both natives and foreigners (cf. Lev. 24.22 and Num. 15.16). Likewise, it is not clear how the resident foreigner of v. 48 is related to the '(cultural-religious) foreigner' of v. 43 and the 'resident alien and day-laborer' of v. 45. The earliest Aramaic translations attempt to fill in the gaps by relating Exodus 12 to the situation of pagan proselytes to Judaism in the Diaspora. For its part, Targum *Pseudo-Jonathan* underlines circumcision's religious significance, which both draws a boundary and makes possible the overcoming of the boundary, by interpreting the resident foreigner of v. 48 as a convert (Targ. *Pseudo-J.* 12.48; cf. Targ. *Onq.* Exod. 12.43).

e. *Circumcision as the Fixing of Gender*
In Lev. 12.3, the commandment to circumcise interrupts the purity rules for the parturient, shifting the reader's attention from the mother to her male offspring. Circumcision here obviously does not signal the transition

---

36. According to Cohen, *The Beginnings of Jewishness*, 189–217, one post-Talmudic text does not include circumcision as part of the conversion ritual; it requires only the immersion.

37. Targum *Onkelos* takes this Hebrew term to mean 'an Israelite who has deserted his faith'; in contrast to Exod. 12.43, Num. 9.14 permits 'any alien residing among you' to keep the Passover, without mentioning a circumcision requirement (cf. Crüsemann, *Tora*, 347).

38. Cf. J. Kidd, *Alterity and Identity in Israel: The 'ger' in the Old Testament*, BZAW 283 (Berlin: de Gruyter, 1999).

39. גֵּר connotes not so much foreign nationality as the fact that one is living in a place in which one was not born (2 Sam. 4.3) and where one therefore enjoys fewer rights.

from childhood to manhood, as it does implicitly in the case of Ishmael, who was circumcised at the age of thirteen (Gen. 17.25). Nevertheless, it is a performative act that unequivocally determines the infant's male gender identity. As a birth rite it anticipates the initiation rite and in a sense repeats it throughout life through a form of fictive memory. Circumcision thus becomes a token of male identity.

The purity regulations in Leviticus 12 codify sexual difference at childbirth even apart from circumcision, but circumcision heightens this difference by emphasizing the male sex.[40]

Circumcision at such an early stage thus counterbalances the identity-connection to the mother created by the sheer fact of birth. It sketches a masculine genealogical line, linking the infant male's circumcision to those of his forefathers.[41]

Genesis 17 repeatedly states that all males shall be circumcised, thereby emphasizing that this marker is reserved for men (vv. 10, 12). Philo of Alexandria was very likely among the first Jews to wonder why only Jewish men (and not also Jewish women) are circumcised. Internal Jewish arguments to the effect that women were thus excluded from the covenant[42] were echoed by early Christian polemics against circumcision. The Hebrew Bible has no analogous ritual for fixing the gender and religious identity of girls and women. The circumcision of male offspring ritually reinforces gender and body constructs that are implicit in concepts of cultic im/purity.

f. Circumcision of the Heart
Deuteronomy 10.16; 30.6, and Jer. 4.4 allude to circumcision, but not in terms of the commandment in Leviticus 12. Rather, they attempt to rival circumcision.[43] According to these passages, the physical marking of the male member is no longer adequate and must be complemented by an inscription upon the heart. 'Heart' in this context denotes the center of human intention and action. The new covenant or *torah* is transferred

---

40. In primary religions, circumcision is understood as the removal of traces of the other sex (cf. Beidelmann, 'Circumcision', 513). To express this transition to one's 'permanent' sex and the shedding of the opposite one, Muslim custom in Egypt, for example, has adolescent boys approach circumcision in girl's clothes and then remove the clothes after the ritual is completed (cf. 'ḴHITĀN', 5:21).

41. Eilberg-Schwartz, *The Savage*, 174, writes in this connection of circumcision as a second birth.

42. Cf. J. Plaskow, *Standing Again at Sinai: Judaism from a Feminist Perspective* (New York: HarperSanFransisco, 1990), 25–36, 58–59, 65–66, 82–83.

43. Deuteronomy has no circumcision commandment.

to the innermost space, 'written' on the heart (Jer. 31.33). For Jeremiah, true circumcision includes the removal of 'the foreskin of the heart'. The *parallelismus membrorum* of Jer. 4.4 expresses it this way:

> Circumcise yourselves for YHWH,
> and remove the foreskin of your hearts,
> O men of Judah and inhabitants of Jerusalem.

The expression 'for (ל) YHWH'[44] suggests that circumcision is a consecration or transfer of oneself to God. In the Hebrew Bible, circumcision of the heart does not supersede circumcision of the male member, but rather presupposes it. Of course, this type of circumcision transcends the concrete life-situation of an eight-day-old male child. Deuteronomy 30.6 heightens the drama by portraying God himself as the one performing the procedure, which makes circumcision an inscription by God into the human body.

The didactic texts adopt the conceptuality reflected in the technical term מול ('circumcise'). Even the anatomical details of the male 'flesh' are transferred to the human heart: multiple texts speak of 'a foreskin (or foreskins) of the heart' (cf. Jer. 4.4; Ezek. 44.7) – while Deut. 30.6 mentions only the heart itself.[45] Ezekiel 44.7, 9 mentions circumcision of the heart and of the penis in the same breath, because in his eyes they are equivalent. Jeremiah 9.24 stands out because of its claim that circumcision, which always bears a positive connotation elsewhere, is not adequate for salvation: both circumcised and uncircumcised face the judgment.

The writings of Paul extend this line of thought[46] by arguing that neither uncircumcision nor circumcision matters; only the keeping of commandments does (1 Cor. 7.18–19; Rom. 2.25–29; Gal. 5.2). Circumcision is of value only if one fulfills the *torah*; otherwise, it becomes equivalent to uncircumcision (Rom. 2.25). In Rom. 4.11 Paul is able to speak of 'the sign of circumcision as a seal on the righteousness of faith (received while) in uncircumcision', stressing in vv. 9–10 that Abraham is the father

---

44. With a passive verb, ל can also denote the subject, so that here, YHWH himself could be seen as performing the circumcision (cf. GK §121f; KBL³, 485).

45. The foreskin metaphor is also applied to the world of plants (Lev. 19.23–25). Similarly, other human body parts described as being 'uncircumcised' include lips (Exod. 6.12, 30, symbolizing clumsiness in speech) and ears (Jer. 6.10, unreceptiveness to prophecy). It is interesting to note that in Hebrew, the term denoting 'uncircumcision' is not simply, as in English, a grammatical negation; rather, the uncircumcised are described as 'the foreskinned ones' (cf. Blaschke, *Beschneidung*, 50–53).

46. Cf. the title of Boyarin's monograph, *A Radical Jew*, a work in which he stresses the agreements between Philo and Paul (ibid., 14–15, 19, 25–26). See also the exposition of Paul's position in Blaschke, *Beschneidung*, 361–425.

even of uncircumcised believers, since righteousness was reckoned to Abraham before he was circumcised. Circumcision – external alteration of the flesh – is nothing; only circumcision of the heart – in the spirit – counts (Rom. 2.28–29; cf. Acts 7.51). Although Rom. 2.29 can be read as commentary on such passages as Jer. 4.4, and Deut. 10.16, which speak of circumcising the heart, for Paul this also means that physical circumcision should be completely abandoned.

Philo of Alexandria argues similar when he states (in *Quaest in Exod.* 2.2) that a proselyte is not someone whose foreskin has been circumcised, but rather someone whose soul has been circumcised of its lusts, desires, and other passions. Unlike his contemporary Paul, however, Philo does not abolish the physical circumcision of proselytes. Paul's approach leads in the end to a negation and loss of physicality. Paul no longer sees circumcision as a physical act, but rather as a purely spiritual one (κατὰ πνεῦμα).[47] Accordingly Gal. 3.28 reads: 'There is no longer Jew nor Greek, there is no longer slave nor free, there is no longer male nor female; for all of you are one in Christ Jesus'. Together with the ethnic-religious boundary between Jews and Greeks, not only does gender duality appear to be overcome, but also physicality itself.[48]

g. *A Distinguishing Mark on the (Male) Body*

We may conclude that neither in Leviticus 12 nor in Genesis 17 do the instructions concerning circumcision contain any details about how the procedure is to be performed. The commandment in Lev. 12.3 offers no formula for a ritual, even though circumcision is clearly a rite. And it is striking that, in contrast to the Hebrew Bible's treatment of menstruation, Leviticus 12 and Genesis 17 say nothing about the blood that flows during circumcision. A tension exists between an embodied and a disembodied manner of description, between the body's visibility and invisibility in these texts.

The fact that circumcision is to occur on the eighth day following birth (Lev. 12.3) seems to relate it to purity concerns, since the mother's postpartum impurity lasts seven days (v. 2).[49] Despite what is implied in

---

47. Cf. Boyarin, *Carnal Israel*, 233.

48. Cf. Boyarin, *A Radical Jew*, 22–24, for whom this passage in the letter to the Galatians becomes an interpretive key: 'For Paul male-and-female means neither male nor female in the non-corporeal body of the risen Christ' (24).

49. Isa. 52.1 juxtaposes the uncircumcised (foreskinned ones) with the impure because both are ritually taboo. This does not imply identity of the two concepts. By contrast, Lev. 19.23–25 LXX characterizes the foreskin as impure and thus sees circumcision as a purifying ritual.

the first chapter of Luke's Gospel, however, the impurity attaches only to the mother, not to the child.

The decision by early Christian leaders to dispense with circumcision as an initiation rite was a key factor both in the relationship to Judaism and the dissemination of the Christian message. In the Hebrew Bible, the uncircumcision of the Philistines makes them the archetypal Gentiles (barbarians), whereas for Greco-Roman civilization, the fact that Jews were circumcised caused them to be seen as barbarians. Circumcision can thus be seen to function analogously to sexual taboos as a means of distinguishing one's culture from 'the other'; it is a physical marker of religious and political difference. Paradoxically for Jews, Greco-Roman culture reversed the polarity and made the Jews into the 'other', reducing them to their physicality.

As was already indicated, the requirement to circumcise occupies no independent literary space in the Hebrew Bible; it has no chapter devoted to it within the purity code of Leviticus. The literary location of the practice in the patriarchal and matriarchal history ties circumcision to Israel's beginnings as a people. In Leviticus 12, the laws concerning childbirth, a notice is inserted reminding of the necessity to circumcise a male descendant on the eighth day. Leviticus 12.3 must therefore be read against the background of Genesis 17.

Our linguistic analysis of the Hebrew term בָּשָׂר in biblical writings yields a history of discourse about the human body, in which contextual factors, such as the addition of specifying prepositions, inscribe gender difference onto the body. In this sense, circumcision is itself a discursive praxis. It is a (written) sign that irrevocably represents both the covenant and God in the male body. It not only marks physically; it functions as a sign (of the covenant), as in Gen. 17.10–12. Sign, the thing signified, and signification thus merge into one. The male בָּשָׂר becomes a sign that points in two directions: toward the covenant, i.e., toward God, and toward the male body itself, thus uniting transcendence and immanence in the body (בָּשָׂר). Circumcision sets a seal on the differentiation of the sexes (*act of gendering*), despite the fact that בָּשָׂר is a general term that seems to convey a gender-neutral concept of 'body'.

Chapter 5

BODILY FLUIDS

Three secretions from sexual bodies appear in Leviticus 12 and 15: genital discharge, semen, and blood. Analyzing these physiological phenomena allows us to see how the texts discursively construct male and female bodies.

I. *Genital Discharge*

Leviticus 15 introduced the noun זוֹב (flow/discharge) as the overarching term for genital discharges of both men and women (cf. vv. 2, 3, 13, 19, 25, 26, 28, 30, 33). The masculine participle זָב (vv. 2, 4, 6, 7, 8, 9, 11, 12, 13, 32, 33), or in one place the feminine participle זָבָה (v. 19), is the *terminus technicus* for a male or female person, respectively, who has a discharge.[1] Along with this, there are forms of the cognate verb in vv. 4, 11, 25 that denote the process of flowing. Interestingly, this verb is not used in the verses dealing with semen (Lev. 15.16, 32, see also 2 Sam. 5.29). That the text uses a single term for both genders has been obscured by such sex-specific translations of זוֹב as either '1. male mucosal discharge' (which some interpreters specify as a sign of *Gonorrhoea benigna*[2]) and '2. menstrual blood flow'.[3] Both translations reflect the interpreters' use of a medical framework, as a result of which they distinguish sharply between male and female bodies. At the same time, such interpreters seemingly fail to notice that a single category can encompass various secretions, both the genital (mucus) discharges of the male and the blood flows of the female (whether the normal monthly flow or an abnormally prolonged one). That being said, it is true that the text does not use the noun or the participle in a consistently gender-neutral way, since

---

1. Cf. Milgrom, *Leviticus 1–16*, 906: 'It is clear from this chapter that *zāb/zābâ*, literally, "the discharging one", is a technical term for 'the one with a discharge'.
2. Cf. ibid., 907, and KBL³, 255. Levine, *Leviticus*, 215, posits an infection of the urinary system.
3. GesB¹⁷, 195; cf. KBL³, 255.

v. 19, which introduces the section on women's discharges, makes it clear that a particular type of discharge, namely menstrual bleeding, is meant, in that it specifies the composition of the discharge (blood).

To describe genital discharges, the writer has chosen a root (זוב) that captures the idea of flowing. The verb's other main use in the Hebrew Bible is in the phrase 'a land flowing with milk and honey'.[4] The physiological process comes into view most vividly in Lev. 15.3, which mentions both flowing (רָר, a transitive *hapax legomenon* qal of the root ריר whose direct object is the discharge, אֶת־זוֹבוֹ)[5] and blockage (חתם hiphil, 'to seal up'). The blockage, most likely of urination, is caused by the discharge, which is the object of the preposition מִן ('from' or 'because of'). The hiphil form of חתם and the verb ריר both occur only here. Both context and construction aid in recovering the technical meaning: 'to have an obstruction'.[6]

Other biblical texts in which זוב occurs as a *terminus technicus* (Num. 5.2-3; Lev. 22.4; 2 Sam. 3.29) presuppose the term's use in Leviticus 15. Of these, only 2 Sam. 3.28-29 is part of a narrative rather than a legal text: David pronounces a curse on Joab and Joab's house that includes skin disease, genital discharge, lameness, violent death, and famine. In this context, skin disease and discharge are not primarily cultic concerns, as they are in Leviticus 13-15, but rather disturbances of the individual's social and physical equilibrium and that of his community.

In the rules for the wilderness camp given in Num. 5.2, the active masculine participle זָב is used for both men and women, as the subsequent verse specifies:[7]

> [2] Instruct the descendants of Israel to remove from camp anyone with an eruption or a discharge and anyone defiled by a corpse. [3] Remove male and female alike; put them outside the camp so that they do not defile the camp of those in whose midst I dwell.

This text is unique in its demand for the exclusion from the camp (and thus from community life) of persons having a discharge. Numbers 5.2 uses the participle זָב just as Lev. 15.33 does, namely, as a gender-inclusive

---

4. Cf. Exod. 3.8, 17; 13.5; 33.3; Lev. 20.24; Num. 13.27; 14.8; 16.14; Deut. 6.3; 11.9; 26.9, 15; 27.3, 31.20; Josh. 5.6; Jer. 11.5; 32.22; Ezek. 20.6, 15.

5. The cognate noun רִיר ('spittle, mucus') of this *hapax legomenon* is found in 1 Sam. 21.14 and Job 6.6.

6. Cf. Hartley, *Leviticus*, 203.

7. KBL³, 266, assigns all occurrences other than those in Lev. 15.19-21 to the section on men; as does GesB¹⁷, 195.

expression for persons (female or male) with genital discharges. As Num. 5.3b makes clear, certain conditions of the human body exclude the divine presence. Physical integrity is the presupposition; with the Holy affects men and women equally in their embodiedness. It affects men and women equally in their embodiedness, without emphasis on sex.

The regulations found in Lev. 22.2–6, which correspond to those of Num. 5.1–4, have as their intended audience the (male) descendants of Aaron, the priestly caste. Nevertheless, the text should not be understood as applying only to priests, but rather to the entire priestly clan (including mothers, wives, and daughters), since the sacred offerings were allotted not only to priests but also to their families.[8] Leviticus 22.2–6 commands:

> [2] Instruct Aaron and his descendants:... [3] Say to them:
> Throughout the ages, if any man among your offspring, while in a state of cultic impurity, partakes of any sacred donation that the descendants of Israel may consecrate to YHWH, that person shall be cut off from before me: I am YHWH.
> [4] No man of Aaron's offspring who has an eruption or a discharge shall eat of the sacred donations until he is pure. If one touches anything made unclean by a corpse, or if a man has an emission of semen [5] or if a man touches any swarming thing by which he is made impure – whatever his uncleanness – [6] the person who touches such shall be impure until evening and shall not eat of the sacred donations unless he has washed his body in water.

It is not immediately clear which of these regulations apply only to the male descendants and which apply to all members of the priestly family. The word בְּנֵי in v. 2, for example, may be understood either gender-exclusively (sons) or gender-inclusively (descendants).[9] Likewise, the Hebrew word אִישׁ in vv. 3, 4 and 5 need not be translated 'man', since it too is capable of designating human beings in general; note that in v. 3b and v. 6, the more encompassing term נֶפֶשׁ is used synonymously[10] and that in v. 4, the distributive construction אִישׁ אִישׁ is employed. Does זָב therefore denote only a man with a genital discharge, or can it also refer to a female member of the priestly household? Subsequent verses lend strength to the latter possibility, as it becomes clear that the sacred offerings are food for the entire priestly household.

---

8. In v. 6 the subject seems to be people in general (נֶפֶשׁ), so that the intended audience appears to be wider, possibly even including those outside the priestly clan (thus Noth, *Das dritte Buch Mose*, 139), or at least the women inside that clan.

9. See Chapter 2, section III.a.

10. Elliger, *Leviticus*, 293.

Commentaries do not give much consideration to the nongendered body model that the conceptual field of זוב suggests. Rather, they direct most of their attention to the regulations concerning female bodies,[11] which constitute a special case. A similar tendency is apparent in the text itself at Lev. 15.32–33:

> [32] This is the instruction concerning the one who has a discharge, and for him who has a seminal emission, such that he becomes ritually impure,
> [33] and concerning her in the unstable condition of her menstrual state, and concerning the one who has a discharge, whether male or female, and concerning a man who lies with a ritually impure woman.

In the summation found in Lev. 15.32, the term זָב ('the one who has a discharge') does not include the menstruating woman in v. 32, even though it did so earlier in the chapter (v. 19). The text is, however, ambiguous, and it is possible to see זָב in v. 32 as comprising all persons (male or female) who have any kind of genital discharge, not just men. The masculine participle הַזָּב appears again in v. 33. This time, the text clearly intends a gender-neutral meaning, by explicitly stating it ('the one who has a discharge, be it a man or a woman'). Hence the masculine participle of the root זוב is often used in a gender-neutral way, even though its initial alignment is with the male body.

Especially when one reads Leviticus 15 against the background of Numbers 5, one gets the strong impression that the conceptual field of זָב provides a symmetrical description independent of sex, even though sex-specific processes are involved. The man's urinary system and the woman's internal genitalia are understood as analogues, though the neutral reference point of the regulations is the male body. Only in the case of the woman, however, is the composition of the discharge more closely defined.

II. *Seed*

In the Hebrew Bible, the substantive זֶרַע can designate vegetable, animal, or human seed. The extended sense of זֶרַע as 'progeny' predominates (Gen. 3.15; 7.3; 13.6; 16.10; 22.17, 18; 26.3, 4, 24; Ezra 2.59; 9.2).[12] Only in rare instances does it denote sperm: Num. 5.28 (together with the

---

11. Cf. section A, 'The Menstruant concerning the woman's outflow', in Milgrom, *Leviticus 1–16*, 948–53. Gerstenberger, *Leviticus*, 205–7, focuses on women's everyday reality.

12. Cf. BDB, 282–83: '4. seed = offspring'.

cognate verb in the niphal) and in the formula שִׁכְבַת־זֶרַע in Lev. 15.16, 17, 18, 32; 19.20; 22.4 and Num. 5.13. The noun, denoting semen, always occurs in these passages in this specific construct chain, which supports the idea that זֶרַע by itself does not denote semen.[13] Only in two other passages does it do so: Gen. 38.9 speaks of זֶרַע ('semen') that is spilled on the ground, whereas in Lev. 15.17, the construct chain שִׁכְבַת־זֶרַע denotes semen that has come to rest on objects.

We will now consider both ways in which the root זרע is used in the purity regulations, namely, (1) as a verb in the hiphal stem meaning 'to produce seed' (Lev. 12), and (2) the expression 'emission (or outpouring) of seed' (Lev. 15).

a. *The Female Seed*
Theories of reproduction prevalent in the ancient Near East and in classical antiquity help to shed light on an expression found in Lev. 12.2, זרע hiphal, which denotes the production of seed by the woman.[14]

An objection to interpreting the hiphal of זרע in a causative sense ('bring forth/produce seed') is that the Hebrew Bible, like the ancient Near East in general, lacked a concept of a female seed or egg cell.[15] In Sumerian, the sign for 'pregnant' (*peš₄*) consists two signs: ša ('placenta', 'inner part') and *a* ('sperm', 'water').[16] In many cultures, one finds the metaphor of 'plowing a field', whereby the woman is the field which is sown with the man's seed.[17] Aristotle taught that woman is matter and therefore plays

---

13. Orlinsky, 'The Hebrew Root ŠKB'.

14. Cf. D. Erbele, 'Gender Trouble in the Old Testament: Three Models of the Relation between Sex and Gender', *SJOT* 13, no. 1 (1999): 131–41, and H. Liss, 'Ritual Purity and the Construction of Identity', in Römer, ed., *The Books of Leviticus and Numbers*, 329–54.

15. C. Delaney, 'Abraham and the Seeds of Patriarchy', in *Genesis*, ed. A. Brenner, A Feminist Companion to the Bible, Second Series (Sheffield: Sheffield Academic, 1998), 129–49 (139–40); R. Biggs, 'Conception, Contraception, and Abortion in Ancient Mesopotamia', in *Wisdom, Gods and Literature: Studies in Assyriology in Honour of W. G. Lambert*, ed. G. Finkel (Winona Lake, IN: Eisenbrauns, 2000), 1–13 (1–2, 13), and G. Leick, *Sex and Eroticism in Mesopotamian Literature* (London: Routledge, 1994), 29, 48–49. For Ancient Egypt, cf. E. Feucht, *Das Kind im Alten Ägypten: Die Stellung des Kindes in Familie und Gesellschaft nach altägyptischen Texten und Darstellungen* (Frankfurt am Main: Campus, 1995), 93.

16. A word that can mean 'water', 'seed', and 'descendants', according to Stol, *Birth*, 4–5.

17. Cf. Leick, *Sex and Eroticism*, 31–32, and Whitekettle, *Levitical Thought*, 384. Cf. as well Num. 5.28; Sir. 26.20–21, and Qur'an 2.223.

only a passive role in the reproductive process.[18] This biological ranking of the sexes has served as the basis for socially constructed gender hierarchies. Sperm is thought of as a form of blood, like the menses but more complex. Sperm plays the decisive role in reproduction, transforming the feminine 'matter' into a new living being.

However, competing conceptual models of reproduction have also been noted in antiquity. Certain curses found in Egyptian and Mesopotamian documents that threaten infertility against men and barrenness against women show that childlessness could be attributed to either partner.[19] A Mesopotamian omen text describes conception as the woman's ability to receive sperm into herself.[20] In Babylon, the concept may have existed of a female seed (*rehû*).[21] Ugaritic texts ascribe an active role to the woman in procreation.[22] The *Corpus Hippocraticum* attributes sperm production to men and women alike;[23] the couple's ability to experience pleasure simultaneously depends upon the timing of the woman's loss of seed (*Genit.* 4.1). That children often resemble their mothers points to the existence of a female seed (*Genit.* 8.1). A child's gender is determined by the relative strength of the male and female seeds.

This Hippocratic two-seed doctrine finds an echo, in altered form, in rabbinical commentaries: according to *b. Nid.* 31a, male children are fruit of the woman, female children fruit of the man. Based on rabbinic texts such as *m. Nid.* 9.11 and *b. Nid.* 64b, Tirza Meachem concludes that '[u]terine blood was seen as female seed, the parallel to male semen'.[24] Ramban (1194–1270 CE), commenting on a rabbinic teaching on Lev. 12.2

18. Cf. E. Cantarella, *Pandora's Daughters: The Role and Status of Women in Greek and Roman Antiquity* (Baltimore: The Johns Hopkins University Press, 1987), 59–61, and O'Grady, 'The Semantics of Taboo', 8.

19. This point is conceded by Feucht, *Das Kind im Alten Ägypten*, 47, 93, despite her preliminary assumption of a monogenetic theory of reproduction in Egypt. Cf. Stol, *Birth*, 6. The blessing formula in Deut. 7.14 demonstrates awareness that the male partner can also be infertile.

20. Cited by Stol, *Birth*, 5: 'her innards accept the semen'.

21. Cf. ibid., 8.

22. *KTU* 1.17.I.39–42; Cf. Marsman, *Women in Ugarit and Israel*, 213–14.

23. *Genit.* 5.6.7.8 (Littré 7:476–78) and *Nat. puer.* 12.1 (Littré 7:486); A. Rousselle, 'Observation féminine et idéologie masculine. Le corps de la femme d'après les médecins grecs', *Annales ESC* 35 (Paris: Colin, 1980), 1089–115; L. Dean-Jones, *Women's Bodies in Classical Greek Science* (Oxford: Clarendon, 1996), 148–60.

24. T. Z. Meachem, 'An Abbreviated History of the Development of the Jewish Menstrual Laws', in *Women and Water: Menstruation in Jewish Life and Law*, ed. Rahel R. Wasserfall (Hanover, NH: University Press of New England, 1999), 25.

to the effect that 'if the woman emits seed first, she will bear a son',[25] wrote that this did not mean that the child was formed from the female seed, since that seed consists of blood. But in this connection, he also adduces the contrary (Greek) notion that the child's substance does indeed consist entirely of the woman's blood, the man's contribution being simply the formative power: 'And if so, the word *tazria* will be like..."as the garden causeth the seeds that are sown in it to spring forth"'.[26]

The nature metaphors implicit in the use of *tazria* in Genesis 1 and Lev. 12.2 may also be reflected in images of a twig- or earth-goddess found on stamp-seals from the MB II B period in Palestine. The iconography is of a woman (goddess) facing forward with feet turned outward. The head is sometimes turned to the side. The woman holds twigs in her hand, and twigs also grow from her pubic triangle.[27] The twigs are therefore commonly seen as symbols of fertility. Thus the notion expressed in Lev. 12.2 about a woman 'bringing forth seed' acquires even greater resonance in light of other manifestations from the cultural background.

b. *Seminal Ejaculation*

As for men, seed is examined in the context of ejaculation, שִׁכְבַת־זֶרַע. This construct chain[28] is confined to a single literary strand (Lev. 15.16, 17, 18, 32; 19.20; 22.4 and Num. 5.13). Two possible etymologies have been considered for the first member of the chain: either from שכב, 'to lie (down)', which would be synecdochic for sexual intercourse, or from a homonymic root meaning 'to pour out'.[29] If the first derivation is correct, then שכב is being used euphemistically, in which case one would have to explain how an expression that combines a euphemism ('to lie down' for sexual intercourse) with a concrete term (semen) is to be understood.

---

25. Ramban (Nachmanides), *Commentary on the Torah: Leviticus*, trans. and annotated by Charles B. Chavel (New York: Shilo, 1974), 156.

26. Cf. Ramban, *Commentary on the Torah Leviticus*, 157, and Cooper, 'A Medieval Jewish Version of Original Sin', 454.

27. Cf. S. Schroer, 'Die Göttin auf den Stempelsiegeln', in *Studien zu den Stempelsiegeln aus Palästina/Israel*, ed. Othmar Keel and Hildi Leu, OBO 88 (Freiburg, Schweiz: Universitätsverlag, 1989), 89–207 (96–98, 123–25).

28. Hartley, *Leviticus*, 203, speaks of an 'adverbial gen[itive]' or a 'gen[itive] of effect'.

29. GesB[17], 825, leans in this direction: '1. Lagerung and 2. m. זֶרַע wahrsch. das Ausgießen' (thus also KBL[3], 1379). By contrast, Orlinsky, 'The Hebrew Root ŠKB', 37, assumes a single meaning for all occurrences of the word, namely 'outpouring'. Milgrom, *Leviticus 1–16*, 927, 'literally, an outpouring of seed'. Cf. Schorch, *Euphemismen*, 206–7, for further discussion.

In the passages referenced above, שׁכב synecdochically denotes the sexual behavior of a man in relation to a woman, to a male partner (Lev. 18.22; 20.13), or to an animal (Exod. 22.18; Deut. 27.21). The 'lying' or 'sleeping' represents an aspect of the overall sexual encounter. Through its connection to זֶרַע in the construct chain as well as from the various contexts, the term acquires a sexual meaning. Genesis 19 explicitly counterposes its antonym קום ('to arise') and uses שׁכב both for 'lying down' (v. 33) and for intercourse (v. 33). Only in Gen. 19.33, 35 and in 2 Sam. 13.11 (in Amnon's exhortation to Tamar) is the root שׁכב used in a sexual sense for a female subject.

As with other expressions for sexual intercourse, a certain ambiguity can arise in unclear contexts or with variant formulations, as for example in Ruth 3.4, 7, where Ruth lies down at Boaz's 'feet'.[30] The concept of שׁכב occurs frequently in legal texts: in Leviticus 15 to denote a source of contamination, and in the list of sexual taboos in Leviticus 20 it is used analogously to לקח ('to take, marry'), as the latter term's occurrence in the parallel context in Leviticus 18 demonstrates. In Lev. 20.18 it parallels an expression meaning 'to uncover shame' (cf. Deut. 27.20, 21, 22, 23). For these literary strands it represents a technical term.

By contrast, if we assume that שִׁכְבָה in שִׁכְבַת־זֶרַע derives from the homonymic root שׁכב ('to pour out'), then the resulting expression 'outpouring of seed' is literal rather than euphemistic. Also in favor of this interpretation is that one passage (Lev. 15.16, 17) uses שִׁכְבַת־זֶרַע to denote not sexual intercourse, but ejaculation in the absence of a partner; in two others (Lev. 15.32 and 22.4), שִׁכְבַת־זֶרַע is used 'summarily and generally for ejaculation'.[31] In Lev. 15.16, 32 and 22.4 the expression is used with the verb 'to go out from' independently of whether the secretion occurs during the sexual act, thus emphasizing ejaculation. By contrast, in Lev. 15.18; 19.20 and Num. 5.13 שִׁכְבַת־זֶרַע occurs in contexts that emphasize sexual congress; in the two latter cases, in connection with prohibited relations.

The regulations for proper behavior in the war camp in Deut. 23.11 also concern themselves with pollution from bodily emissions. Besides emissions of semen (vv. 11–12), human excrement (vv. 13–15) is singled out as harmful for the camp. Because God is present there, the camp must be kept holy (v. 15). The text speaks of a 'nocturnal event' (קְרֵה־לָיְלָה), the only occurrence of this euphemism in the Bible.[32] Men affected by an

30. Brenner, *Intercourse of Knowledge*, 22–23, 37.
31. Schorch, *Euphemismen*, 207.
32. Cf. GesB[17], 727, and Schorch, *Euphemismen*, 192.

emission of semen must leave the camp and bathe, and they may return the following evening. This passage shares certain presuppositions with Leviticus 15, but it casts them in a different linguistic form. It is not possible to know for certain whether the cognate noun מִקְרֶה in 1 Sam. 20.26 refers to an emission of semen; Saul reasons to himself that David's absence at the feast may be due to an event that rendered him unclean. According to Leviticus 15, however, such an occurrence would certainly require avoidance of cultic areas.

Yet another noun to consider is שְׁכֹבֶת (Lev. 18.20, 23; 20.15 and Num. 5.20), which always occurs with the verb נתן.[33] In three passages, the feminine object of a man's sexual attentions is appended with the preposition בְּ: either an animal (Lev. 18.23 and 20.15) or a woman (Num. 5.20). The act expressed by this construction can be performed only by males on females. The noun שְׁכֹבֶת has been assigned two different meanings depending upon the proposed etymology of שׁכב: (1) 'cohabitation', (2) 'outpouring'. It could represent an abbreviation of a euphemistic phrase that omits mention of the material substance, since the substance is implied by the accompanying verb נתן ('to give'). The particular way in which the construction is used in both Leviticus 18 and 20 also argues for understanding שְׁכֹבֶת as euphemistic for 'emission of seed'.

A review of the ways in which the construct chain שִׁכְבַת־זֶרַע is used in Lev. 15.16, 17, 18, 32 makes clear that it can mean both sexual intercourse and ejaculation. In Lev. 15.16, 17 it is used exclusively for the emission of semen. It represents a technical expression that focuses on the cultic consequence of a loss of semen, namely, that the affected man becomes ritually impure for a day, as do the objects upon which his semen falls or the woman with whom he has had relations. The texts do not attempt to explain why loss of semen creates impurity. It is noteworthy that in texts dealing with reproduction, the noun זֶרַע in its meaning of male seed is not in the foreground. Finally, through its use of the causative stem (hiphil) of זרע to mean 'bring forth seed', Lev. 12.2 brings to expression that the woman also occupies a substantive role in human reproduction.

III. *Blood*

The noun דָּם ('blood') is used approximately 360 times in the Old Testament, most densely in Leviticus, which has 88 occurrences.[34] The plural דָּמִים has as its primary meaning the violent shedding of blood.

---

33. Cf. Milgrom, *Leviticus 1–16*, 927.
34. See Gerleman, 'דָּם *dām* Blut', *THAT* 1:448.

Blood constitutes a central element in the various forms of sacrificial offering,[35] although even in the case of the חַטָּאת it may be replaced by a plant-based donation (Lev. 5.11–13). The instructions for the whole burnt offering (Lev 1) state at the beginning that the animal's blood must be offered (Lev. 1.5). In the עֹלָה and the אָשָׁם the blood is sprinkled upon the altar (זרק; cf. Exod. 29.16; Lev. 1.5, 11; 3.2, 8, 13; 7.2, 14; 8.19, 24; 9.12, 18; 17.6; Num. 18.7). In the חַטָּאת the priest brings the blood to the entrance of the Tent of Meeting, dips his finger in it, and casts it seven times upon the entrance curtain of the sanctuary (Lev. 4.6, 17), after which he applies some to the horns of the altar. The remainder is poured out at the altar's base (Lev. 4.7, 18, 25, 30, 34; 14.41; 17.4, 13). On the Day of Atonement, the blood is sprinkled in the direction of the place of atonement (הַכַּפֹּרֶת) inside the Holy of Holies (Lev. 16.14–15). In priestly ordination, blood is applied to the ordinand's right earlobe (Exod. 29.20; Lev. 8.23). A person who has recovered from eczema is sprinkled with the blood of a slaughtered bird, after which the priest declares the person pure (Lev. 14.4–6, 51–53). Overall, blood's ritually purifying function is central to the rites involving its sprinkling and smearing. In addition, an apotropaic function may be discerned: in Exod. 12.7 the Passover blood deflects harm (as does the blood of circumcision in Exod. 4.24–26).

The regulations in Leviticus 15 speak of women's blood, whereas in the treatment of circumcision in Leviticus 12, no blood is mentioned. The texts do not claim that the woman's cultic ineligibility is due to her blood loss. Further, blood in itself is never described as 'impure' (טָמֵא); it can cause both cultic impurity (Lev. 15.19–21; Isa. 59.3) and cultic purity (Lev. 14.14, 49–52).[36] In Lev. 12.4, 5 the expression 'blood of (her) purification'[37] is used in connection with a period of cultic ineligibility for the woman, which points toward a cleansing power in blood.

When a woman's discharge of blood lasts longer than her usual monthly flow, she becomes impure (Lev. 15.25). The woman's genital discharge is characterized in terms of its substance: thus v. 19 reads, 'blood is her discharge', and v. 25, with reference to unusually long-lasting flows, mentions her 'flow of blood'.

---

35. Cf. Eberhart, *Studien zur Bedeutung der Opfer*, 222–88.
36. Cf. G. J. Wenham, *The Book of Leviticus*, NICOT (Grand Rapids: Eerdmans, 1979), 188: 'blood is at once the most effective ritual cleanser...and the most polluting substance when it is in the wrong place'.
37. Cf. *DCH* 3:348–49, '*blood of*, perh. requiring, *purification*'.

a. *The Life Is in the Blood*

Blood is the substance that transports life and vitality. The law given in Deut. 12.23–25, after permitting profane slaughter, prohibits the eating of blood, giving as justification the simple equation, 'for the blood is the life' (v. 23a). The flesh may be eaten but not the blood, because blood is נֶפֶשׁ, i.e., 'life' (or 'life force', 'vitality'). Other passages which prohibit the consumption of blood are Gen. 9.4, Lev. 17.10–14, and Lev. 19.26, along with Lev. 3.17 and 7.26–27, which additionally forbid the consumption of fat.[38] Leviticus 17.10–14 represents a Sinaitic appendix to the primeval, universally applicable prohibition in Genesis 9, which is interested in a partial restitution of creation. The multiple attempts that Leviticus 17 makes to rationalize the blood prohibition are elaborations and variations of the interrelations of נֶפֶשׁ, דָּם and בָּשָׂר. The argument takes chiastic form:

> [10] And if anyone of the house of Israel or of the strangers who reside among them ingest any blood; I will set my face against the person who partakes of the blood. And I will cut him off from his kin.
> [11] For the life of the flesh is in the blood. And I have placed it upon the altar for making reconciliation and purification for your lives. It is the blood that effects reconciliation and purification by means of life.
> [12] Therefore I say to the descendants of Israel: No person among you shall ingest blood, nor shall the stranger who resides among you ingest blood...
> [14] For the life of all flesh – its blood is its life. Therefore I say to the descendants of Israel: You shall not ingest the blood of any flesh, for the life of all flesh is its blood. Anyone who ingests of it shall be cut off.[39]

The simplest predication appears to be in v. 11aα, whose interpretation admittedly depends upon how one translates the preposition בְּ.[40] The LXX took the preposition as a *beth essentiae* and thereby assimilated v. 11a to v. 14b, surely not least because of the equation in v. 14a of דָּם and נֶפֶשׁ.[41] If instead the preposition is understood as a *beth instrumentii*

---

38. The prohibition against consuming blood is believed to be unique to Israel in the ancient Near East; cf. M. Vervenne, '"The Blood Is the Life and the Life Is the Blood": Blood as a Symbol of Life and Death in Biblical Tradition (Gen 9,4)', in *Ritual and Sacrifice in the Ancient Near East*, ed. Jan Quaegebeur, OLA 55 (Leuven: Peeters, 1993), 451–70 (456, 458). Ancient Greece is the only other culture in which blood is recognized as material for sacrifice (cf. B. Bergquist, 'Bronze Age Sacrificial Koine in the Eastern Mediterranean? A Study of Animal Sacrifice in the Ancient Near East', in Quaegebeur, ed., *Ritual and Sacrifice in the Ancient Near East*, 11–43 [13, 23]).

39. Translation is a slightly changed version of the JPS.

40. Cf. Eberhart, *Studien zur Bedeutung der Opfer*, 259–60.

41. Likewise Vervenne, '"The Blood Is the Life"', 467.

('by means of'), then blood is not life itself but rather life's locus or seat.⁴² This interpretation is supported by the lack of any statement in the verse about blood's material composition; rather, the verse expresses a cultic or functional regulation.

Seen in the light of these explanations of the prohibition against consuming blood, the shedding of blood in animal sacrifice (vv. 3–5 and chs. 1–7) could be taken to represent a return to God of the life that the blood contains.⁴³ But human beings are not the owners of the blood, even though as offerers of sacrifice they pour it out at the altar; rather, as v. 11b emphasizes (in its literal translation), YHWH himself places it upon the altar (an action that is usually performed by priests), so that atonement may be made for the life of the offerers. The idea that sacrifice is a return to God by the worshiper of what belongs to God (i.e., the life) must also take into consideration the statement of v. 11b, namely, that God himself has placed the blood upon the altar.⁴⁴ The argument in v. 11 includes two כִּי clauses: the blood stands for life, and it has been instituted by YHWH as the medium for purification and atonement.⁴⁵ Thus the pouring out of the blood on the altar guarantees what the prohibition of eating blood implies, namely, that the blood is given back to God.

The rationale for the prohibition against eating blood is repeated in v. 14 in two nearly identical כִּי clauses, in the context of killing animals during a hunt. The entire discussion is then compressed into an extremely terse equation: life is blood.⁴⁶ When (much) blood is spilled, death can result.

---

42. Cf. Janowski, *Sühne*, 245–46; J. Milgrom, *Leviticus 17–22*, AB 3A (New York: Doubleday, 2000), 1478; and B. J. Schwartz, 'The Prohibitions Concerning the "Eating" of Blood in Leviticus 17', in Anderson and Olyan, eds., *Priesthood and Cult in Ancient Israel*, 34–63 (47–48).

43. Cf. Milgrom, *Leviticus 1–16*, 1003: 'Sacrifice...means returning life to its creator. This is the underlying postulate of the blood prohibitions as well... Herein lies the link between the two major corpora in P's Leviticus, sacrifices (chaps. 1–10) and impurities (chaps. 11–16).'

44. This action is usually ascribed to a priest (cf. Exod. 29.12; Lev. 8.15; 16.8).

45. Milgrom, *Leviticus 1–22*, 1474–75, argues that this law concerns only the offering of well-being, even though elsewhere no expiatory function is attributed to it. For critiques of this view, cf. R. Rendtorff, *Leviticus*, BKAT III/1 (Neukirchen-Vluyn: Neukirchener, 1985), 168–69, and Janowski, *Sühne*, 242–43.

46. Cf. R. Rendtorff, 'Another Prolegomenon to Leviticus 17:11', in *Pomegranates and Golden Bells: Studies in Biblical, Jewish, and Near Eastern Ritual, Law, and Literature in Honor of Jacob Milgrom*, ed. David Wright et al. (Winona Lake, IN: Eisenbrauns, 1995), 23–28 (25), on Lev. 17.11, 14a, 14b: 'the *nepeš* in the blood – the blood in the *nepeš* – *nepeš* equals blood. All three of these formulations revolve around the same idea'. See also Schwartz, 'Prohibitions Concerning Eating', 63.

By contrast, in the context of ritual, blood loss signifies life. Although some interpreters characterize blood as a *symbol* for life, Leviticus 17 formulates it more concretely: דָּם and נֶפֶשׁ, blood and life, are equated; i.e., blood *is* life. Corresponding to the loss of blood is a loss of life ('loss of vitality'[47]). Of course, this idea cannot be simply transferred to the blood loss of menstruation, since the latter is a prerequisite for reproductivity.[48] In the interpretation of Levitcus 15, it is precisely the reproductive power, i.e. the fertility[49] and thus the gender of menstrual blood, that must be considered. We shall return to this issue under the heading 'Impurity as a Marker of the Gender Boundary' (Chapter 7, section I.c).

b. *Physiology and Symbolic System*
The texts sketch a physiology of bodily fluids with the help of a symbolic system that draws boundaries between the sexes, between inside and outside. Nevertheless, in spite of the differentiation into two sexes, a tendency is discernible to describe the male and female bodies analogously. In its application of participial and verbal forms of the root זוב to both men and women, the text establishes an analogy between male and female genital secretions. Genital secretions bear gender-neutral characteristics, with women's secretions constituting a special case. This also holds true about the uses of דָּם, since blood is mentioned only in relation to women's secretions.

The question dealt with in this chapter has been how language gives rise to body and gender. Like the term בָּשָׂר that was elucidated in the preceding chapter (Chapter 4), the word-family of 'flow' has proved to be equally ambivalent in relation to perceptions of the sexual body, in that the Bible's language depicts both a 'one-body model' and sexual difference. According to Leviticus 15, it is not the sex act as such that renders one impure. In the unusual construction 'outpouring of seed' it is not the material substance that stands in the foreground. While the noun 'seed' is applied only to the male body, the use of the related verb זרע hiphil in Lev. 12.2 for the female body suggests a bisexual doctrine of seed.

---

47. G. J. Wenham, 'Why Does Sexual Intercourse Defile (Lev 15:18)?', *ZAW* 95 (1983): 432–34 (434).
48. Cf. Milgrom, *Leviticus 1–16*, 1002: 'Vaginal blood and semen represent the forces of life; their loss – death'.
49. A. Gottlieb, 'Menstrual Cosmology Among the Beng of Ivory Coast', in *Blood Magic: The Anthropology of Menstruation*, ed. T. Buckley and A. Gottlieb (Berkeley: University of California Press, 1988), 73, states regarding the West-African Beng: 'Rather, menstrual blood is viewed as a symbol of human fertility'.

Blood is the locus of the life force. The common ethnological theory that (menstrual) blood is connected with deep-seated fears finds no echo in Leviticus.[50] Within the Hebrew Bible's symbol system, blood loss resulting from specific violations of the body's boundaries can cause impurity. The blood that is spilled in circumcision is differentiated from menstrual blood, which causes impurity. The sex of the blood plays a role. Nor is blood fundamentally impure;[51] as in the case of a bleeding wound. Only menstrual blood and a woman's unusually prolonged bleeding cause impurity. At the same time, blood in itself is not seen as impure; on the contrary, Leviticus 12 contains the expression 'blood of purification'. The question of conceptions of bodily purity will be pursued in Chapter 7. But first an analysis will be performed of how menstruation is characterized (Chapter 6).

50. Claude Lévi-Strauss points out that among many peoples the blood is felt to be a danger primarily to the woman herself and not to others (*Les structures élémentaires de la parenté*, 2nd ed. [Paris: La Haye, 1967], 24–25).
51. For its purifying role, see Milgrom, *Leviticus 1–16*, 254–55.

Chapter 6

MENSTRUATION

The purity regulations bring women's bodies into relation with the cult. Leviticus 12 and 15 describes the female body with the help of two lexemes: the substantive נִדָּה (*niddah*) and the root דוה, the former being the most influential in the reception history. The term *niddah* has assumed the role of a technical term for the condition into which women are placed by their menstrual cycle. In the exegetical discussion, seemingly little notice has been taken that *niddah* and דוה are used in diverse contexts. We shall analyze how the words' cultic uses relate to other instances. This will include a review of dictionaries and translations that frequently ascribe repugnant connotations to the terms which will lead us to revised translations.

The intertextual analysis at the end of this chapters examines how the phenomenon of menstruation is treated in narrative texts. Through the comparison with the narrative texts the specific traits of the cultic conception of menstruation becomes apparent. This chapter thus offers a comprehensive view of menstruation in the Hebrew Bible.[1]

I. *Menstruation as Separation*

a. *What Do Menstruating Women and the Land of Israel Have in Common?*
This strange question arises because, in God's discourse in Ezek. 36.17, both are described as unclean and related to one another:

> Mortal, when the house of Israel lived on their own land, they defiled it by their ways and their deeds. Their ways before me were like the uncleanness of a woman in her menstrual period (כְּטֻמְאַת הַנִּדָּה).

---

1. For earlier works on menstruation, see Klee, *Menstruation*, and Philip, *Menstruation and Childbirth*.

The connection of the term *niddah* with uncleanness in Ezekiel 36 led to the identification of these two words. This idea found repercussions in lexica,[2] commentaries[3], monographs[4] and translations of the Bible. The 17th edition of Gesenius indicates the core meaning of *niddah* as abhorrent impurity.[5] The entry is subdivided into (1) impurity of the female bleeding and (2) impurity in general. Thus different levels are confused: the physical description of the blood flow and its possible religious or cultic implications. The dictionary passes a moral and religious judgment on the blood flow. In the Hebrew–Aramaic Lexicon (KBL[3]), the entry on *niddah* is divided in two subsections: (1) bleeding, menstruation of a woman, and (2) separation, abomination, defilement.[6] The *Dictionary of Classical Hebrew* mentions *niddah* as 'impurity (unless…flow of blood)' and 'flow of blood (unless…impurity)', leaving it up to the reader of the dictionary to decide.[7] Uncleanness is considered to be the specific and dominant aspect of the definition.

An etymological point of view does not provide a satisfying answer to the meaning of *niddah* either: it is deduced from the root 'to abandon, to flee' or from 'to migrate, to flee', but the actual meaning varies very little. If *niddah* is understood as the flow of blood, the attached meaning of impurity remains puzzling. *Niddah* is often understood as seclusion, but whether this seclusion is perceived in a physical, social or cultic manner is not specified.

However, is there evidence in the text to support this assimilation of impurity and menstruation? In the purity-*torot* this term is only once connected with uncleanness in Lev. 15.26. In Lev. 15.33 the adjective טמא is used for the woman during her menstruation. Finally, *niddah* נִדָּה in the genitive construction מֵי נִדָּה ('water of the *niddah*', Num. 19.9, 13.20–21; 31.23) cannot be understood as something impure against

---

2. Cf. GesB[17], 487, and G. Feld, 'Menstruation I (AT)', *NBL* 2: 773–76 (773).

3. Cf. Milgrom, *Leviticus 1–16*, 744; M. Gruber, 'Purity and Impurity in Halakic Sources', in de Troyer et al., eds., *Wholly Woman*, 65–76 (71): '*niddah* in its basic meaning of "impurity"'.

4. Cf. W. Paschen, *Rein und Unrein: Untersuchung zur biblischen Wortgeschichte*, StANT 24 (Munich: Kösel, 1970), 27–28; Wright, 'Unclean – Clean', 729. Philip, *Menstruation und Childbirth*, 72: 'The inherent nature of the impurity of menstrual blood is accepted in all priestly writings'.

5. GesB[17], 487.

6. KBL[3], 635–36.

7. Cf. *DCH* 5:621–24.

the background of its use as a cleansing substance.⁸ Moreover, it should be noted that Hebrew usually employs the semantic field of טָמְאָה to describe impurity.

b. *Bodily, Social, or Cultic Separation?*

The two main etymological models of נִדָּה that have been discussed present yet another question: Is *niddah* to be understood as a social or a physiological separation? It is derived either from the geminate נדד qal ('leave, flee'⁹) or from the piel form of נדה, 'avoid, flee'. Independent of the root preferred, the meanings only vary slightly and are practically synonymous.¹⁰ נִדָּה is understood as rejection, distancing, and separation. Moshe Bar-Asher suggests an alternative interpretation: נִדָּה reflecting two homonyms – one as an abstract noun for the impurity during menstruation, and a second designating a female person like in Mishnaic Hebrew.¹¹

The intercultural comparison and, similarly, the later rabbinic texts have led to the general conclusion that woman in ancient Israel were excluded from social life during their period of menstruation.¹² This thesis then serves in the discussion concerning the kind of separation as a circular argument in favor of understanding *niddah* as social separation. Referring to the taboo related to menstruation risks obscuring the nuances in the text. These stereotypes largely influenced the sense attributed to this Hebrew root for its linguistic usage in the Bible. In regard to the times of the First and Second Temple, there is no proof of such an isolation of women during or consequent to menstruation.

---

8. Differently Ruane, *Sacrifice and Gender*, 145: 'P's unusual use of the term *niddâ* in Num 19 to describe the impurity of death, as well as its unusual choice of a female animal, relates death impurity to the objectively unrelated impurity of reproduction'.

9. Cf. GesB¹⁷, 487; likewise Moshe Greenberg, 'The Etymology of *nidda* "(Menstrual) Impurity"', in *Solving Riddles and Untying Knots: Biblical, Epigraphic, and Semitic Studies in Honor of J. C. Greenfield*, ed. Ziony Zevit *et al.* (Winona Lake, IN: Eisenbrauns, 1995), 69–77 (71).

10. Cf. Milgrom, *Leviticus 1–16*, 744–45.

11. Cf. M. Bar Asher, 'The *Qal* Passive Participle of Geminate Verbs in Biblical Hebrew', in *Biblical Hebrew in Its Northwest Semitic Setting: Typological and Historical Perspectives*, ed. Steven E. Fassberg and Avi Hurvitz (Jerusalem: Hebrew University/Magnes, 2006), 11–25.

12. E. Püschel, *Die Menstruation und ihre Tabus* (Stuttgart: Schattauer, 1988); K. van der Toorn, *Van haar wieg tot haar graf: De rol van de godsdienst in het leven van de Israëlitische en Babylonische vrouw* (Baarn: Ten Have, 1987), 46–49.

If the underlying verb 'reject/abandon' represents the physical process this term (נדד or נדה) would then describe the bleeding (the separation of the blood),[13] as expressed in Lev. 15.19.

On the basis of this understanding of the lexeme נִדָּה as '(blood) flow', the postulated variant of the meaning 'impure' is inconceivable. The meaning of *niddah* cannot therefore be clearly determined by etymology alone; this is only possible through analysis of the contexts in which the word appears. We will now deal with the questions raised by the review of the lexica by analyzing the passages containing *niddah*. This will reveal the semantic spectrum of the term.

c. Niddah *as a Cultic Term*

The purity-*torot* relative to sexual discharges of the woman in Leviticus 15 is the starting point of the study, since this chapter contains not only the largest number of occurrences (nine out of fifteen in Leviticus; altogether it is only used 27 times in the Hebrew Bible) but also forges the use of *niddah* with respect to the cultic state during the menstruation. The introductory verse about women in Lev. 15.19 reads:

> And a woman, when she has a discharge, her discharge being blood in her body, seven days she is in her menstrual state. Whoever touches her is ritually impure until evening.

The Hebrew text uses different expressions to describe the situation of a menstruating woman. The words 'her discharge being blood' indicate a physical phenomenon, whereas *niddah* is more of a cultic description. The statements in v. 25 on a discharge of blood that would last exceptionally long – 'many days, not at the time of her menstrual separation (*niddah*)' and 'beyond her period of menstrual separation (*niddah*)' – stress the temporal aspect of *niddah*. *Niddah* will last for a specific period of time (seven days, see Lev. 12.2), whereas the period of blood loss may be shorter or longer. *Niddah*, in this context, is a technical term for the cultic position caused by blood flow lasting for seven days. In English, there is no equivalent of this. The authors of the early Greek translation, the LXX, already had to deal with the same problem: the lack of a specific cultic term. Therefore, Greek translation uses a term from the medical literature of antiquity (ἄφεδρος), losing thus the cultic dimension. Likewise, *niddah* adopts a medical connotation when it is translated as 'monthly flow'

---

13. Levine, *Leviticus*, 97: 'It does not connote impurity in and of itself but, rather, describes the physiological process of the flow of blood'. See also Levine, *Numbers 1–20*, 464: '*niddāh* literally means, as applied to a menstruating woman, "one who is spilling" blood'.

or 'menstruation'. *Niddah* cannot be translated as 'menstruation' in all cases, since the duration of the blood flow is variable, while *niddah*, by definition, lasts for seven days. *Niddah*, understood as the exclusion from the sacred, refers to a situation caused by the blood flow but presupposing a cultic understanding.

The question now is in what sense the body, especially the loss of blood, matters. The term *niddah* in Leviticus may refer to the bleeding, but blood as such is never called 'unclean' and the period of *niddah* has been fixed at seven days, regardless of the actual length of the menstruation. The period during which women are regarded as a danger to the sanctuary, or, the other way round, women are endangered by the sanctuary, is independent of the actual length of blood loss.

Leviticus 15.19 does not state directly that a menstruating woman is unclean. She causes cultic impurity towards others. However, impurity is not the basic meaning of *niddah*: 'Such a woman [a menstruating one] was declared to be impure during her period, but it is not the word *niddāh* that, by itself, connotes that impurity!'[14] *Niddah* indicates the cultic position caused by the menstrual cycle and not so much a physical concept.

This excludes impurity as the primary sense of *niddah*. Impurity, in the context of menstruation, is therefore evoked only through the combination of the two semantic fields. Thus it becomes clear that the lexica and commentaries adopted the secondary meanings as the primary one. How and why this happened will be discussed in what follows.

d. Niddah *as a Socio-religious Term*

The common feature of the following passages is that, while considering the menstruating woman, her state was seen not only as a cultic issue but also implying ethical questions. In the catalogue of sexual prohibitions in Lev. 18.19, in addition to a man's mother and sister, a woman during her menstruation is listed as a forbidden sexual partner: 'Do not come near a woman during her menstrual period of impurity to uncover her nakedness'.[15]

In Leviticus 18, *niddah* is discussed not in a cultic but an ethical context, and, in contrast to Lev. 15.29, the text speaks of the total exclusion from the community, which actually means the death of both man and woman. The abstention from a woman in her *niddah*, serves as a distinguishing marker between Israel and their neighboring peoples (Lev. 18.3).

---

14. Levine, *Numbers 1–20*, 464.
15. Cf. *The Contemporary Torah: A Gender-Sensitive Adaptation of the JPS Translation*, ed. D. E. S. Stein (Philadelphia: Jewish Publication Society, 2006).

The juridical speech in Ezek. 22.10 reiterates the list of taboos:

> In you they uncover their fathers' nakedness; in you they violate women in their menstrual periods. (NRSV)

Because the verb that is used refers to a violent and illegitimate sexual contact (ענה[16]), this text appears to guard women against violation. While Leviticus 15 has the purpose of protecting the sanctuary and other people from unclean contact, the moral lesson of Ezekiel 22 gives no indications of a negative appreciation of a menstruating woman. Stemming from priestly circles, the prophet Ezekiel uses the language and ideas of the so-called priestly book of Leviticus, yet in a rather loose way and with a different intention. In Ezekiel 18 and 22, the catalogue of prohibited sexual relations of Leviticus 18 is transformed into a question of justice and ethics. On other instances in Ezekiel, the cultic term of *niddah* even develops into a polemic concept.

e. Niddah *as Pejorative and Polemical Term*

In Leviticus 20, Ezra 9, Ezekiel 7 and 36 and 1 Chronicles 29, *niddah* is used to denote religious, cultural and ethical differences. These texts all originated in the wake of the post-Babylonian exilic period and were completed during the Persian or Hellenistic period. During the latter, *niddah* becomes a literary indication of what is outside the system, suggesting that clear-cut boundaries could be set.

In the list of the sexual contacts to be condemned and punished in Lev. 20.2, *niddah* is used in a devaluating tone:

> If a man takes a wife of his brother, it is a situation like in times of menstruation (נִדָּה).

The logic is inverted in comparison with ch. 18. While Lev. 18.19 condemns sexual intercourse with a woman during menstruation (*niddah*) in Leviticus 20 sexual intercourse with the wife of one's brother is said to constitute נִדָּה. A term that is employed as a neutral technical cultic expression for menstruation in Lev. 12.2, 4; 15.19, 24-26 is used for 'confusion of the levels of order' (Lev. 20.12) or 'shame' (Lev. 20.14) implying disqualification.[17]

---

16. Cf. T. Frymer-Kensky, 'Law and Philosophy: The Case of Sex in the Hebrew Bible', *Semeia* 45 (1989): 89–102 (93), for the piel form of ענה being used for illegitimate sexual intercourse.

17. Cf. Milgrom, *Leviticus 17–22*, 1758: 'However, it should be apparent that H uses this term metaphorically; it is a foul, odious, repulsive act. Here H parts with P's specific, cultic *niddâ*, menstrual impurity (15:19, 20, 26).'

Toward the end of the penitential prayer in Ezra 9, in which the people are exhorted, we read:

> The land that you are entering to possess is a contaminated land unclean with the pollutions (*niddah*) of the peoples of the lands, with their abominations (*niddah*). They have filled it from end to end with their uncleanness. (v. 11)

Here *niddah* appears in a context of abomination and impurity, often used for the very translation of the concept.[18] The people returning from Babylonian captivity conceive the homeland (Israel) as a woman during her menstruation. The catastrophe of the exile is considered as the consequence of religious and cultural pollutions, while the immoral situation of the country is compared to a woman during her monthly blood flow. Menstruating women are equated with impurity, while the land deserving harsh judgment is presented as a menstruating woman. In this sense, impurity becomes a feminine concept and impurity as such is associated with women.

In what sense was the land contaminated in the exilic period? As Klawans states, 'That menstrual impurity is the concern of Ezra 9.11 is out of the question: Israelite women too are subject to menstrual impurity, and this impurity does not defile the land'.[19] After all the land is not stained with menstrual blood. The technical term becomes a simile for the lamentable moral state of the land as it is compared to a woman during her menstruation (*niddah*). This text establishes boundaries in the Persian period, not only between peoples and their cultures and religions (the Hebrews vs. the Egyptians, Canaanites, Babylonians, and Greeks), but between the sexes as well.

Likewise, Ezek. 7.19–20 uses *niddah* as an accusation against the common religious policy, trying to draw a demarcation line back through an expansive exegesis of purity language:

> [19] They shall fling their silver into the streets, their gold shall be treated as contaminated (נִדָּה). Their silver and gold cannot save them on the day of the wrath of YHWH.
> They shall not satisfy their hunger. Or fill their stomach with it. For it was the stumbling block of their iniquity. [20] From their beautiful ornament, in which they took pride. They made their abominable images, their detestable things. Therefore I will make of it an object of contamination (נִדָּה).

---

18. Philip, *Menstruation and Childbirth*, 37, calls this a metaphorical usage of *niddah* which implies that menstruation and impurity are taken as synonyms: 'One kind of impurity, the impurity of menstruation, now represents impurity itself'.

19. Klawans, *Impurity and Sin*, 44.

The term *niddah* is used in parallel with what is outside: those attached with *niddah* must be thrown out and separated from the realm of the holy. Both Ezek. 36.17 and 7.19 as part of a prophetic accusation stress the impurity of the land. The conduct of the people in the sight of God was like the impurity of a woman in her menstrual period. Hence on these instances in Ezekiel *niddah* has been translated with contamination. This usage harks back to the cultic ideology of Leviticus, even though it has been transformed into a moral and sociopolitical symbolic system. In Ezra and Ezekiel menstruation becomes a curse.

In a similar vein 2 Chron. 29.5 argues to purge the holy place from all which is contaminated (נִדָּה) referring implicitly to iconic cultic objects (cf. 2 Kgs. 18.4). The aspect of purging comes to the forefront. If, according to Leviticus 15, a woman is temporarily cultic impure during her menstruation, then in the above mentioned postexilic texts she actually becomes the symbol of impurity.

There is no evidence of a linear development; instead, divergent uses appear. The polemical, pejorative aspect of *niddah* was very efficacious. The use of נִדָּה in Ezek. 7.19 marks a decisive point in the transformation of the meaning, for the lexeme passed, through metaphorical use, from being a technical term designating a woman's state in relation to the cult to signifying a menstruating woman in the Hebrew of the Mishnah.

f. *Discourse on Menstruation as a Boundary Marker*

Rereading the exegetical findings with the work of the cultural anthropologist Mary Douglas in mind sheds further light on their implications for the relation between the body and the sacred and its social dimensions. She understands the human body as a microcosm that reflects the macrocosm that is the social and religious community. 'The danger', Douglas writes, 'which is risked by boundary transgression is power. Those vulnerable margins and those attacking forces which threaten to destroy good order represent the powers inhering in the cosmos'.[20]

Having stated this, the discourse on menstruation can be explained in spatial terms serving to draw borders. Symbolic patterns implied in such concepts as impurity and pollution reinforce social practices. Through the female body, the texts in Ezra and Ezekiel strive to control borders and enforce purity laws. Their interpretations of the purity regulations deploy the female body to create a situation that is unattainable by the social body. The female body is used as a symbol of the community and of socio-religious representations, which are in turn formed by rituals and purity laws. In these texts the female body becomes the instrument to set

20. Douglas, *Purity and Danger*, 161.

religious and cultic boundaries. Obviously, *niddah* as a spatial concept functions on various levels as a system of symbols by which boundaries are set.

(1) Niddah *as a cultic boundary marker*. *Niddah* was coined in Leviticus 12 and 15 as a technical cultic term for the description of a woman's state due to menstruation that obliged her to stay away from the sanctuary. This condition of incompatibility with the cult lasted for seven days. The female cycle and the cult were therefore mutually related to each other through the term. This fundamental cultic meaning of the term is also reflected in its polemical use in Ezek. 7.19–20 where it is said that everything affected by *niddah* must be removed from the sanctuary.

(2) Niddah *as physical boundary marker*. The body serves as a boundary marker: everything which trespasses the boundary of the human body can cause pollution. In this sense, sexual fluids become symbolic expressions of cosmic transgressions. Leviticus 12 and 15 do not bother about tears, urine or pus.

The physiological details found in the texts relating to *niddah* are sparse. Leviticus gives no indication of the duration of the complete female cycle or of the duration between the bleedings. Furthermore, the bleeding does not necessarily continue for seven days; only the condition created by the bleeding in relation to the cult lasts for seven days. Cultic impurity can arise independently from concrete material impurities, even after the bleeding has stopped. *Niddah* is therefore fundamentally not a physiological category. This is illustrated by the designation of a postpartum woman (i.e., after childbirth) as *niddah*. Nevertheless, at the same time, symbolic boundaries are inscribed on the woman's body.

(3) Niddah *as gender boundary marker*. The concept of *niddah* is reserved exclusively, in its use by the Hebrew Bible, for the description of women or female gendered personifications. Subsequently, in the Mishnah and in the Talmud, *niddah* designates the menstruation itself. In Qumran (CD 12.1–2; 4QMMT 45.10; 11QT^a/11Q19 45.10) this specifically female concept is likewise used with respect to the man, where the nocturnal emission is described as an impurity comparable to *niddah*.[21] In Leviticus,

---

21. Cf. Gruber, 'Purity and Impurity', 65–76, 71–72; M. Himmelfarb, 'Sexual Relations and Purity in the Temple Scroll and the Book of Jubilees', *DSD* 6 (1999): 11–36 (18). W. Loader, *The Dead Sea Scrolls on Sexuality: Attitudes Towards Sexuality in Sectarian and Related Literature at Qumran* (Grand Rapids: Eerdmans, 2009), 349–51, stresses that the term is likewise used for moral impurities.

however, only impurity of the female body is doubly marked and designated with a particular term, which leads to the othering of the woman. *Niddah* represents a one-sided category that establishes a boundary between the genders that comes to play a role in the constitution of identity, since the laws concerning purity reflect the life cycle on a ritual level.

(4) Niddah *as ethnical and interreligious boundary marker*. The designation of the land as *niddah* in Ezra 9 is used to establish the prohibition of mixing between cultures and ethnics. In Ezekiel 7 the concept of *niddah* serves to stigmatize the women of a specific historical situation. This postexilic Diaspora literature puts boundaries, not only between the sexes but between peoples, their cultures and religions as well.

This kind of literature is a rhetorical response to the social crisis of the exilic or postexilic Persian period whereby boundaries must be introduced with reference to the notions of impurity from Leviticus.

(5) Niddah *as boundary marker in marital sexual life*. The purity regulations in Leviticus 15 themselves may already be understood as a discussion about the praxis of the purity regulations – they are self-reflexive. Not all of them are equally detailed, as for instance the ejaculation of a man is treated more extensively (Lev. 15.2–15) than the regulations for a woman (Lev. 15.19–30). In later times these will be explained as guidelines for everyday life: the regulations about the ejaculation of a man get extended so as to include the blood flow of a woman.[22]

The specifications in rabbinic and talmudic literature reflect a change in the perception of the purity-*torot*. In late medieval Jewish commentaries these texts also invite theological reflection on the anthropology of wo/men.[23] Marital intercourse is forbidden for fifteen days out of each month – the period of the actual blood loss plus seven so-called white days. For the majority of women, resuming sexual activity coincides with the ovulation, the beginning of their fertile period. The Talmud offers an explanation of these rules: the sexual abstinence should inflame the husband's desire towards his wife after *niddah* (*b. Nid.* 31b). While the rules in Leviticus 15 about women during her period affect all people around her, in Talmudic times they are only related to the husband. In the Mishnah, the regulations for women include – besides lifting a portion of dough and lighting the candles to mark the beginning of the festivals and the Shabbat – rules for *niddah*, that is, marital sexual abstinence during

22. Cf. Wright, *The Disposal of Impurities*.
23. Cf. Cooper, 'A Medieval Jewish Version of Original Sin'.

menstruation and subsequent ritual cleansing. However, these rabbinical writings on the purity laws do not aim at a social and religious exclusion of women. In the course of the history of reception of the purity-*torot* in Leviticus 12 and 15, they became so-called family laws[24] which concentrated on the regulations of the married couple.[25] Recognized as negative markers aimed at the exclusion of women from male-dominated sacred places, the menstruation regulations are valued for creating a safe space for female practices.[26]

To conclude, conceptualizing purity in spatial terms has proved helpful for explaining the different meanings of *niddah*. The laws focus on secretions related to sexuality and/or reproduction as they have the potential to cause trouble in social relations especially in patrilineal societies, as Douglas has stressed. In the course of the reception history, the female body as a body undergoing menstruation is used for ethnic, religious and cultic demarcation. It seems to be that the gender issue pervades all the other aspects of identity construction.[27] In Leviticus 20, Ezra 9, Ezekiel 7 and 36 and 2 Chronicles 29, the Hebrew word for menstruation is used in a metaphorical and political sense to denote differences creating an androcentric ideology. In these texts (beyond Lev. 12 and 15) moral conceptions and cultic ideas about purity go hand-in-hand. We shall turn now to the second term used to denote menstruation in the purity-*torot*, namely דוה.

II. *Menstruation as Destabilization*

a. *What Do Menstruation and Sickness Have in Common?*
The woman who has given birth is characterized in Lev. 12.2 as being both in her *niddah* and as one who is 'in the period of her unstable condition' (כִּימֵי נִדַּת דְּוֹתָהּ; cf. Lev. 15.33). The verb דוה occurs as a construct infinitive with a pronominal suffix (דְּוֹתָהּ). This term is frequently left untranslated

---

24. Cf. E. Marienberg, *Niddah: Lorsque les juifs conceptualisent la menstruation* (Paris: Belles lettres, 2003), 40–41, 147–56, 275–79.

25. Cf. ibid.; B. Greenberg, 'Female Sexuality and Bodily Functions in the Jewish Tradition', in *Women, Religion and Sexuality*, ed. J. Becher (Geneva: Trinity, 1990), 1–44 (28–29); and Biale, *Women and Jewish Law*, 148, 158, 173–74.

26. Fonrobert, *Menstrual Purity*, 214: 'To practice forms of menstrual abstention…allowed women to engage in the continuous observance of Torah, with and in their bodies'.

27. Cf. the assessment of C. Camp, 'Feminist and Gender-Critical Perspectives on the Biblical Ideology of Intermarriage', in *Mixed Marriages: Intermarriage and Group Identity in the Second Temple Period*, ed. C. Frevel, LHBOTS 47 (London: T&T Clark International, 2011), 303–15 (314–15).

or merged with *niddah*.²⁸ When translated, it is usually rendered with a term connoting sickness. Thus, for example, the terms for the menstruating woman in Lev. 15.33 is translated as being 'in the infirmity of her period' (הַדָּוָה בְּנִדָּתָהּ).²⁹

The word field דוה describes the menstruating woman in one further instance in Leviticus: among the sexual taboos in Lev. 20.18 the adjectival form specifies the condition of the female participant in a forbidden sexual encounter (אִשָּׁה דָוָה), which, as the second part of the verse makes clear by speaking of 'the uncovering of her flow of blood', it identifies as menstruation.

Should we conclude, then, that these Leviticus passages associate menstruation with illness or indisposition, and finally birth with sickness?³⁰ It would seem then that the application of the root דוה to the menstruant expresses a negative evaluation of bodily processes and discrimination against women.³¹ The implication is that one should understand menstruation as a feminine illness.³² Jacob Milgrom affirms this, arguing from the Akkadian root *dawû* and its Ugaritic cognate *dwy*: 'Thus philology confirms experience: menstruation is associated with illness. Hence, *niddâ* and *dāwâ* are related.'³³ 'Sickness' seems for these interpreters to be the umbrella term.

What remains unclear is whether the root דוה connotes a state of bodily sickness experienced by the female person herself (female gendered word), or whether it serves as a social label.³⁴ Besides defining דוה as illness, dictionaries and commentaries also conflate it (just as they do *niddah*) with טָמֵא ('impure'): GesB¹⁷ translates דָוֶה as '1. impure'.³⁵ The

28. Milgrom, *Leviticus 1–16*, 742, translates in Lev. 12.2: 'during her period of her menstrual infirmity'.

29. See the translation by Elliger, *Leviticus*, 192. The English translation given here is that of the NRSV.

30. According to Philip, *Menstruation and Childbirth*, 29, this is the case: 'The root דוה as a name for the menstruant reflects the idea that menstruation was seen as a kind of sickness'.

31. Cf. D. Ellens, 'Menstrual Impurity and Innovation in Leviticus 15', in de Troyer et al., eds., *Wholly Woman*, 29–44 (30–34, 42). According to Ellens, the text stigmatizes menstruation as unhealthy.

32. KBL³, 207; Cf. Elliger, *Leviticus*, 276. According to Ellens, 'Menstrual Impurity', 30, the text stigmatizes menstruation as unhealthy. As we shall show, the term 'infirmity' (Levine, *Leviticus*) is better than 'sickness' or 'poor health'.

33. Milgrom, *Leviticus 1–16*, 746.

34. For the cultural construction of illness in antiquity, cf. Weissenrieder, *Images of Illness in the Gospel of Luke*.

35. GesB¹⁷, 158.

revised entry in GesB[18] gives as the first definition of the adjective דוה 'menstruating', followed by '2. impure', and finally '3. sad, miserable'.[36] On the one hand, this shows a mistaken extension of the meanings of טָמֵא to other contexts and terms, while on the other, the relations between the different definitions remain unexplained.

However, the passages in question (Lev. 12.2; 15.33; 20.18) establish no connection between menstruation and illness. The word field דוה, it appears, has become associated with illness as a result of other texts. In Deut. 7.15; 28.60, for example, the noun מַדְוֶה refers to the plagues and diseases of Egypt. The synonymy of the two word fields דוה and חֳלִי ('illness') is thought to be established by their parallel use in Ps. 41.4 and Isa. 1.5 of the heart. In Isaiah 1, the context connects the adjectival form with a condition of general weakness caused by injuries and abuse. Next to menstruation, lament is a major referent for the root דוה. This hints to a different direction for the understanding of דוה as weakness and destabilization of the general state. This said, we shall take 'destabilization' in what follows as a first translation, before going on to see whether this might be the term's core meaning.

b. *Destabilization of Physical, Emotional, and Mental Balance*

Derivatives of the lexeme דָּוֶה that are used in Leviticus 12 and 15 for the menstruating woman are often employed, in contexts of plight and lament, to express the sorrow of the heart (Isa. 1.5; Lam. 1.22; 5.17), implying a state of physical and emotional distress. Our first task is therefore to survey these contexts to determine the connection between the two senses and whether the sense in Leviticus can be characterized as euphemistic or metaphorical.

By equating דוה with חֳלִי, the prayer in Ps. 41.4 establishes a parallel between 'sickbed' and 'bed of illness': 'YHWH sustains him on his sickbed; you restore him from his bed of illness'.

In the subsequent verse, the psalmist asks for healing, further strengthening the connection. From Psalm 41 as a whole it becomes clear that the illness depicted has many layers: bodily pain goes along with social and psychic affliction, and, what is most important, the sufferer's physiological destabilization afflicts the relationship with God. Through words of lament the singer tries to express his[37] painful bodily sensations (cf. Lam. 5.17).

---

36. Ges[18], 244-45.
37. Does the use of דוה signal that a woman is speaking?

In Lamentations, the first song, which bemoans the plight of Jerusalem and its inhabitants, twice puts a word derived from the root דוה (Lam. 1.13, 22) into the mouth of Lady Zion:

> He [YHWH] has turned me into a desolate place (שְׁמֵמָה) / all day long faint (דָּוָה). (v. 13)

> For my groans are many and my heart is destabilized (וְלִבִּי דַוָּי). (v. 22c)

That it is a woman who speaks here – a woman introduced in v. 1 as a widow – lends a face to these plaintive, even accusatory, words. A conceptual field beyond any specific gender assignment appears to qualify דוה more narrowly.

Besides Lam. 1.22, there are two other biblical passages in which the heart is characterized as confused, disturbed, raw, even shattered: Isa. 1.5 complains: 'the whole head is sick, the whole heart is destabilized (דַּוָּי)'. Head and heart represent, *pars pro toto*, the person. In Jer. 8.18, we hear a voice lamenting the plight of destroyed Jerusalem. The obscure first half-verse reflects the brokenness that so pains the speaker: 'Incurable sorrow overtakes me, my heart is destabilized (לִבִּי דַוָּי)'.

In all these passages, one must not think of the heart as merely the seat of emotion, which is its meaning in modern Western languages; rather, in Hebrew thought the heart is the locus of thinking, planning, and willing – the point where this lamentation crystallizes.[38] Pain and fear render such a heart narrow and destabilized (Ps. 25.17). The adjectives דָּוֶה and דַּוָּי serve to express the speaker's destabilized condition. In the biblical lamentation literature, no clearly defined physical ailment is in view; rather, lament brings the overall brokenness of body and spirit to expression. Thus, it does not seem correct to make illness the primary association of דוה; rather, the root serves as the affective expression of a destabilization of bodily experience and, as such, a destabilization of the entire person. In the next section, we shall examine whether 'destabilization' as a translation might be used in that sense likewise in the purity-*torot*.

---

38. Cf. M. Smith, 'The Heart and Innards in Israelite Emotional Expressions: Notes from Anthropology and Psychobiology', *JBL* 117, no. 3 (1998): 427–36, and B. Janowski, 'Das Herz – ein Beziehungsorgan. Zum Personenverständnis im Alten Testament', in *Dimensionen der Leiblichkeit. Theologische Zugänge*, ed. Bernd Janowski and Christoph Schwöbel (Neukirchen-Vluyn: Neukirchener Theologie, 2015), 1–39.

c. *Destabilization of Cultic Status*
In contrast to the lamentation texts just considered, chs. 12, 15 and 20 of Leviticus are cultic prescriptions whose primary concern is to classify phenomena. The final verse (v. 33) of Leviticus 15 summarizes the chapter, and in the course of doing so it characterizes the menstruant as 'the unstable one in her menstruation'. In both Lev. 12.2 and 15.33, the word field דוה is introduced along with the technical term נִדָּה to describe the woman's condition. Does this mean that, for Leviticus, the word field דוה has become a similarly technical term for the woman's destabilization with regard to the cult, or does it bring an element of women's experiences into play?[39]

In Lev. 20.18, דוה is used alone to denote the woman's menstruating condition. The context signals a shift in the term's meaning from neutral to pejorative. Leviticus 20 stipulates that a man's sexual intercourse with a menstruating woman renders him impure, and not just for seven days, as Leviticus 15 prescribes; instead, it results in his permanent exclusion from cult and community and thus in death – this despite the fact that Leviticus 15 does not use דוה as synonym for ritual impurity. As we shall see in the next section, two other passages (Job 6.7 and Isa. 30.22) make the same connection that Lev. 20.18 appears to make between דוה and impurity.

d. *Destabilization of Aesthetic and Religious Sensibilities*
Job 6.7 associates דְּוֵי with revulsion: 'But the very things my appetite revolts at are now my food as in sickness (כִּדְוֵי)'. In the face of his misery, Job experiences distaste for everything edible, which leads him to reach for the comparison just quoted. Isaiah 30.22 brings דוה into connection with cultically impure objects in the context of a polemic against images of (alien) gods:

> Then you will defile your silver-covered graven images and your gold-plated molten images.
> You will scatter them as things that destabilize (דָּוָה); / you will say to them: Dung!

The sequence of events in Isa. 30.18–26 reaches its turning point when the people discard their human-crafted idols as something out of bounds. In contrast to Leviticus, where excrement is not mentioned as a cultic contaminant, this passage drastically links the idols to excrement in order to emphasize the severity of the contamination that emanates from them. This comparison recalls the use of נִדָּה in Ezra 9.11 and 2 Chr. 29.5 as

---

39. Cf. the suggestion made by Ellens, *Women in the Sex Laws*, 71.

a blanket term for impurity in general. Physiological processes in the female body become loaded with negativity. Apparently, a singular shift in meaning for דוה has taken place against the background of the use of נִדָּה: the word field serves here polemical uses.

In a concluding section, we now consider the differing meanings of the word field דוה – cult and impurity, physical weakness or destabilization along with the specific experiences of women – by means of an analysis of Lamentations 1, another text besides Leviticus in which דוה and נִדָּה are used together. This shall serve to take up the discussion in the first part of this chapter on *niddah*.

e. *Women's Experiences?*

In the course of a song of lament, the first chapter of Lamentations[40] portrays Israel as a woman. To Jerusalem and its inhabitants, the writer ascribes a female body on which their guilt as well as their wounds are displayed. It seems that, in order fully to express the catastrophic impact of war and exile on both women and men, the writer sees no literary means other than to draw upon women's experiences. With this, however, the woman's body and even the woman herself threaten to become the targets of accusation.

First, a speaker bemoans the widow's misery (Lam. 1.1–11). From v. 9 on, the victim's own voice becomes increasingly audible; she survives in her lament. From v. 12 onward, she herself becomes the speaker, interrupted only by v. 17. In the alternation of voices we may see a reflection of a dramatic staging of the text that exposes varying perspectives on what has occurred. Readers and listeners to the text thus lament with the woman in v. 13:

> From on high he [YHWH] sent fire; it went deep into my bones; he spread a net for my feet; he turned me back; he has left me stunned, destabilized (דָּוָה) all day long.

Sighing deeply once again (v. 22), Lady Zion reaches back to her earlier choice of words (v. 13):[41]

> For my groans are countless and my heart is destabilized (וְלִבִּי דַוָּי).

---

40. Cf. X. Pham, *Mourning in the Ancient Near East and the Hebrew Bible*, JSOTSup 302 (Sheffield: Sheffield Academic, 1999), 37–95.

41. Cf. ibid., 194: 'The adjectives דוה (v.13c) and דוי (v.22c) refer to the state of being weakened to the point of fainting, even of death, due to much sorrow and weeping'.

Only in the parts in which the woman is spoken of rather than speaking does נִדָּה appear as something that elicits disgust and exclusion, as in v. 17:

> Zion stretches out her hands, but there is no one to comfort her;
> YHWH has commanded against Jacob that his neighbors should become his foes;
> Jerusalem has become as something contaminated (נִדָּה) among them.

These laments introduce the city as a widow (Lam. 1.1), not, as is often the case with the prophetic literature, as an unfaithful woman. Nevertheless the woman's body is stigmatized. Prophetic denunciations seem to alternate with, and interrupt, laments over suffered humiliations. A significantly different use of both נִדָּה and דוה can be detected: from outside (woman as object), the woman's body is something that renders (her) unclean, while in her own laments (woman as subject), her body is the site of the wounds of which she complains. On the one hand, the woman bemoans her condition; on the other, she is an object of ostracism. In this process, the text thematizes women's painful and degrading experiences during war; the general, public trauma is sketched with a female face and narrated largely by a woman's voice. The peculiar experiences deriving from women's personal and social roles condense in the use of the word field דוה ('destabilization').[42] Jerusalem, the holy city, is contaminated. From a distance we hear the strains of the cultic language, in which the term נִדָּה designates the status of cultic incompatibility caused by menstruation.

If we conclude that the association of menstruation with illness in Leviticus 15 'may be a function of the implicit and unconscious assumption of the writer's worldview',[43] we should not neglect the specific focalization menstruation receives through such a linguistic designation.

III. *Menstruation in Narrative Texts*

The following section undertakes an intertextual analysis to determine how the Bible's narrative texts reflect the priestly notion of the female body's uncleanness during menstruation. Behind this question looms

---

42. A. Berlin, *Lamentations: A Commentary*, OTL (Louisville, KY: Westminster John Knox, 2002), 7, maintains that, due to differing experiential perspectives, experiences of suffering can be sex or gender specific. Dijk-Hemmes, *On Gendering Texts*, 85–86, surmises that this text expresses feminine perspectives.

43. Ellens, *Women in the Sex Texts*, 70, concluding her paragraph 'Menstruation as Illness': 'His [the author's] conscious decision, therefore, to treat menstruation as if normal is all the more stunning'.

the larger one of whether the purity regulations are at least implicit in the writings that deal with women's daily lives. As we shall see in the discussion of the narrative texts, menstrual bleeding and the female play only a marginal role in the relevant narrative texts (Gen. 18.11; 31.35; 2 Sam. 11.2–5); furthermore, the linguistic usage of the purity regulations of Leviticus is foreign to them.

a. *'The way of women is upon me' (Genesis 31.35)*
In order to hide the stolen *teraphim* (the household gods of her father Laban), Rachel sits on them. When her father comes searching, she asks to be excused for not standing up. The text (Gen. 31.35b) lets Rachel use an ambiguous formulation: 'the way of women is upon me' (דֶּרֶךְ נָשִׁים לִי). If this is a euphemism for menstrual bleeding,[44] then Rachel's figurative way of speaking suggests a taboo around menstruation. דֶּרֶךְ refers to a customary experience, or condition.[45] With reference to Leviticus 15, most commentators adopt this interpretation. Hence, afraid of losing his ritual purity by touching the things that Rachel is sitting on,[46] Laban avoids them and does not order Rachel to rise from her seat. For him (as well for Rachel), it would be inconceivable to keep the *teraphim*, obviously of vital significance for all, in an unclean place.

However, the text gives no clear hint that Rachel is having her period. In fact, she utters not a single word about her being in an impure state. Moreover, if Laban is afraid of contact with contamination, why does he later give his daughter a goodbye kiss (Gen. 32.1) or, for that matter, continue searching her tent after being greeted by her? According to Lev. 15.19–21, either of these actions (searching and kissing Rachel goodbye) would have been enough to render Laban impure. In essence, an informed reader of Leviticus does expect Laban to obey the rules of Leviticus 15 when Rachel informs him of her condition. Rachel's explanation may make use of a cliché concerning menstruation and it most likely simply means what it says, that she cannot stand up 'because the way of the women' is upon her. Thus although her feigned inability draws its plausibility from an accepted belief about menstruation (e.g. weakness, general indisposition), it draws none of its relevance from Leviticus 15. Laban, and thus the writer of the story, is either ignorant of or indifferent to the purity regulations.

---

44. Cf. Schorch, *Euphemismen*, 110.
45. Cf. BDB, 203.
46. Van der Toorn, *Van haar wieg*, 52–53.

b. 'The way corresponding to women' (Genesis 18.11)

Sara's laughter in response to the promise of a child would be comprehensible simply from her advanced age and the age of her even more elderly husband. However, the narrator adds this further explanation: 'The way corresponding to women (אֹרַח כַּנָּשִׁים) had ceased to be for Sara' (Gen. 18.11).

In contrast to the passage just examined, the word used is not דֶּרֶךְ, but אֹרַח ('way'), a substantive related in meaning but more typical of poetic and wisdom texts. Analogously to Gen. 31.35, the expression here is to be understood as a euphemism for menstruation. It relates, however, not simply to the menstrual period, but also to the overall capacity for fertility, as is shown by Sara's doubt, expressed in Gen. 12.12, that she can still experience sexual pleasure and is thus still fertile. This verse transmits the idea that the female orgasm is precondition for conception.[47] As another reason for doubt, Sara notes that her husband is very old (v. 12c).

Does this cessation of 'the way corresponding to women' imply that Sara has therefore ceased to be a woman?[48] In that case, womanhood would be defined physiologically, i.e., endocrinologically. However, the story's sequel upsets expectation: although things no longer happen to Sara corresponding to the way of women, she becomes pregnant and gives birth to a child, as the messenger foretold (Gen. 21.1–2). From this no case can be made for arguing that the expression 'the way corresponding to women' alludes to the regulations for menstruating women in Leviticus.

c. 'She was purifying herself from her impurity' (2 Samuel 11.4)

In 2 Samuel 11 we see, through David's eyes, a beautiful woman bathing on the roof of a house not far from the king's palace (2 Sam. 11.2). A few verses later, after the account of David's sexual union with this woman (Bathsheba, wife of Uriah), the text states, 'Now she was purifying (קדש hithpael) herself from her impurity (טֻמְאָה)' (v. 4). Due to its position, this notice most likely refers, not to the rooftop bathing that David observed before sex, but rather to a post-coital bath by Bathsheba. The term for purification used here recalls the priestly world only vaguely, as Leviticus 15 does not use the hithpael form of the verb קדש for the concept of purification.

---

47. For Ugarit, see Marsman, *Women in Ugarit and Israel*, 459.
48. Philip, *Menstruation and Childbirth*, 20: 'in a certain way, a woman who does not have "the way as it is for women" is no longer a woman'.

Supposing, however, that the expression does concern a purificatory bath following menstruation, it would still not provide a direct link to Leviticus 15, since the text there does not prescribe purification after menstruation; that was an innovation of post-biblical literature. A reference here to a post-menstrual purificatory bath (which many, if not most modern interpreters take it to be) could be a subtle hint that Bathsheba could not have been pregnant prior to her liaison with David, since she had just had her period, and that therefore the child could not be Uriah's.

The rule derived from Leviticus 15 stipulating that, after the expiration of the seven-day period of the unsuitability for the cult, the woman must wash is in conflict with Bathsheba's immediate pregnancy following a single act of intercourse, which is improbable at that moment. Nothing in the text suggests that 2 Samuel 11, like the Mishnah, presupposes another seven days of separation following the end of *niddah*.

At first sight, 2 Samuel 11 seems to evoke a context shaped by the purity code of Leviticus, but as has been shown, the references are not specific. Although the term used, טֻמְאָה ('cultic uncleanness'), does stem from cultic literature, it is not found there in combination with purification. Perhaps the writer of 2 Samuel 11 was attempting to apply a generic term from the realm of the sacred to everyday and private life. In summary, the text makes unclear references to the symbolic system in Leviticus 15.

d. *Narrative Texts Beyond the Conceptual World of the Purity-*torot
At best only a negative conclusion can be drawn from the narrative texts concerning the application of the laws of purity from Leviticus 15: the cultic language and ideas of Leviticus are not applied or used. The two sets of texts do not share terminology. The expressions used in Genesis 18 and 31, as we saw above, represent euphemisms, although precisely what the euphemisms represent is unclear, since neither expression can be taken to refer unambiguously to the actual process of menstruation. That fact, of course, may be due to a linguistic taboo surrounding menstruation, but at the very least the expressions refer to some kind of physiological phenomenon.[49]

Not only does the vocabulary of the narrative texts differ greatly from that of the purity regulations in Leviticus and from the prophetic texts the latter have influenced, but also the conceptual worlds are different.

---

49. Cf. D. Erbele-Küster, 'Comment dire l'interdit? Le tabou linguistique et social des la menstruation en Lévitique 11–20', in *Tabou et transgressions. Actes du colloque organisé par le Collège de France, Paris, les 11–12 avril 2012*, ed. J.-M. Durand et al., OBO 274 (Göttingen: Vandenhoeck & Ruprecht, 2015), 181–90.

Consequently, neither the Genesis passages nor the account in 2 Samuel 11 represents an interpretation of the legal texts. Moreover, the passages do not reflect a seclusion of women during their menstruation. The narrative texts do not draw any of their relevance from Leviticus 15. This silence could, despite our conclusions above, be due to some indirect (intertextual) influence by Leviticus 15, but even if we discount that, it is remarkable that the everyday life of women during menstruation does not appear in these texts, despite the text's being narrative rather than legal.

The primary texts for understanding the lexeme נִדָּה are the purity-*torot* of Leviticus 12 and 15, where the term is used in a neutral, descriptive way to describe a woman whose cultic status is conditioned by her menstruation. Although the use of נִדָּה in Lev. 18.19 and Ezek. 18.6 and 22.10 derives from the regulations in Leviticus 11–15, the term acquires an extended sense that is pejorative. Thus the biblical use of this term oscillates between two poles.

In the foregoing pages, we have investigated the employment of the root דוה in the cultic-technical texts of Leviticus. Terms suggesting illness and the treatment of illness are absent; even in the case of bleeding that continues beyond the normal period (v. 25), the text speaks only of an excessively long flow of blood. Besides Lamentations 1, where the two word fields נִדָּה and דוה are used twice by a lamenting woman to describe herself (vv. 17, 22), דוה is used in three passages in Leviticus in its discourse concerning the female body (chs. 12; 15 and 20), so that overall it appears to express experiences proper to the female body. If that is the case, however, it is possible to ask why, then, both roots are not also used in the narrative texts about menstruation.

Chapter 7

THE CULTIC PERSPECTIVE

In this final chapter of the discussion of anthropological concepts, we will reexamine the notions of 'pure' and 'impure' (the Hebrew roots טמא and טהר) as used in Leviticus, particularly in chs. 11–15. Purity is the encompassing perspective of Leviticus and hence seems like a suitable key for unlocking its conceptual world as a whole. It is striking enough that in the scholarly field issues of purity and issues of gender are often discussed separately. Therefore this chapter serves at least a threefold purpose: (1) to define the meanings of these central terms by analyzing the spectrum of their use; (2) to understand their rhetorical function within the purity regulations in constructing body and gender; and (3) to unravel the discourse history of these terms. Hence it correlates the three main areas of research that were identified in Chapter 1: the specific language Leviticus used for the (gendered) body and its rhetoric, as well as the understanding of the purity concept using the concept of boundaries, as in the case of menstruation (*niddah*) unfolded in the previous chapter. This shall lead to the reevaluation of the life–death paradigm to explain the purity system of Leviticus.

I will argue that these roots טמא and טהר are used in Leviticus to describe and distinguish between bodies that comply with cultic prescriptions, and bodies that do not. The chapter discusses the interpretation and the rendering of these terms describing the (gendered) body. Impurity seems to be a question of gender,[1] since, as according to the postpartum prescription in Leviticus 12, the length of the time a woman is impure after the delivery of a female child she must abstain from the cult, twice as long as after that of a male.

---

1. Cf. D. Erbele-Küster, 'Gender and Cult: "Pure" and "Impure" as Gender-relevant Categories', in *Torah*, ed I. Fischer and M. Navarro Puerto, The Bible and Women 1 (Atlanta: SBL, 2011), 375–406.

In numerous studies on the subject, attention is paid primarily to impurity.² This corresponds to the prescriptions in Leviticus, which hardly have anything to say about purity – almost as if purity were merely the absence of impurity.³ However, the semantics of the two Hebrew roots טמא ('impure') and טהר ('pure') is more complex than the antithetical couplet of the renderings would suggest. The roots are completely unrelated. In many studies, 'the antithetical linguistic construction pure/impure'⁴ follows the Greek Bible, which distinguishes between καθαρός ('pure') and ἀκάθαρτος ('impure').⁵ Pure, in this representation, is the fundamental category while impure, marked by the privative prefix, is its negation. For the Hebrew language the situation is different. Hence, the couple impure/pure is not appropriate as a rendering of טמא/טהר.⁶ In what follows, I will make a case for alternative renderings.

Actually, the two Hebrew terms only make sense in relation to a third category, which is holiness: 'Everything that is in opposition to God's realm is impure' and 'purity makes it possible to enter this realm'.⁷ Consequently, purity can be parallel to the holy (Lev. 10.10; Ezek. 22.26). The holy, however, can also be described in analogy to the impure as a dynamic reality, as opposed to purity which is static.⁸ Even if, at first sight, holiness appears to be the absolute opposite of impurity, both have similar structures; they share a common base. Like the impure, the holy can have

---

2. Cf. L'Hour, 'L'Impur et le Saint I': As the title indicates, impurity is seen here as the dominant category for Leviticus. Cf. also Wright, 'Unclean – Clean'. Also in *NBL*, the lemma 'Rein' ('pure') is mainly about impurity. The studies by Douglas likewise are concerned mainly with the sources of impurity. Paschen, *Rein und Unrein*, 19–21, first discusses notions of purity. See the survey of research in Klawans, *Impurity*, 3–20.

3. Cf. Milgrom, *The Dynamics of Purity*, 29: 'Purity is the absence of impurity'.

4. Paschen, *Rein und Unrein*, 13.

5. Cf. the explanation of these terms in M. Vahrenhorst, 'Levitikon/Levitikus/Das dritte Buch Mose', in *Septuaginta Deutsch. Erläuterungen und Kommentare I: Genesis bis Makkabäer* (Stuttgart: Deutsche Bibelgesellschaft, 2011), 325–430 (366–71).

6. Cf. Willi-Plein, *Opfer und Kult*, 38.

7. H.-J. Hermisson, *Sprache und Ritus im altisraelitischen Kult: Zur "Spiritualisierung" der Kultbegriffe im Alten Testament*, WMANT 19 (Neukirchen-Vluyn: Neukirchener, 1965), 89.

8. J. Milgrom, 'The Dynamics of Purity in the Priestly System', in *Purity and Holiness: The Heritage of Leviticus*, ed. M. Poorthuis and J. Schwartz, Jewish and Christian Perspectives Series (Leiden: Brill, 2000), 29–32 (29): 'In the priestly system of the Bible purity is inert, but purification is dynamic'. Cf. L'Hour, '*L'Impur et le Saint* I', 532, and Hermisson, *Sprache und Ritus*, 88.

a contaminating effect (Lev. 16.27–28; Num. 19.7). Nevertheless, the holy and the impure constitute a contrasting pair. The main task of the priestly lineage, according to Leviticus, is to separate the 'pure' (טהר) from the 'impure' (טמא) according to Lev. 10.10 (cf. 11.47; 20.25).

Interestingly, in noncultic texts, טהר ('pure') appears to be the dominant category, with impurity conceived of as the absence of purity. Several types of negation are attested: לֹא טְהֹרָה in Gen. 7.2 (cf. Deut. 23.11); אֵינֶנָּה טְהֹרָה in Gen. 7.8; בִּלְתִּי טָהוֹר in 1 Sam. 20.26. As a result, these texts exhibit less formulaic usage than the book of Leviticus, while there is a stronger notion of bipolarity here. In these texts outside Leviticus purity constitutes the background against which the opposite condition is qualified.

While the root טהר with its derivatives ('purity') is the dominant category in noncultic texts, in the cultic texts the root טמא ('impure') has this function. Purity is secondary because, unlike ritual impurity, it is not contagious. Impurity, by contrast, represents a power and a dynamic which the prescriptions attempt to neutralize in the chapters under discussion in this study.

We will now seek to demonstrate how the concepts of טמא and טהר define the body even if they are not so much about material, physical conditions of hygiene and cleanness. Rather, the texts revolve around the concept of (dis)ability for the cult, or (non)compliance with cultic requirements. This is the framework for a proper understanding of these terms.

I. *Impurity as Cultic Disability*

a. *Is Impurity Material?*

Expressions such as 'the discharge of her impurity'[9] in Lev. 15.25b, 30b or 'his impurity is on/over him' in Lev. 7.20 would suggest that impurity has a distinctly material quality. Likewise, verbs of the root טמא, constructed with the preposition ב ('to defile oneself with, to become impure through') would seem to refer to physical contact with a concrete substance. On closer scrutiny, however, it turns out that the preposition – more specifically, the suffixed third person pronoun it always carries in this context in Leviticus – can refer to many different things: to (human) impurity as such in a rather unspecific, abstract way (Lev. 5.3), to all the animals that swarm upon the earth (Lev. 11.43), to an emission of semen (Lev. 15.32), to genital discharge (Lev. 15.3), to one's neighbor's

---

9. Cf. Gerstenberger, *Leviticus*, 196: 'all the days of her impurity flow'; Milgrom, *Leviticus 1–16*, 903: 'her impure discharge'.

wife (Lev. 18.20), to copulation with an animal (Lev. 18.23), summarily to multiple impurities at once (Lev. 18.24), to ghosts and spirits (Lev. 19.31), and to torn animal carcasses (Lev. 22.8). In some of these cases, the pronoun refers to a 'substance' that caused the impurity – or rather, cultic non-compliance. In other cases there is a certain ambiguity, where the pronoun might not be referring exclusively to a physical entity but also to some action. In Lev. 18.20 it is actually not so much the neighbor's wife herself, but rather the act of having sex with her which disqualifies a man from participating in the cult. The preposition ב is of course to be understood as a *beth causae*, indicating that the impurity is somehow caused or conditioned by something. It does not, however, by itself imply physical contact.[10]

Likewise, in the description in Leviticus 12 of a woman's condition after childbirth (seven days of impurity after giving birth to a boy, fourteen days with a girl), it cannot be the blood itself or the physical bleeding which functions as the point of reference for the impurity, since the duration of the postpartum bleeding varies from one instance to another and is not conditioned by the sex of the new-born child.[11] Rabbinic tradition does take the duration of the bleeding as starting point and adds to it a certain time period of cultic impurity. As the talmudic tractate *Niddah* stipulates: 'she has to be cult-abstinent during the time of the bleeding and the subsequent seven days'.[12] In Leviticus 12 the impurity seems to be constructed in reference to the woman's body, but without direct consideration of physiological processes. Thus rather than labeling the pollutions as physical ones[13] which holds true to a certain degree in our investigation we shall unfold how the concept of impurity serves to construct the body. Alluding to the term 'purity regulations' (*Reinheitsbestimmungen*), I have labeled these chapter earlier as 'body regulations' (*Körperbestimmungen*) playing on the German term *bestimmen* ('to define').[14] The impurity is not (primarily) material however constitutes the perception and construction of the gendered body, as we shall see below. First its cultic character will be highlighted.

---

10. Cf. Jenni, *Die Hebräischen Präpositionen*, 228–30.
11. Cf. Whitekettle, 'Leviticus 12 and the Israelite Women', 397–99.
12. Cf. Marienberg, *Niddah*, 31–32, 133–34.
13. Nihan, 'Forms and Functions of Purity', 321–23, distinguishes in Leviticus as a whole between two main types of impurity according to the source of pollution: physical (or biological) and moral, understanding them as complementary and unified into one system of purification.
14. Cf. Erbele-Küster, 'Körperbestimmungen'.

b. *Impurity as a Technical Cultic Term*

More than half of the biblical occurrences of derivations from the root טמא are found in the book of Leviticus, particularly chs. 11, 13 and 15.[15] טמא in the priestly-cultic texts, as we will argue, is a technical and rather functional term[16] concerning cultic non-compliance.

The moral evaluation of the term is only secondary: 'There is no onus attached to these pollutions...no "guilt" attributed to the impure'.[17] In this respect, however, the book of Leviticus attests to several diverging opinions. In Lev. 15.24, sexual contact with a woman during her menstruation only results in the status of *niddah* being temporarily transferred to the man. In Leviticus 18 and 20, the same action is a capital offense entailing exclusion from the community, as it pollutes the land. Does this mean that categories are blurred, as questions of cultic fitness are dealt with *as if* they were about sexual morality? Not really. It seems to me that Leviticus has cultic and moral regulations next to each other, both aimed at preventing the crossing of boundaries aiming at the holiness of the sanctuary.

To conclude: In Leviticus 11–15, טמא is a functional category that describes the status of an object or a person with respect to the cult and the sanctuary. As Mary Douglas puts it: 'Unclean is not a term of psychological horror and disgust, it is a technical term for the cult... To import feelings into the translation falsifies, and creates more puzzles.'[18] This is what the suggested renderings of טמא such as 'unsuitable for the cult', 'unclean in a ritual respect', 'compromising the cult', 'cult-abstinent', 'cult-disabled', 'ritual noncompliance', 'cultic disqualification', 'in conflict with the cult' – are intended to express. These renderings try to make visible the cultic notion of impurity in Leviticus 11–15 in contrast to the moral usage elsewhere as 'unless we supply our own descriptive terminology, confusion about the nature of the relationship between impurity and sin will continue'.[19]

c. *Impurity as a Marker of the Gender Boundary*

We will now pursue our argument that the laws on impurity implement boundaries not only between life and death, between inside and outside,

---

15. Cf. Paschen, *Rein und Unrein*, 27; L'Hour, 'L'Impur et le Saint', 526.

16. Cf. Klawans, *Impurity and Sin*, and T. Seidl, 'Rein und Unrein: (I) AT', *NBL* 2:315-21 (317).

17. Frymer-Kensky, 'Pollution, Purification', 403.

18. Cf. Douglas, *Leviticus as Literature*, 151, and the critique of this stance in Bachmann, 'Die biblische Vorstellungswelt', 6.

19. Klawans, *Impurity and Sin*, 22.

but ultimately also between the genders.[20] It has been claimed by several scholars that the regulations in Leviticus 11–15 essentially concern the border between life and death. Accordingly, impurity is seen as a life-threatening condition, belonging to the realm of death.[21] Even if death is no theme of its own in the system of the purity regulations in Leviticus 11–15,[22] life and death may be considered as important elements in how commentators read these chapters: since the God of Israel is a God of life, the regulations seek to contain the realm of death. The main concern of Leviticus 11 is respect for life.[23] The animals listed there as unfit for consumption constitute a realization of the primordial order of creation as described in Genesis 1, a text belonging to the same priestly system. The prohibition on the consumption of blood, under this order, concerns animal and human blood alike.[24] Regarding Leviticus 15, Milgrom states: 'The loss of vaginal blood and semen, both containing seed, meant the diminution of life and, if unchecked, destruction and death. And it was a process unalterably opposed by Israel's God, the source of its life.'[25]

Thus, a theological foundation is provided for an interpretation of the purity-*torot* as a system that draws the line between life and death. Body excretions, the touching of corpses, and the skin condition known as צרעת are all incorporated in this system. However, the mentioning in Leviticus 13–14 of eczema-like symptoms – not only of the skin but also in textiles and in the walls of houses – cannot be completely explained from the life-and-death paradigm, as these symptoms are not lethal. צרעת, therefore, is seen in this analysis as part of the cultic system rather than as a medical condition.[26] In the life-and-death paradigm, the impurity caused by the

20. See Chapter 1 for the interpretive models of purity in general; see aso Chapter 5, section III.

21. Cf. Wenham, *Purity*, 385–86; Paschen, *Rein und Unrein*, 60–64; Milgrom, *Leviticus 1–16*, 766–67, 1000–1004; L'Hour, 'L'impur et le pur', 532; Ellens, *Women in the Sex Texts*, 62–70.

22. The handling of dead bodies is only mentioned in Lev. 10.4–5; 21.11; 22.4; Num. 6.6–7, 9; 9.6–11; 19.14; 31.19–20, 24.

23. Cf. Milgrom, *Leviticus 1–16*, 735: 'Its purpose is to teach the Israelites reverence for life'.

24. Cf. Douglas, *Leviticus as Literature*, 151: 'the case of the animal's blood and the case of the human's blood are parallel. Ritual impurity imposes God's order on his creation.'

25. Milgrom, *Leviticus 1–16*, 767. Cf. L'Hour, 'L'Impur et le Saint I', 532: 'tout ce qui est expression de mort est source d'impureté. Ainsi en est-il du sang, porteur de vie, quand il s'écoule hors du corps.' For a critical reading of this position, cf. Ruane, *Sacrifice and Gender in Biblical Law*, 151–55.

26. Cf. Milgrom, *Leviticus 1–16*, 817–19.

loss of semen is explained in terms of loss of life. But then it remains unclear why the ejaculation of semen during sexual intercourse should cause impurity (Lev. 15.18), as it may result in new life. In addition, as it is the man who loses semen, why should the woman become impure? As to the impurity caused by vaginal loss of blood, it is often claimed that this is due to the life which is contained in blood (as mentioned, e.g., in the prohibition on the consumption of blood, Lev. 17.10–14).[27] However, were this true, the implication would be that blood which is shed as a result of injury would likewise render impure,[28] which is not the case. In sum, the life–death paradigm appears to be insufficient as an explanation for these regulations.

In another line of reasoning, it is held that the bodily discharges have a polluting effect because body orifices are weak points on the border between inside and outside. The laws on purity try to define and conserve the order; as Mary Douglas has stated, 'Purity is the enemy of change, of ambiguity and compromise'.[29] More recently it has been argued that the loss of social control over human bodies is the decisive point.[30] The regulations deal with basic physiological processes involving border-crossings as well as trespassing biographical borders in the sense of ritual passages.[31] However, this analysis fails to account for the fact that not all body excretions are mentioned in the purity regulations of Leviticus. Substances such as tears, sweat, urine, and feces are not even hinted at in this context.

It would seem, then, that it is notions of sex and gender which play the ultimate decisive role in the selection and evaluation of body excretions in the Leviticus passages.[32] Tears, for instance, are hardly relevant in that context, which makes them less useful as symbols of social relations. It is not blood as such which renders impure (or rather, causes cultic non-compliance), but blood which is related to the reproductive process (menstruation, postpartum discharge);[33] hence only gendered blood is of

27. Ibid., 767.
28. Cf. Paschen, *Rein und Unrein*, 61.
29. Douglas, *Purity and Danger*, 191.
30. Cf. Nihan, 'Forms and Functions of Purity', taking up ideas of Eilberg-Schwartz, *The Savage in Judaism* and others.
31. Cf. Van Gennep, *Rites de passage*.
32. Cf. Eilberg-Schwartz, *The Savage in Judaism*, 174 and 186; Ruane, *Sacrifice and Gender in Biblical Law*, 175, 183, 185.
33. Marx, 'L'impureté selon P', 361, 370–73, 381–82, mentions sexuality as a cause of impurity within the system of the priestly codex, while acknowledging the normality and necessity of sexuality. However, his explanatory preference differs from ours, which stresses the two factors: gender construction and reproductive system.

interest. And in fact, nowhere is blood itself characterized as impure – it has a stronger association with the concept of purity. Likewise these regulations make use of the gendered body. They serve to construct and define the gender identities within its model of society focused on the temple and its priestly discourse of power.[34] This could be understood against the backdrop of the Persian period where the priestly competence seeks to define social matters by making use of the (female) gender, for example, concerning the marriage laws.

II. *Purity as Cultic Ability*

a. *Is Purity Material?*

In modern day-to-day usage, the word 'pure' has the meaning of 'clean', as opposed to 'dirty'. The Hebrew adjective טָהוֹר as it is found in the book of Exodus (accounting for about one third of all biblical occurrences) also seems to refer to physical, material cleanness. It is used of gold, for example, as an evocation of its purity and sparkle (e.g. Exod. 25.11, 17, 24, 29, 31, 36, 39; 30.3). The basic meaning of טָהוֹר is usually related to its Ugaritic cognate, referring to the purity, integrity and cleanness of an object.[35] In Leviticus, the root טהר occurs mainly in verbs that have the performative meaning of declaring something (an object, a person or an animal) to be pure in cultic respect.

The question remains, then, whether or not this purity is (primarily) material. In some passages this would in fact seem to be the case. Leviticus 15.13 mentions the man that is or becomes טָהוֹר of his discharge (cf. 15.28 and Lev. 12.7). Some commentators use the term 'healed of'[36] as a rendering here, which reflects a physical or medical understanding of this verb – as opposed to their rather more cultic reading of exactly the same verb at the end of the verse.[37] In many cases it is not that obvious, however. In a metaphorical sense, one can be clean (or cleansed) from sins (Lev. 16.30; Prov. 20.9) or from impurity (Ezek. 24.13; 36.25).

Also in Leviticus 12, the woman's 'blood of purification' (בִּדְמֵי טָהֳרָה) after childbirth is not restricted to a material understanding of purity.

---

34. Cf. J. Schaper, 'Priestly Purity and Social Organisation in Persian Period Judah', *BN* 108 (2003): 51–57, who tries to relate the priestly purity concept to the social reality of Achaemenid Judah focusing on the role the verb to separate plays within the binary system of pure and impure.

35. Cf. KBL³, 354; L'Hour, 'L'Impur et le Saint I', 527.

36. Cf. Milgrom, *Leviticus 1–16*, 902–3, 921, and Gerstenberger, *Leviticus*, 195–96.

37. Péter-Contesse, *Lévitique 1–16*, 236.

This passage is not about the length of the bleedings, nor about the physical characteristics of the blood. The central issue here is the numerical symbolism in the periods of restriction. The purity regulations codify and, to a certain extent, actually constitute the gender of the child. A woman is to remain in a state of cultic non-compliance for 33 or 66 days, dependent on the sex of the child, not on the length of her postpartum bleeding. Nor is blood as such located on the side of the impure. Already during the period of cultic disqualification, mention is made of the 'blood of purification' referred to above (Lev. 12.4, 5).

It would seem, then, that even if there is a physical, material side to the concept of purity, its realization is independent from the material or even beyond it. In Leviticus 11–15, טָהוֹר, like טָמֵא, functions as an essentially cultic term.

b. *Purification or Purity?*
In Leviticus 12 we find the expressions 'blood of purification/purity' and 'the days of her purification'. How are these expressions, particularly the root טהר, to be understood? Do they refer to a process of purification, to a state of purity, or to a ritual declaration of purity? Actually, they are the feminine and masculine variants of a single noun. Nine out of thirteen occurrences of the feminine variant are in the context of purity regulations: eight in Leviticus 12–15, one in Num. 6.9. The masculine form is found only in Lev. 12.4, 6 and Exod. 24.10. Let us first take a look at the occurrences outside the purity regulations.

One of the tasks assigned to the Levites according to 1 Chr. 23.28 is the טָהֳרָה ('purification') of everything which is holy. According to 2 Chr. 30.19, some of those present at the celebration of the Passover festival under Hezekiah were not 'in accordance with the טָהֳרָה of the sanctuary'. In Neh. 12.45, the story of the dedication of the wall of Jerusalem, טָהֳרָה, the keeping of the regulations of purity, is mentioned as one of the charges of the priests and Levites.[38] In Ezek. 44.26, the priest of the future temple is requested to wait for seven days 'after his טָהֳרָה' – most probably, a declaration of cultic purity – before entering the sanctuary.

Thus, outside the priestly purity regulations, the noun טָהֳרָה appears to have three semantic dimensions: first of all, the process of purification (1 Chr. 23.28), second, the state of purity (2 Chr. 30.19; Neh. 12.45), and third, the (ritual) declaration of a state of purity (Ezek. 44.26).

---

38. GesB[17], 272; Ges[18], 417, renders it in this passage as 'declaration of cultic purity'.

We shall now turn to the other occurrences which are all part of the purity regulations of Leviticus 12–15, with one further occurrence in Numbers 6. In a passage such as Lev. 14.2, where mention is made of 'the day of someone's purification', the intended meaning appears to be the ritual declaration of purity:[39] 'This is the *torah* concerning the person with a contagious skin-disease on the day of his purification ritual (טָהֳרָה)'.

Likewise, we have 'the eighth day of his purification' in Lev. 14.23. In Num. 6.9, on the vow of the Nazirite, the expression 'the day of his טָהֳרָה' (cf. Ezek. 44.26) refers to the day on which the Nazirite becomes cultic compliant again after contact with a corpse.[40] In Lev. 13.35, on the possible reappearance of a scab on one's skin, the expression 'after his טָהֳרָה' apparently refers to the purification/cleansing procedure and the priestly declaration of purity outlined in the preceding verse. Leviticus 13.7 is yet another instance where טָהֳרָה seems best rendered as 'purification ritual'. In Lev. 14.32, it seems to include the offering involved in the ritual:

> This is the *torah* concerning the person with a contagious skin-disease who cannot afford the means of his טָהֳרָה (purification ritual).

Leviticus 15.13 mentions someone who has become clean of his discharge. He must count seven days 'until his purification ritual'. Then, having washed his body and his clothes with fresh water, 'he shall be clean'. Remarkably, this concluding formula (in the usual *waw* perfect form) occurs before the offering mentioned in v. 14 has taken place – whereas in Lev. 12.7, 8, the regulations on the woman after childbirth, it comes after the priestly ritual. It can be said both of the man in Leviticus 15 and the woman in Leviticus 12 that their status is in fact ambiguous. It would seem that the meaning of טָהֳרָה in Leviticus 12–15 and in Numbers 6 focuses on the process of purification (the first of the three dimensions just presented). The most adequate rendering in Lev. 12.4, therefore, is 'blood of purification', as it expresses the ambiguity of the process. The (ritual) declaration of cultic compliance is a performative act in itself, in which the state of purity and the process of purification merge.

---

39. Regarding Lev. 13.7 and 14.2, Seidl, 'Rein und Unrein', 320, speaks of 'declarations of purity'.

40. Cf. Levine, *Numbers 1–20*, 222.

In Lev. 12.4b, 6 we find the expression 'the days of her purity', using the masculine noun.[41] The only further occurrence of this noun is Exod. 24.10, where it denotes purity and a shining quality (here, of sapphire). In Lev. 12.4, 6, by contrast, the preceding specifications of the number of 'the days of her purity/purification' (33 and 66 days, respectively) underline the idea of a process. The suffixed personal pronoun establishes a firm link between this process and the woman.

As it turns out, the three semantic dimensions outlined above – process of purification, declaration of purity, and state of purity – are all represented among the occurrences of טָהֳרָה within the regulations on purity Leviticus 12–15. In addition, we discerned a specific component of meaning through which טָהֳרָה develops into the technical term for the purification ritual (Lev. 13.7; 14.2, 23; 15.13). The declaration of purity is no single act in itself. It is closely connected with a process of purification (cf. Lev. 12.4, 6; 13.35; 15.13).[42] In many of its occurrences in Leviticus, the noun טָהֳרָה appears to refer to a process of purification, with a view towards a concluding declaration of purity. Thus, even if purity is essentially static, the noun טָהֳרָה in these passages allows for a dynamic interpretation.[43]

c. *Declarative Formulae*

Returning once more to the roots טמא and טהר, we observe that in Leviticus 11–15 their derivatives are typically used in stereotyped phrases. Each of these chapters features its own specific usage, expressing a specific idea.

The phrase טָמֵא הוּא לָכֶם ('it is unclean in a cultic respect for you') occurs only in the regulations on the consumption of flesh, Leviticus 11 (vv. 4, 5, 6, 7, 8, 26, 27, 38; in a slightly different form in v. 35b, as a heading and a conclusion in vv. 29, 31). Specific categories of animals are defined here as טמא, the specification 'for you' (cf. Deut. 14.7, 8, 10, 19) indicating that this is no general statement. The animals are not inherently unclean, but they are to be shunned as unclean by Israel in particular.[44]

---

41. The form is analyzed by some as an infinitive construct (e.g. Milgrom, *Leviticus 1–16*, 755; cf. GesB[17], 272: 'Reinwerden/Reinigung').

42. *DCH* 3:348: '1. usu. (process of) purification, purification ritual...period of purification'; according to Milgrom, *Leviticus 1–16*, 749, טָהֳרָה is a nominal form meaning 'purity'.

43. Cf. the title of Milgrom's contribution: 'The Dynamics of Purity in the Priestly System'.

44. Douglas, *Leviticus as Literature*, 144: 'Thus the rules of impurity are not a way of promoting a universal hygienic principle or pronouncing a general health warning'. Cf. L'Hour, 'L'Impur et le Saint I', 533, and Marx, 'L'impureté selon P', 368–70.

Inherent to the notion of cultic (dis)qualification is a certain amount of arbitrariness which in principle allows for other classifications. All attempts to explain the regulations of Leviticus 11 in (seemingly objective) terms of health and hygiene miss this crucial point. The promise of Gen. 9.8–11 that all animals are part of God's covenant is in no way compromised by Leviticus 11.[45]

In Lev. 13.11, 15, 36, 44, 46, 51, 55; 14.44; 15.2, 3, 25 we find the declarative formula טָמֵא הוּא, which in its wording is analogous to the opposite declaration טָהוֹר הוּא of Lev. 11.37; and Leviticus 13 (vv. 13, 17, 34, 37, 39, 40, 41, 58). Through these formulae, which typically occur at the conclusion of an examination by the priest, the text establishes a person's (dis)qualification for the cult. It is important to note that the formulae in Leviticus 15 are not uttered as direct speech by the priest. It is the text itself that proclaims a person to be cultically (dis)qualified – and, through the act of reading, it is the reader who does so. A case in point is the regulation on eczema in Leviticus 13. Similarly, the formula צָרַעַת הוּא ('it is eczema') in vv. 3, 8, 11, 15, 20, 25, 27, 30, 42 might well constitute a form of literary, not medical diagnosis.

Another type of declarative formula uses perfect tense verbal forms built on the root טהר with the qal: Lev. 12.7, 8; 13.34; 14.19, 53. These are likewise concluding statements on the purity of a person or an object, which are best rendered 'to be pure', rather than 'to become pure'. To reflect the performative character of the formulae, a rendering 'to be regarded as cultically pure' would also be suitable.[46]

Throughout Leviticus 15, the verbal formula 'and he/she/it is unclean until the evening' serves to underline the temporary nature of cultic non-compliance. Most of the occurrences have the *waw*-perfect tense form (vv. 5, 6, 7, 8, 10b, 11, 16, 18, 22, 27). This form marks the impurity as being the result of that which was mentioned previously; it also expresses the durative aspect of the situation.[47] In a few cases, however, the text uses the imperfect tense ('he/she/it becomes/will be impure until the evening', as in Lev. 11.27, 31, 39 and Lev. 15.10a, 19b, 23).

The piel form of the verb טהר occurs in ch. 13 (vv. 6, 13, 17, 23, 28, 34, 37, 59) and ch. 14 (vv. 7, 11, 48), as does the piel form of the verb טמא in ch. 13 (vv. 8, 11, 17, 20, 22, 25, 27, 30, 44, 59). Both verbs have

---

45. Cf. Douglas, *Leviticus as Literature*, 134–36.
46. *DCH* 3:344: טהר qal, 'be (regarded as) pure, be purified, be (regarded as) clean, cleansed'.
47. Cf. the translation by Gerstenberger, *Leviticus*, 179–80, and Milgrom, *Leviticus 1–16*, 902–3: 'to remain impure'.

a declarative meaning: to declare 'pure' and 'impure', respectively.[48] They contain performative statements on cultic qualification, made by the priest, the grammatical subject. The use of the piel highlights the result of the declarative act. By implication, the cultic status of the person under consideration remains unclear as long as no declaration has been made. The use of the declarative or factitive piel, particularly in Leviticus 13, reflects the notion that a *state* of impurity requires a *declaration* of impurity. This meaning of the terms can be grasped only from a cultic perspective.

As to the relation between טמא and טהר, we may conclude that they represent different concepts, even if they are used in similar expressions. Purity, in Leviticus 11–15, signifies the suspension or the absence of anything that might compromise the cult. In case of doubt, a person is seen as a hazard to the cult, until he or she has been cleared by the priest. But cultic hazard is equally discursive, as it arises out of its priestly declaration. Essentially, the notions of im/purity constitute a classification instrument. Declarations of im/purity are used to draw borders – specifically between impurity (טמא) as a condition of cultic hazard implying cultic abstinence, and purity (טהר) as a neutral condition allowing cultic participation.

This final analytical chapter has highlighted the conceptual underpinnings of impurity, mainly in Leviticus, as it serves as a general notion relating and defining body and gender. In Leviticus 12 and 15, the impurities, i.e., the threats posed to the cult, are gender specific. The occurrences of the roots טהר and טמא in Leviticus 11–15 have one particular feature in common: they denote conditions which are ritually declared from outside, by the priest – and in the end, by the text as such and its readers. 'Purity' and 'impurity' are no intrinsic qualities of (gendered) persons, they are brought about through acts of attribution and they last only for specific periods of time. Purity in Leviticus 11–15 is thus a performative concept.

---

48. Cf. Milgrom, *Leviticus 1–16*, 778; Joüon and Muraoka, *Grammar of Biblical Hebrew*, §52d.

Chapter 8

PROSPECTS

My reading of Leviticus 12 and 15 has sought to correlate different areas of research that were identified at the outset in Chapter 1: source-critical approaches of the chapters in question, the specific (gendered) language they use for the body, and interpretations of their underlying conceptions of purity. The goal was to sketch how gender and gender relations, concepts of body and purity emerge from and are standardized in discourse. This final chapter provides in a first step a summary of it. Finally, I will outline the prospective of the discourse analysis for the purity regulations in general and Leviticus as a whole. The analysis has potentially wide-reaching implications for our understanding of the purity-*torot*, namely that the writing and reading of the texts sketch out the body and, in so doing, open up a (virtual) survival space.

My approach has recast the old problem of finding a conceptual model to explain the texts' purity concerns: specifically, I have shown how the texts themselves create the purity categories and how cultic (dis)ability is constructed by talking about the body in gendered ways. Spatial concepts have been useful on several levels for explaining cultic disability. One important outcome has been that gender is not a category which can be treated separately. Likewise interpreting the concept of purity cannot be done without dealing the role gender plays in the purity regulations.

I. *Textual Conceptions and Their Performative Practices*

a. *Discourse and Translation History*
Translations play an important role in the history of discourse and interpretation – including in the work of exegetes. This became particularly clear through our examination of the Greek translation of Leviticus, which was one of the first translations to be performed. The Greek version of the purity-*torot* had a recursive effect on interpretations of the Hebrew text. For example, the translation of the Hebrew term טמא as 'impure' owes more to the Greek term ἀκάθαρτος than it does to the Hebrew concept, which is best understood in terms of endangerment of the cult or abstinence from it. The Greek translation introduces the privative concept of

im/purity, and this continued to affect the formation of vocabulary of the body into the modern period. In this way, the Greek text has exercised an implicit influence on the reception of the Hebrew text.

A comparison of the MT with the Greek makes the shaping of body images through culture and language particularly apparent. The LXX gives expression to a reception of the text that developed its own specific language of the body, as for example for the bodily secretions. But it found no suitable term for the woman's cultic status that was comparable to the Hebraic concept of *niddah*. We may infer from this that, within the Hellenistic context, *niddah* was an untranslatable concept.

For other Hebrew expressions with which they had difficulty, the early Greek translators coined neologisms. But they also reached back to medical literature for some terms, as a result of which the depiction of the body in Leviticus 15 LXX has less of a cultic than a physiological character.[1] By contrast, the Hebrew text attributes no significance to the cyclical character of the woman's impurity. Its sole interest is in the seven-day period of abstinence from the cult that menstruation makes necessary.[2]

Our analysis of the concepts נִדָּה and דָוֶה, the two main terms concerned with the menstruating woman's condition, makes apparent that in Leviticus 12 and 15 these terms express no aversion to the menstruating woman. Rather, in those chapters *niddah* connotes the setting of a boundary in response to her menstruation. Only when other discourses were superimposed did a devaluation arise, with the result that *niddah* (נִדָּה) became a synonym for repulsiveness beyond Leviticus 12 and 15. The uncovering of the reception history of the term deconstructs the misogynistic body images that are bound up with it.

For Ezra and Ezekiel, the *niddah*, a condition caused by menstruation, is a symbol for the decline of society. The woman stands *pars pro toto* for all of society. In prophetic literature the same images serve to express sorrow over the land's distress and to exhort its hearers to cleanse the land of contaminations and disgrace. The female body thus becomes a symbol for boundary in crisis situations, in general.

This view became formative in the interpretation history of Leviticus 15. The Jewish and Christian inheritors of the purity regulations focused

---

1. In turn, medical texts from Greek antiquity influenced rabbinic texts; cf. M. Morgenstern, *Übersetzung des Talmud Yerushalmi: Nidda – Die Menstruierende* Bd. VI/1 (Tübingen: Mohr & Siebeck 2006), 191–93.

2. It is even possible that menstruation's cyclical nature was not fully appreciated, since the menses of women in ancient Israel may have been irregular or even absent over longer periods due to malnutrition and hard physical labor, as well as to frequent pregnancies and the subsequent periods of nursing.

not on the man's impurity (through semen) but rather on the woman's, conditioned by menstruation.³ If Leviticus 15 is concerned with restoring the purity (i.e., the cultic ability) of those who have come into contact with a person with a secretion, the interpretation-history of the chapter has directed its attention primarily to the woman as the source of the contamination. It appears that it is solely in the female body and in its cultic and social praxis that the purity regulations have been inscribed.

The body is much talked about in Leviticus, and yet it alludes only peripherally to concrete physical experiences. The term נִדָּה (cf. as well דָוֶה) refers thus not to the body in its materiality; rather, it sketches out the body in discursive praxis in a way that transcends physiology. Applying a gender perspective to the history of discourse about the body, as exemplified in the discussion of *niddah*, we were able to break through existing patterns of reception. This showed us that standard dictionaries and common translations must be revised to acknowledge the intertwining of body, language and gender.

b. *Leviticus 12 and 15 as Performative Regulations Creating Body, Gender and Purity*

In taking up the title of the monograph, I want to stress the intertwinedness of the categories. In what follows the circular construction of these categories will be highlighted, starting with the gender duality in body conceptions. Language, through such features as grammar, word choice, and syntax, constructs body, gender and purity. Gender differences, like the body itself, come to being in discourse. Circumcision and menstruation – these two concepts mark gender. No biblical text explicitly correlates them; in Leviticus 12 circumcision is simply inserted into the rules for a menstruating woman.

In Leviticus, a particular terminology inscribes gender duality of the body: in Lev. 12.4, 5 and Lev. 15.19, *niddah* (נִדָּה) designates the woman's cleansing process of secretion. While she is in this condition, she is seen

---

3. Even the writings of the Qumran community, which according to mainstream view consisted of celibate males, discuss the purity regulations for menstruating women (cf. Harrington, *The Purity Texts*, 100–103). Differently T. Ilan, 'Reading for Women in 1QSa (Serekh ha-Edah)', in *The Dead Sea Scrolls in Context: Integrating the Dead Sea Scrolls in the Study of Ancient Texts, Languages, and Cultures*, ed. Armin Lange, Emanuel Tov and Matthias Weigold (Leiden: Brill, 2011), 61–76 (61): 'Before the 1990s there were no women in Qumran. All agreed (and most continue to agree) that the Qumranites were Josephus' Essenes, and these were male celibates'. However she takes the female skeletons found in the Qumran cemetery as counter-evidence.

as endangering the cult, though at the same time her body stands in relation to the cult. This polarity of cult-endangerment vs. cleansing is held together by the concept of *niddah*.

The mother's body determines a newborn child's gender through the duration of the mother's impurity (Lev. 12.2, 4, 5). Leviticus 15 describes men's and women's bodies both in a gender-neutral way as well in a gender-specific one. Both men's and women's genital secretions are designated by the same semantic root, as if the processes were physiologically comparable, but only the woman's secretion is further specified through the application of the term *niddah* (נִדָּה) and the identification of the substance being secreted, i.e., blood. Through the use of identical terms and analogous expressions for both men's and women's gendered bodies the chapter creates, to a certain degree, a one-gender body.

In tension with the textual space's gender symmetry in Leviticus 15, however, as well as with its interest in describing men's and women's bodies analogously, stands the asymmetry of gendered bodies in terms of their details, through which gender differences arise, which then are elaborated into gender hierarchies in the reception history.

Through its structure, Leviticus 15 parallels the man's ejaculation of semen with the woman's menstruation. Since Leviticus 12 refers to the male child's circumcision, that chapter may also appear to be concerned with both genders; however, redaction criticism considers the reference to circumcision to be a later insertion.

A man who has sexual contact with a woman during her menstrual period is subsumed with her into the condition of *niddah* (Lev. 15.24). Given that נִדָּה was coined specifically to differentiate woman, its application to man causes a confusion of genders. Leviticus 18.19 insists that such confusion must absolutely be avoided, and as punishment it prescribes permanent exclusion from society. The gender dynamics are mirrored in the language: *niddah* is a gender-specific term used in the Hebrew Bible solely for woman. The texts mark the woman's gender with *niddah*, while for man the fixing of gender identity occurs through circumcision.

Most biblical texts that deal with circumcision usually do not mention the blood that is shed; in a medieval rabbinic text it is designated as 'the blood of the covenant' and set in parallel with menstrual blood: 'Since God commanded the males, and not the females, we may deduce that God commanded to seal the covenant on the place of maleness. The blood of menstruation that women observe by telling their husbands of the onset of their period – this for them is the blood of the covenant.'[4]

---

4. From a commentary by the twelfth-century Rabbi Joseph Bekhor Shor, cited in Cohen, 'A Brief History', 40.

8. *Prospects*

The difference in the Hebrew Bible's construction of body and gender can best be exemplified by comparing the circumcision command to the menstruation regulations: whereas the male body's relation to God, to the cult, is inscribed permanently through the one-time act of circumcision, for the female body, this relationship is repeatedly renewed through observance of the purity-*torot*.

Analogously, circumcision may be understood as a physical sign of difference with religious significance. As a distinctive mark of identity it is reserved for men. By contract, neither the purity-*torot* nor the Hebrew Bible as a whole has a ritual for women that fixes their gender and religious identity.

Finally, I turn to the concept of purity. As the analyses of the purity-*torot* (especially in Lev. 12 and 15) made clear, the body is not an object but rather a concept that is mediated and standardized by discourse, and by doing so shaping the concept of purity. According to Leviticus 13, cultic ineligibility can adhere to a person based on a specific appearance of his skin, but it requires a performance, namely the reading of the text, in order for the person to be declared (and thus to become) cultically ineligible. In other words, according to Leviticus 13–14, cultic ineligibility in the case of certain skin conditions is not automatic, but dependent on the confirmation of the condition's presence. Cultic ineligibility is not objective, even though it may be traceable back to physical phenomena. If the texts performatively ascribe purity (cultic ability) and impurity (cultic disability) to persons and objects, this means that the purity regulations qualify neither women nor men as ontologically impure.

The texts do not correlate impurity directly with physiological phenomena such as loss of bodily fluids through secretion. The woman after childbirth is *both* cultically impure *and* losing 'the blood of purification' (Lev. 12.4, 5). This is part of the purification process. The woman who loses blood after giving birth is not impure on account of the flow of blood; rather, it is precisely by this flow that she is purified. Some interpreters have attempted to express this ambivalence of the woman's condition after giving birth through phrases such as 'positieve onreinheid'[5] or the title of the essay collection *Wholly Woman – Holy Blood*. Perceptions of physiology are interwoven with the construction of symbolic systems, as is apparent in the fact that the *niddah* lasts seven days irrespective of the duration of blood flow. Im/purity as an organizing category retains some relationship to physiology while remaining substantially detached from it.

---

5. A. Noordtzij, *Het Boek Leviticus*, Korte Verklaring der Heilige Schrift (Kampen: Kok, 1940), 131.

Though the interests of the purity-*torot* are clearly not physiological, their program is not disembodied.

Deciphering the interrelatedness of the constructions of these three concepts (body, gender and purity) has been eminently helpful to understand each of them and how they function together: Leviticus 12 and 15 both *de*scribe and *in*scribe:[6] they *pre*scribe social relations and cultic connections and thereby standardize the body and its gender.

c. *From Practice to Theory of the Purity-*torot *and Back*

According to standard interpretations, the instructions in Leviticus 11–15 were either drawn from the realm of everyday and domestic life and then re-composed for a cultic context, or they were native to a priestly context but repurposed after the exile as rules for everyday life (see Chapter 1). My study's discourse-analytic procedure opens up another possibility: Leviticus 12 and 15 are performative regulations that actively create the body and gender through their discourse. The text's communicative structure also functions at a time and in a situation that has no experience of the priestly office or has lost the experience of it, since the way in which the regulations are to be practiced reveals itself in the structure of the text (see below). This is evident from the texts' discursive structure, as for example in the gaps, but also in the almost nonexistent intertextual reflections in narrative texts from the Hebrew Bible as well as in extra-textual finds. In short, the regulations in Leviticus 12 and 15 do not support any conclusions about real-world cultic-ritual praxis. The praxis of the texts is realized first of all in the fact that the gendered body is produced through discourse.

Thus the regulations shape one's perception of reality and allow the body to come into being through the performativity of the texts, as was explained regarding various passages of the purity-*torot*. On the textual level, a person or an object is declared by the priest to be cultically eligible or cult-endangering, without it being the case that this status is traceable back to a specific physical condition; for example, objects within a house that is stricken with eczema become unclean only once the house is declared by a priest to be unclean (Lev. 14.36). The designation of uncleanness does not adhere before the priest applies it. The woman's period of purification after the birth of a girl is twice as long as after the

---

6. Cf. C. E. Hayes, *Gentile Impurities and Jewish Identities: Intermarriage and Conversion from the Bible to the Talmud* (Oxford: Oxford University Press, 2002), 3: 'I argue that in ancient Jewish culture, the paired terms "pure" and "impure" were employed in various ways not to describe but also to inscribe sociocultural boundaries between Jews and Gentile others'.

birth of a boy (Lev. 12), although this has no basis in the actual duration of the postpartum bleeding. The *niddah* lasts seven days regardless of how long the monthly bleeding endures (Lev. 15). The analyzed purity regulations are not descriptions of physiological processes; rather, with the aid of the body, they construct cultic dis-ability.

The purity regulations do not deal with concrete experiences of men and women as such; at most, those of women reverberate in the use of the root דוה. The purpose of the regulations in Leviticus 12–15 is not primarily to regulate the (cultic) life of everyday women and men; it is much more the case that they use the body as a projective surface upon which to inscribe the cultic (dis)ability of persons with specific characteristics.

Persons who are experiencing a bodily discharge are not the intended (direct) audience for the instructions in Leviticus 15. Except for the second person plural hortatory formula in Lev. 15.31, the instructions are not formulated as prescriptions but as descriptions; as such, they derive from a form-critical perspective, not (ritual) instructions. Rather, attention is focused on those who have come into contact with such a person with a bodily discharge. By contrast, the exposition in Leviticus 12 revolves exclusively around the woman who has recently given birth. Chapter 15 sets forth what must be done in case other people or inanimate objects are exposed to their impurity, so that the cult-endangering contamination does not spread any further and the impure condition can be eliminated. Only in special cases does the priest have any role to play. The text does not attest or transmit any priestly pronouncements such as 'You are clean' or 'You are unclean'. On the literary plane, the direction of communication runs within the textual space; we overhear no direct utterances by the priest. These observations cause Erhard Gerstenberger to wonder whether 'this absence of any verbatim declaratory formula…indicate[s] that this text does not represent genuine ritual instructions after all, but rather something more like illustrative material for a worship lectionary'.[7] This raises the further question: What is the relationship between the text's content and priestly declarations of im/purity, which the text prescribes in certain cases? In my view, the absence of any verbatim declaratory formula for the priest and the corresponding presence of a textual statement on the literary level indicates that what we have before us is not a ritual text but a text for reading.[8] The utopic character becomes visible in the text's literary and communicative structure. Further evidence for this

7. Cf. Gerstenberger, *Leviticus*, 159, regarding Lev. 13.
8. Cf. Gorman, 'Pagans and Priests', 109: 'In such a view, reading and hearing (and writing?) become ritual practices, acts of textual ritualizing, critical to the experiential engagement with the cultic reality of the texts' (see below).

is the observation that the objects necessary for performance of the rituals remain unmentioned[9] and that the rituals are accomplished noiselessly in the process of reading.[10] Leviticus gives a theological orientation as the body is sketched out in relation to the sanctuary.

It is also remarkable that Leviticus as well as other priestly texts report neither that nor how the purity regulations were translated into practice. The tension between the regulations and their implementation is anticipated on the textual level. The programmatic character of the purity regulations – what I would call the fictional character (see the next section) – is likewise visible in the Greek version, which, however, gave Leviticus 12 and 15 a more physiological character by taking up ancient medical concepts. This caused a shift in the subsequent interpretive history. It appears as if later interpreters were determined to re-invest the text with physical meaning, to make them more realistic. Rituals undergo change in the course of history in terms of their performance, and their function. Social history and discourse history must therefore be correlated.

That a woman should wash herself after menstruation is not something that the regulations in Leviticus 15 demand. Specific ritual facilities for washing are neither prescribed by Leviticus 15, nor are they mentioned in other biblical texts. By contrast, the Mishnah recognizes particular installations, i.e., the *mikvot*, which gives us the key for understanding certain stone artifacts from the centuries before and after the turn of the era. Interpretations of the regulations in Qumran do enforce the regulations found in Leviticus 15, placing the *niddah* and with it the female body and the absolute purity of the temple/community at the center of interest. Protecting the temple is no longer a consideration, since it had been destroyed.[11] But even the rabbinic interpretation of *niddah* cannot be reduced to mere instructions for behavior.[12] It is in such mediated ways that the literary texts affect everyday life even up through the present, as is shown by revived discussion among the different streams of Judaism regarding their practices.

---

9. Cf. Levine, *Leviticus*, xxxix.

10. This phenomenon is captured in the title of I. Knohl's *The Sanctuary of Silence: The Priestly Torah and the Holiness School* (Minneapolis: Fortress, 1995).

11. But even before the Second Temple was destroyed, evidence exists that a household Judaism was beginning to develop (cf. Berlin, 'Jewish Life Before the Revolt'; I. Werret, 'The Evolution of Purity at Qumran', in *Ritual Purity and the Dead Sea Scrolls* (Leiden: Brill, 2007), 493–518, and see above in Chapter 1).

12. Cf. Fonrobert, *Menstrual Purity*, 22–24, and D. Boyarin, *Intertextuality and the Reading of Midrash* (Bloomington: Indianapolis University Press, 1990).

II. *Leviticus and Body Practices as Survival Space in Exilic and Persian Times*

Leviticus occupies an in-between space in the narrative of the exodus community, both textually and thematically. It establishes a peculiar domain within a literary cosmos and opens up a reading space. My suggestion that Leviticus may have served as reading book is underlined by its later reception history, where it has become the exemplary book, according to the Tannaitic commentary on Leviticus, *Sifra* – Aramaic for 'the book'.[13] As I have outlined above, the text's ritual practice is subject to reshaping in the course of history and can be realized beyond bodily practices. Impurity, i.e., cultic disability, realizes itself in writing, reading, and interpreting of the text.

a. *Fictionality and Normativity*

As was noted in the introductory chapter, fictional should not be understood in the sense of unreal, not truthful. Fictionality[14] as a literary tool is a positive textual function, as it opens up realms of experience. Nor is fictionality detrimental to the biblical texts' validity. On the contrary, the Bible's character as literature, including its fictionality, is crucial to its canonical status. Fictionality and normativity are not mutually exclusive. It is precisely such characteristics of fiction as stylized introductory notices,[15] abstraction of place, gaps,[16] rhetorical structure[17] and intertextual references that lend durability to a text and allow it to become canonical. The informational gaps[18] might indicate that the priestly texts were written for reading and not enacting.

---

13. See G. Stemberger, 'Leviticus in Sifra', in *Encyclopedia of Midrash*, ed. J. Neusner and A. J. Avery Peck, Biblical Interpretation in Formative Judaism (Leiden: Brill, 2005), 429–47; L. Schiffman, 'From Text to Tradition', cited 6 May 2011, online: http://cojs.org/cojswiki/Other_Tannaitic_Texts.

14. Cf. W. Iser, 'Akte des Fingierens. Oder: Was ist das Fiktive im fiktionalen Text?', in *Funktionen des Fiktiven*, ed. D. Henrich and W. Iser (Munich: Fink, 1983), 121–51.

15. For Luciani, *Sainteté et Pardon I*, 10, the introductory divine-speech formulas constitute the primary indicators of the literary structure of the book.

16. Cf. Liss, 'Ritual Purity', 334–35. Bibb, *Ritual Words*, 95–99, makes similar observations regarding Lev. 1–7.

17. Watts, 'Ritual Rhetoric in the Pentateuch', emphasizes that the Torah's rhetorical strategies serve to reinforce its authority.

18. Gorman, 'Pagans and Priests', 108.

To read Leviticus as literature in the technical sense entails taking into account its fictional character; in received terminology, this would be referred to as the book's utopian, eschatological character.[19] In contrast to source- and form-critical approaches that we sketched at the outset and that classify Leviticus 11–15 as ritual texts, we have read these chapters as literary texts distinguished by their fictionality.[20]

Like the purity regulations in general, Leviticus 12 and 15 are staged as God's speech to Moses (and to Aaron). Missing from chs. 13 and 14 but present here is the requirement that the regulations be handed on to Israel's descendants. The practice of the regulations is an event that is immanent to the text, while their performance is realized already in reading and in hearing. Many exegetes have faced the difficulty of balancing awareness of the regulations' programmatic and fictive character with the need to understand them as part of Israel's religious and social history. Through discourse analysis, the programmatic as well as the socially and culturally formative character of the chapters has become apparent. 'Through reading, hearing, copying or commenting upon Leviticus, the ancient audience was gradually educated in a distinctive model of society that, by construing the related oppositions between the sacred and profane and between clean and unclean as central oppositions, subordinates social organization to the temple' and confer to the Israelites 'a degree of priestly competency in the domestic sphere'.[21] In the intertwinedness of inside the text and outside the text, of reading and living, of body and language, the dualism between textuality and materiality is overcome.[22] In this way, we were able to uncover both the fictional and normative character of the texts in Leviticus.

b. *Leviticus as a Reading Space*
As the third book of the Torah, Leviticus constitutes its own space in the heart of the Torah: a niche between the books Genesis to Exodus and Numbers to Deuteronomy. Through its specific idiom, Leviticus adds a new dimension to the narrative in contrast with Exodus's theme of liberation, namely, Israel's atoning encounter with God.[23] Action ceases.[24]

---

19. Cf. Marx, 'Les recherches sur le Lévitique', and Knohl, *The Sanctuary of Silence*, 156.

20. Liss, 'The Imaginary Sanctuary', uses the term 'fictional' for the priestly writings in general and the chapters on the tent of meeting in Exodus in particular.

21. Nihan, 'Forms and Functions of Purity', 362.

22. Cf. Boyarin, *Intertextuality and the Reading of Midrash*, 117–29.

23. Cf. Berthil Oosting, *Verzoening als Verleiding: Een nieuwe toegang tot de wondere woorden van het boek Leviticus* (Vught: Skandalon, 2004), 47–50.

24. Cf. Levine, 'Leviticus: Its Literary', 23: 'In Leviticus there is no movement'.

In an unmediated way and without identifying the subject the book begins: 'And he called to Moses'. The book opens with a *waw* consecutive, suggesting on a formal level that it continues what stands before – the book Exodus. It is only in the second half of the verse that we learn who the speaker is: YHWH. The instructions issue forth 'from the Tent of Meeting', in which, at the end of Exodus, God's glory had taken up residence. By directing our attention to the entrance to the Tent, Lev. 1.1 achieves both a narrowing and an abstraction of the place.[25] The time remains unnamed. The book's historical location is thus presented in a decidedly abstract manner, which makes the concrete communicative situation difficult to infer. God's presence is conceived in spatial categories.

The focus is upon the entrance to the sanctuary. The book's instructions otherwise apply 'in all your settlements' (Lev. 3.17; 7.26; 23.3, 14, 21, 31), which could allude to a scattering of Israel's descendants in the diaspora or to the fact that the regulations can be detached from the temple and applied in different locations. Does Leviticus therefore record the transcript of an exiled elite's diaspora theology, for example, a concealed countermodel to Babylonian–Persian culture, politics, and religion? In this view, Leviticus is an exilic project that demonstrates its relevance in the diaspora down to the present day and that, as text, assures the project's survival by furnishing it with a literary home. In the exile and after the destruction of the temple, all that remained of the community's ritual inheritance was the performance of bodies and of texts, in which the relationship to the cult can be imaginarily depicted.

Therefore, along with Watts I have been favoring a rhetorical interpretation underlying the twofold structure of the texts in Leviticus: 'P's rhetorical goals may include the validation of the ritual and its form on the basis of ostensibly ancient textual authority, and/or persuasion to motivate performance of rituals, and/or persuasion to accept the whole text's authority (Torah) because of its authoritative instruction on ritual performance.'[26] One part of this process described could be labeled as 'textualization of ritual'[27] or 'scripturalization of cult'.[28]

---

25. On space as decisive category in the openings of Leviticus and Numbers, cf. Zenger and Frevel, 'Die Bücher Levitikus und Numeri als Teile der Pentateuchkomposition', 53–55.
26. Watts, *Ritual and Rhetoric in Leviticus*, 309.
27. Cf. Bell, *Ritual*, 202–5.
28. G. Anderson, 'Sacrifice and Sacrificial Offerings: Old Testament', *ABD* 5:882–85 (873).

And with the recording and literary shaping of the purity regulations in Leviticus, a preservation of the cult in the word was accomplished. *Leviticus Rabbah* 7.3 implicitly likens the purity regulations to the instructions for sacrifices, in that it claims for both that studying them counts as performing them: when one reads the purity-*torot*, one needs no temple, since holiness is realized in the body and its practices and in the reading of these practices likewise.[29]

As a virtual and at the same time real place, the body is the locus of utopia. Leviticus may therefore be read as a fictional pilgrimage that plays itself out in the imagination of a male or female devotee after the destruction of the temple: 'There is no tabernacle, the faithful are not moving around it, all the movement is in the book that they are reading, or hearing through their ears. Learning the book becomes a way of internalizing the tabernacle.'[30] The texts create a world within a literary space, a reading space.[31] 'The Holy is conserved within the only space that had been left for it, the realm of literature.'[32]

The purity regulations are an attempt to restructure the community's life in exilic time and in the Diaspora, an attempt that assures survival in spaces beyond the cult and the temple. In the *torot*, holiness is described and thus preserved beyond the sanctuary. This preservation ('Aufhebung' in a Hegalian sense) of the body and of the cult is not to be understood in the sense of a negation or an erasure. To characterize this process as a spiritualization of the cult or a discarnation of the body fails to encompass its full reality, since the purity rules (Lev. 11–15) do still employ the category of the body. Purity and holiness are depicted, not in the sanctuary, but realized in the textualized practice of the body. The question of what the texts refer to, and wherein their reality consists, is answered by the textual and theological composition, the discursive structure.

Body assumes significance through discourse. The findings of our exegeses oscillate between the body as performance and the body as material object. The body comes into being through language that is

---

29. Cf., for a similar idea, S. Schreiner, '"Wo man Tora lernt, braucht man keinen Tempel". Einige Anmerkungen zum Problem der Tempelsubstitution im rabbinischen Judentum', in *Gemeinde ohne Tempel/Community without Temple. Zur Substituierung und Transformation des Jerusalemer Tempels und seines Kults im Alten Testament, antiken Judentum und frühen Christentum*, ed. B. Ego *et al.*, WUNT 118 (Tübingen: Mohr Siebeck, 1999), 371–92.

30. Douglas, *Leviticus as Literature*, 230.

31. Cf. Liss, 'Kanon und Fiktion', 32–33.

32. Cf. Liss, 'Ritual Purity and the Construction of Identity', 354.

historically and culturally conditioned. Language depends upon corporeality for its reference, and conversely, the body is graspable only through language. In the discourse of the body in Leviticus 12 and 15, materiality and virtuality coincide. I have discerned the outlines of the textual conceptions of body, gender and purity as it has developed through the (innerbiblical) discourse history, in a way that is decisive for a biblical anthropology in historical perspective.

I have attempted to chart new territory within research of Leviticus and of the body from a gender-informed and cultural perspective. The regulations in Leviticus 11–15 encourage us to redefine the roles of body and sexuality in both ethics and anthropology and to reconstruct the relation between the sacred and everyday life through analysis of textualized bodily practices.

BIBLIOGRAPHY

Anderson, Gary A. 'Sacrifice and Sacrificial Offerings: Old Testament'. *ABD* 5:882–85.
Bachmann, Veronika. 'Die biblische Vorstellungswelt und deren geschlechterpolitische Dimension: Methodologische Überlegungen am Beispiel der ersttestamentlichen Kategorien "rein" und "unrein"'. *lectio difficilior* 2/2003. Online: http://www.lectio.unibe.ch (last accessed 3 November 2013).
Bachmann-Medick, Doris. *Cultural Turns: Neuorientierungen in den Kulturwissenschaften*. Reinbek bei Hamburg: Rowohlt, 2006.
Bailly, Anatole, ed. *Dictionnaire grec – français*. Paris: Hachette, 1961.
Bar Asher, Moshe. 'The *Qal* Passive Participle of Geminate Verbs in Biblical Hebrew'. Pages 11–25 in *Biblical Hebrew in its Northwest Semitic Setting: Typological and Historical Perspectives*. Edited by Steven E. Fassberg and Avi Hurvitz. Jerusalem: Hebrew University Magnes Press, 2006.
Bartor, Assnat. *Reading Law as Narrative: A Study in the Casuistic Laws of the Pentateuch*. Ancient Israel and Its Literature 5. Atlanta: Society of Biblical Literature, 2010.
Bassnett, Susan, and André Lefevre, eds. *Translation, History, Culture*. London: Pinter 1990.
Bauer, Walter. *Griechisch-deutsches Wörterbuch*. 6th ed. Berlin: de Gruyter, 1988.
Bell, Catherine, *Ritual: Perspectives and Dimensions*. New York/Oxford: Oxford University Press, 1997.
Benthien, Claudia, and Christoph Wulf, eds. *Körperteile. Eine kulturelle Anatomie*. Reinbek bei Hamburg: Rowohlt, 2001.
Berequist, Brigitta. 'Bronze Age Sacrificial Koine in the Eastern Mediterranean? A Study of Animal Sacrifice in the Ancient Near East'. Pages 11–43 in *Ritual and Sacrifice in the Ancient Near East*. Edited by Jan Quaegebeur. OLA 55. Leuven: Peeters, 1993.
Bergen, Wesley J. *Reading Ritual: Leviticus in Postmodern Culture*. London: T&T Clark International, 2010.
Berlejung, Angelika, Jan Dietrich, and Joachim F. Quack, eds. *Menschenbilder und Körperkonzepte im Alten Israel, in Ägypten und im Alten Orient*. ORA 9. Tübingen: Mohr Siebeck, 2012.
Berlin, Adele. *Lamentations: A Commentary*. OTL. Louisville, KY: Westminster John Knox, 2002.
Berlin, Andrea M. 'Jewish Life Before the Revolt: The Archeological Evidence'. *JSJ* 36 (2005): 417–70.
Beuken, Willem. 'שָׁכַב *šākab*'. *ThWAT* 6:1306–18.
Biale, Rachel. *Women and Jewish Law: An Exploration of Women's Issues in Halakhic Sources*. New York: Schocken, 1984.
Bibb, Bryan D. *Ritual Words and Narrative Worlds in the Book of Leviticus*. LHBOTS 480. London: Bloomsbury T&T Clark, 2008.
Bienkowski, Piotr. 'Horse'. Page 147 in Bienkowski, ed., *Dictionary of the Ancient Near East*.
———. 'Law'. Pages 175–76 in Bienkowski, ed., *Dictionary of the Ancient Near East*.

Bienkowski, Piotr, ed. *Dictionary of the Ancient Near East*. London: British Museum Press, 2000.
Biggs, Robert D. 'Conception, Contraception, and Abortion in Ancient Mesopotamia'. Pages 1–13 in *Wisdom, Gods and Literature: Studies in Assyriology in Honour of W. G. Lambert*. Edited by Andrew R. George and Irving L. Finkel. Winona Lake, IN: Eisenbrauns, 2000.
Blaschke, Andreas. *Beschneidung: Zeugnisse der Bibel und verwandter Texte*. TANZ. Tübingen: Francke, 1999.
Blum, Erhard. *Studien zur Komposition des Pentateuch*. BZAW 189. Berlin: de Gruyter, 1990.
Boyarin, Daniel. *Carnal Israel: Reading Sex in Talmudic Culture*. The New Historicism 25. Berkeley: University of California Press, 1993.
———. *Intertextuality and the Reading of Midrash*. Bloomington: Indianapolis University Press, 1990.
———. *A Radical Jew: Paul and the Politics of Identity*. Berkeley: University of California Press, 1994.
Bratsiotis, N. P. 'בָּשָׂר *bāśār*', *ThWAT*, 1:850–67.
Brenner, Athalya. *Intercourse of Knowledge: On Gendering Desire and Sexuality in the Hebrew Bible*. BIS 26. Leiden: Brill, 1997.
———. *The Israelite Woman: Social Role and Literary Type in Biblical Narrative*. The Biblical Seminar 2. Sheffield: JSOT, 1985.
Brockelmann, Carl. *Hebräische Syntax*. Neukirchen–Vluyn: Neukirchener, 1956.
Butler, Judith. *Bodies That Matter: On the Discursive Limits of 'Sex'*. New York: Routledge, 1993.
———. *Gender Trouble: Feminism and the Subversion of Identity*. New York: Routledge, 1990.
Camp, Claudia. 'Feminist and Gender-Critical Perspectives on the Biblical Ideology of Intermarriage'. Pages 303–15 in *Mixed Marriages: Intermarriage and Group Identity in the Second Temple Period*. Edited by Christian Frevel. LHBOTS 47. London: T&T Clark International, 2011.
Cantarella, Eva. *Pandora's Daughters: The Role and Status of Women in Greek and Roman Antiquity*. Baltimore: The Johns Hopkins University Press, 1987.
Cohen, Shaye J. D. *The Beginnings of Jewishness: Boundaries, Varieties, Uncertainties*. Berkeley: University of California Press, 1999.
———. 'A Brief History of Jewish Circumcision Blood'. Pages 30–42 in *The Covenant of Circumcision: New Perspectives on an Ancient Jewish Rite*. Edited by Elizabeth Wyner Mark. Hanover: Brandeis University Press, 2003.
Cooper, Alan. 'A Medieval Jewish Version of Original Sin: Ephraim of Luntshits on Leviticus 12'. *Harvard Theological Review* 97 (2004): 445–59.
Crüsemann, Frank. 'Ein israelitisches Ritualbad aus vorexilischer Zeit'. *ZDPV* 94 (1978): 68–75.
———. *Die Tora: Theologie und Sozialgeschichte des alttestamentlichen Gesetzes*. Munich: Kaiser, 1992.
Daniel, Suzanne. *Recherches sur le Vocabulaire du Culte dans la Septante*. Paris: Klincksieck, 1996.
Davies, Philip R. 'Leviticus as a Cultic System in the Second Temple Period: Responses to Hannah K. Harrington'. Pages 230–37 in Sawyer, ed., *Reading Leviticus*.

Dean-Jones, Lesley. 'The Cultural Construct of the Female Body in Classical Greek Science'. Pages 111–37 in *Women's History and Ancient History*. Edited by Sarah B. Pomeroy. Chapel Hill: University of North Carolina Press, 1991.

———. *Women's Bodies in Classical Greek Science*. Oxford: Clarendon, 1996.

Delaney, Carol. 'Abraham and the Seeds of Patriarchy'. Pages 129–49 in *Genesis*. Edited by Athalya Brenner. The Feminist Companion to the Bible, Second Series. Sheffield: Sheffield Academic, 1998.

Dijk-Hemmes, Fokkelien van, and Athalya Brenner. *On Gendering Texts: Female and Male Voices in the Hebrew Bible*. Leiden: Brill, 1996.

Dijkstra, Meindert. 'Schone Handen: Reinheid in de Culturen van de Levant'. *Phoenix* 48, no. 2 (2002): 73–92.

Donner, Herbert, and Wolfgang Röllig. *Kanaanäische und Aramäische Inschriften Bd. II*. Wiesbaden: Harrassowitz, 1964.

Douglas, Mary. 'The Forbidden Animals in Leviticus'. *JSOT* 59 (1992): 3–23.

———. *Leviticus as Literature*. Oxford: Oxford University Press, 1999.

———. *Purity and Danger: An Analysis of the Concepts of Pollution and Taboo*. London: Routledge & Kegan, 1966.

Duden, Barbara. *Geschichte unter der Haut: Ein Eisenacher Arzt und seine Patientinnen um 1730*. Stuttgart: Klett-Cotta, 1970.

Eberhart, Christian. *Studien zur Bedeutung der Opfer im Alten Testament: Die Signifikanz von Blut- und Verbrennungsriten im kultischen Rahmen*. WMANT 94. Neukirchen-Vluyn: Neukirchener, 2002.

Ehrlich, Arnold B. *Randglossen zur Hebräischen Bibel. Textkritisches, Sprachliches und Sachliches*. Hildesheim: Olms, 1968.

Eilberg-Schwartz, Howard. *The Savage in Judaism: An Anthropology of Israelite and Ancient Judaism*. Bloomington: Indiana University Press, 1990.

———, ed. *The People of the Body: Jews and Judaism from an Embodied Perspective*. Albany, NY: State University of New York Press, 1992.

Ellens, Deborah. 'Menstrual Impurity and Innovation in Leviticus 15'. Pages 29–44 in de Troyer et al., eds., *Wholly Woman*.

———. *Women in the Sex Texts of Leviticus and Deuteronomy: A Comparative Conceptual Analysis*. LHBOTS 458. New York: T&T Clark International, 2008.

Elliger, Karl. *Leviticus*. HAT 4. Tübingen: Mohr, 1966.

———. 'Sinn und Ursprung der priesterlichen Geschichtserzählung'. *ZTK* 49 (1952): 121–43.

Erbele, Dorothea. 'Gender Trouble in the Old Testament: Three Models of the Relation between Sex and Gender'. *SJOT* 13, no. 1 (1999): 131–41.

Erbele-Küster, Dorothea. 'Comment dire l'interdit? Le tabou linguistique et social de la menstruation en Lévitique 11–20'. Pages 181–90 in *Tabou et transgressions: Actes du colloque organisé par le Collège de France, Paris, les 11–12 avril 2012*. Edited by Jean-Marie Durand et al. OBO 274. Göttingen: Vandenhoeck & Ruprecht, 2015.

———. 'Der Dienst der Frauen am Eingang des Zeltheiligtums (Exodus 38:8) – Kultisch-religiöse Verortungen von Frauen in Exodus und Leviticus'. Pages 265–81 in *The Interpretation of Exodus: Studies in Honour of Cornelis Houtman*. Edited by Riemer Roukema et al. CBET 44. Leuven: Brill, 2006.

———. 'Gender and Cult: "Pure" and "Impure" as Gender-relevant Categories'. Pages 375–406 in *Torah*. Edited by Irmtraud Fischer and Mercedes Navarro Puerto. The Bible and the Women 1. Atlanta: SBL, 2011.

———. *Körper und Geschlecht. Studien zur Anthropologie von Lev 12 und 15*. WMANT 121. Neukirchen-Vluyn: Neukirchner, 2008.

———. 'Die Körperbestimmungen in Leviticus 11–15'. Pages 209–24 in Berlejung, Dietrich and Quack, eds., *Menschenbilder und Körperkonzepte im Alten Israel*.

———. 'Reading as an Act of Offering: Reconsidering the Genre of Leviticus 1'. Pages 34–46 in *The Actuality of Sacrifice: Past and Present*. Edited by Alberdina Houtman et al. JCP 28. Leiden: Brill, 2014.

———. 'Ungerechte Texte und gerechte Sprache: Überlegungen zur Hermeneutik des Bibelübersetzens'. Pages 222–34 in *Die Bibel – übersetzt in gerechte Sprache? Grundlagen einer neuen Übersetzung*. Edited by Helga Kuhlmann. Gütersloh: Gütersloher Verlagshaus, 2005.

Erbele-Küster, Dorothea, and Elke Toenges. 'Beschneidung'. Pages 47–49 in *Sozialgeschichtliches Wörterbuch*. Edited by Frank Crüsemann et al. Gütersloh: Gütersloher Verlagshaus, 2009.

Eshel, Hanan. 'The Pools of Sepphoris: Ritual Baths or Bathtubs? They Are Not Ritual Baths'. *BAR* 26 (2000): 42–45.

Fabry, Heinz-Josef, and Hans-Winfried Jüngling, eds. *Levitikus als Buch*. BBB 119. Berlin: Philo, 1999.

Feucht, Erika. *Das Kind im Alten Ägypten: Die Stellung des Kindes in Familie und Gesellschaft nach altägyptischen Texten und Darstellungen*. Frankfurt am Main: Campus, 1995.

Fischer, Irmtraud. 'Über Lust und Last, Kinder zu haben: Soziale, genealogische und theologische Aspekte in der Literatur Alt-Israels'. *JBT* 17 (2002): 55–82.

Fishbane, Michael, *Biblical Interpretation in Ancient Israel*. Oxford: Clarendon, 1985.

Fleishman, Joseph. 'On the Significance of a Name Change and Circumcision in Genesis 17'. *JANES* 28 (2002): 19–32.

Fonrobert, Charlotte E. *Menstrual Purity: Rabbinic and Christian Reconstructions of Biblical Gender*. Stanford: Stanford University Press, 2000.

Frevel, Christian, ed. *Biblische Anthropologie: Neue Einsichten aus dem Alten Testament*. QD 237. Freiburg: Herder, 2010.

Frevel, Christian, and Christophe Nihan, eds. *Purity and the Forming of Religious Traditions in the Ancient Mediterranean World and Ancient Judaism*. Leiden: Brill, 2013.

Frymer-Kensky, Tikva. 'Pollution, Purification, and Purgation in Biblical Israel'. Pages 399–414 in *The Word of the Lord Shall Go Forth: Essays in Honor of David Noel Freedman*. Edited by Carol L. Meyers et al. Winona Lake, IN: Eisenbrauns, 1983.

Gane, Roy. *Cult and Character: Purification Offerings, Day of Atonement, and Theodicy*. Winona Lake, IN: Eisenbrauns, 2005.

Gennep, Arnold van. *Les rites de passage*. Paris: Picard, 1909.

Gerlemann, Gillis. 'בָּשָׂר *bāśār* Fleisch'. *THAT* 1:376–79.

———. 'דָּם *dām* Blut'. *THAT* 1:448–51.

Gerstenberger, Erhard S. *Leviticus: A Commentary*. Louisville: Westminster John Knox, 1996.

Gilders, William K. *Blood Ritual in the Hebrew Bible: Meaning and Power*. Baltimore: The Johns Hopkins University Press, 2004.

Gispen, Willem-Hendrik. *Het Boek Leviticus*. COT. Kampen: Kok, 1950.

Gorman, Frank H. *The Ideology of Ritual. Space, Time and Status in the Priestly Theology*. JSOTSup 91. Sheffield: Sheffield Academic, 1991.

———. 'Pagans and Priests: Critical Reflections on Method'. Pages 96–110 in *Perspectives in Purity and Purification in the Bible*. Edited by Baruch Schwartz et al. LHBOTS 474. New York: T&T Clark International, 2008.

Gottlieb, Alma. 'Menstrual Cosmology among the Beng of Ivory Coast'. Pages 55–74 in *Blood Magic: The Anthropology of Menstruation*. Edited by Thomas Buckley and Alma Gottlieb. Berkeley: University of California Press, 1988.

Grabbe, Lester. *Leviticus*. Old Testament Guides. London: T&T Clark International, 1993).

———. 'The Priests in Leviticus – Is the Medium the Message?' Pages 207–24 in Rendtorff and Kugler, eds., *The Book of Leviticus*.

Graf, Karl Heinrich. *Die geschichtlichen Bücher des Alten Testament: Zwei literarisch-kritische Untersuchungen*. Leipzig: Weigel, 1866.

Greenberg, Blue. 'Female Sexuality and Bodily Functions in the Jewish Tradition'. Pages 1–44 in *Women, Religion and Sexuality*. Edited by Jeanne Becher. Geneva: Trinity, 1990.

Greenberg, Moshe. 'The Etymology of *nidda* "(Menstrual) Impurity"'. Pages 69–77 in *Solving Riddles and Untying Knots: Biblical, Epigraphic, and Semitic Studies in Honor of J. C. Greenfield*. Edited by Ziony Zevit et al. Winona Lake, IN: Eisenbrauns, 1995.

Grohmann, Marianne. *Fruchtbarkeit und Geburt in den Psalmen*. FAT 53. Tübingen: Mohr Siebeck, 2007.

Gruber, Mayer I. 'Purity and Impurity in Halakhic Sources and Qumran Law'. Pages 65–76 in de Troyer et al., eds., *Wholly Woman*.

———. 'Women in the Cult according to the Priestly Code'. Pages 35–48 in *Judaic Perspectives on Ancient Israel*. Edited by Jacob Neusner. Philadelphia: Wipf & Stock, 1987.

Hanson, Ann Ellis. 'The Medical Writer's Woman'. Pages 309–37 in *Women's History and Ancient History*. Edited by Sarah B. Pomeroy. Chapel Hill: University of North Carolina Press, 1991.

Haran, Menhahem. *Temples and Temple-Services in Ancient Israel*. Oxford: Clarendon, 1978.

Harlé, Paul, and Didier Pralon, eds. *La Bible d'Alexandrie: Le Lévitique*. Paris: Éditions du Cerf, 1988.

Harrington, Hannah K. *The Impurity Systems of Qumran and the Rabbis: Biblical Foundations*. SBLDS 143. Atlanta: Scholars Press 1993.

———. 'Interpreting Leviticus in the Second Temple Period: Struggling with Ambiguity'. Pages 214–29 in Sawyer, ed., *Reading Leviticus*.

———. *The Purity Texts*. Companion to the Qumran Scrolls 5. London: T&T Clark International, 2004.

Hartley, John E. *Leviticus*. WBC 2. Dallas: Word Books, 1992.

Hayes, Christine E. *Gentile Impurities and Jewish Identities: Intermarriage and Conversion from the Bible to the Talmud*. Oxford: Oxford University Press, 2002.

Hengel, Martin. *Judentum und Hellenismus: Studien zu ihrer Begegnung unter besonderer Berücksichtigung Palästinas bis zur Mitte des 2. Jh.s v. Chr.* WUNT 10. Tübingen: Mohr Siebeck, 1988.

Hermisson, Hans-Jürgen. *Sprache und Ritus im altisraelitischen Kult: Zur „Spiritualisierung" der Kultbegriffe im Alten Testament*. WMANT 19. Neukirchen-Vluyn: Neukirchener, 1965.

Hertog, Cornelis G. 'The Treatment of Relative Clauses in the Greek Leviticus'. Pages 65–97 in *Helsinki Perspectives on the Translation Technique of the Septuagint: Proceedings of the IOSCS Congress in Helsinki 1999*. Helsinki: Finnish Exegetical Society; Göttingen: Vandenhoeck & Ruprecht, 2001.

Hieke, Thomas. *Levitikus*. HThKAT. 2 vols. Freiburg im Breisgau: Herder, 2014.

Himmelfarb, Martha. 'Sexual Relations and Purity in the Temple Scroll and the Book of Jubilees'. *DSD* 6 (1999): 11–36.

Hoffman, Lawrence A. *Covenant of Blood: Circumcision and Gender in Rabbinic Judaism*. Chicago: University of Chicago Press, 1996.

Holzinger, H. *Einleitung in den Hexateuch: Mit Tabellen über die Quellenscheidung*. Freiburg/Leipzig: Mohr Siebeck, 1893.

Houtman, Cornelis. *Exodus* HCOT. 3 vols. Leiden: Brill, 2000.

———. *Der Pentateuch: Die Geschichte seiner Erforschung neben einer Auswertung*. CBET 9. Kampen: Kok, 1994.

Huber, Karl. *Untersuchungen über den Sprachcharakter des griechischen Leviticus*. Giessen: Töpelmann, 1916.

Ilan, T. 'Reading for Women in 1QSa (Serekh ha-Edah)'. Pages 61–76 in *The Dead Sea Scrolls in Context: Integrating the Dead Sea Scrolls in the Study of Ancient Texts, Languages, and Cultures*. Edited by Armin Lange, Emanuel Tov and Matthias Weigold. Leiden: Brill, 2011.

Iser, Wolfgang. 'Akte des Fingierens. Oder: Was ist das Fiktive im fiktionalen Text?' Pages 121–51 in *Funktionen des Fiktiven*. Edited by D. Henrich and W. Iser. Munich: Fink, 1983.

Jacob, Benno. *Das Buch Genesis*. Berlin: Schocken, 1934.

———. *Der Pentateuch*. Leipzig: Veit, 1905.

Janowski, Bernd. 'Das Herz – ein Beziehungsorgan: Zum Personenverständnis im Alten Testament'. Pages 1–39 in *Dimensionen der Leiblichkeit: Theologische Zugänge*. Edited by Bernd Janowski and Christoph Schwöbel. Neukirchen-Vluyn: Neukirchener, 2015.

———. *Sühne als Heilsgeschehen: Studien zur Sühnetheologie der Priesterschrift und zur Wurzel KPR im Alten Orient und im Alten Testament*. WMANT 55/2. Neukirchen-Vluyn: Neukirchener, 2002.

Jenni, Ernst. *Das hebräische Piel: Syntaktisch-semasiologische Untersuchung einer Verbalform im Alten Testament*. Zurich: EVZ-Verlag, 1968.

———. *Die hebräischen Präpositionen*. Bd. 1, *Die Präposition Beth*. Stuttgart: Kohlhammer, 1992.

Joüon, Paul, and Takamitsu Muraoka. *A Grammar of Biblical Hebrew*. Subsidia biblica 279. Rome: Gregorian & Biblical Press, 2006.

Kaufmann, Jehezqël. 'Probleme der israelitisch-jüdischen Religionsgeschichte'. *ZAW* 48 (1930): 23–43.

Kidd, José E. Ramirez. *Alterity and Identity in Israel: The "ger" in the Old Testament*. BZAW 283. Berlin: de Gruyter, 1999.

Kiuchi, Nobuyoshi. *The Purification Offering in the Priestly Literature: Its Meaning and Function*. JSOTSup 56. Sheffield: JSOT, 1987.

Klawans, Jonathan. *Impurity and Sin in Ancient Judaism*. New York: Oxford University Press, 2000.

———. *Purity, Sacrifice, and the Temple: Symbolism and Supersessionism in the Study of Ancient Judaism*. Oxford: Oxford University Press, 2006.

Klee, Deborah. 'Menstruation in the Hebrew Bible'. Ph.D. thesis. Boston University, 1998.
Klingbeil, Gerald A. *Bridging the Gap: Ritual and Ritual Texts in the Bible*. BBRS 1. Winona Lake, IN: Eisenbrauns. 2007.
Knierim, Rolf P. *Text and Concept in Leviticus 1:1–9*. FAT 2. Tübingen: Mohr Siebeck, 1992.
Knohl, Israel. *The Sanctuary of Silence: The Priestly Torah and the Holiness School*. Minneapolis: Fortress, 1995.
Koch, Anne. 'Reasons for the Boom of Body Discourses in the Humanities and the Social Sciences Since the 1980s: A Chapter in European History of Religion'. Pages 3–42 in Berlejung, Dietrich, and Quack, eds., *Menschenbilder und Körperkonzepte im Alten Israel*.
Koch, Klaus. 'Die Eigenart der priesterschriftlichen Sinaigesetzgebung'. *ZTK* 55 (1958): 36–51.
———. *Die Priesterschrift von Exodus 25 bis Leviticus 16. Eine überlieferungsgeschichtliche und literarkritische Untersuchung*. FRLANT NF 53. Göttingen: Vandenhoeck & Ruprecht, 1959.
Köckert, Matthias. 'Leben in Gottes Gegenwart: Zum Verständnis des Gesetzes in der priesterschriftlichen Literatur'. *JBT* 4 (1989): 29–61.
König, Eduard. *Syntax der Hebräischen Sprache, in Historisch-kritisches Lehrgebäude der hebräischen Sprache*. Leipzig: Hinrichs, 1897.
Korpel, Marjo. *A Rift in the Clouds: Ugaritic and Hebrew Descriptions of the Divine*. Münster: Ugarit-Verlag, 1990.
Kratz, Reinhard G. *Die Komposition der erzählenden Bücher des Alten Testaments: Grundwissen der Bibelkritik*. Göttingen: Vandenhoeck & Ruprecht, 2000.
Kraus, Wolfgang, ed. *Septuaginta Deutsch*. Stuttgart: Deutsche Bibelgesellschaft, 2009.
Kuenen, Abraham. *Historisch-kritische Einleitung in die Bücher des Alten Testaments hinsichtlich ihrer Entstehung und Sammlung: Die Entstehung des Hexateuch*, I/1. Autorisierte deutsche Ausgabe. Leipzig: Schulze, 1887.
L'Hour, Jean. 'L'impur et le saint dans le Premier Testament à partir du livre du Lévitique. Partie I: L'impur et le pur'. *ZAW* 115 (2003): 524–37.
Landsberger, Benno. 'Jungfräulichkeit. Ein Beitrag zum Thema "Beilager und Eheschließung"'. Pages 41–65 in *Symbolae Iuridicae et Historicae Martino David dedicatae*. Edited by J. A. Ankum et al. Leiden: Brill, 1968.
Laqueur, Thomas. *Making Sex: Body and Gender from the Greeks to Freud*. Cambridge MA: Harvard University Press, 1990.
Leick, Gwendolyn. *Sex and Eroticism in Mesopotamian Literature*. London: Routledge, 1994.
Lévi-Strauss, Claude. *Les structures élémentaires de la parenté*. 2nd ed. Paris: La Haye, 1967.
Levine, Baruch A. *In the Presence of the Lord: A Study of Cult and Some Cultic Terms in Ancient Israel*. Leiden: Brill, 1974.
———. *Leviticus*. The JPS Torah Commentary. Philadelphia: Jewish Publication Society, 1989.
———. 'Seed versus Womb: Expressions of Male Dominance in Biblical Israel'. Pages 337–43 in *Sex and Gender in the Ancient Near East: Proceedings of the 47th Rencontre Assyriologique Internationale, Part I*. Edited by Simo Parpola and Roger M. Whiting. Helsinki: Neo-Assyrian Text Corpus Project, 2002.

Liss, Hanna. 'The Imaginary Sanctuary: The Priestly Code as an Example of Fictional Literature in the Hebrew Bible'. Pages 663–89 in *Judah and Judeans in the Persian Period*. Edited by Oded Lipschits and Manfred Oeming. Winona Lake, IN: Eisenbrauns 2006.

———. 'Kanon und Fiktion: Zur literarischen Funktion biblischer Rechtstexte'. *BN* NF 121 (2004): 7–38.

———. 'Ritual Purity and the Construction of Identity'. Pages 329–54 in Römer, ed., *The Books of Leviticus and Numbers*.

Løland, Hanne. *Silent or Salient Gender? The Interpretation of Gendered God-language in the Hebrew Bible, Exemplified in Isaiah 42, 46 and 49*. Tübingen: Mohr Siebeck, 2008.

Lorenz, Maren. *Leibhaftige Vergangenheit: Einführung in die Körpergeschichte*. Tübingen: Diskord, 2000).

Luciani, Didier. *Sainteté et Pardon I. Structure littéraire du Lévitique*. BETL 175A. Leuven: Peeters, 2005.

Lust, Johann. *Greek–English Lexicon of the Septuagint*. 2nd ed. Stuttgart: Deutsche Bibelgesellschaft, 2015.

Magonet, Jonathan. '"But if it is a Girl, she is unclean for twice seven days…" The Riddle of Leviticus 12,5'. Pages 144–52 in Sawyer, ed., *Reading Leviticus*.

Maier, Christl. 'Körper und Geschlecht im Alten Testament. Überlegungen zur Geschlechterdifferenz'. Pages 183–208 in Berlejung, Dietrich and Quack, eds., *Menschenbilder und Körperkonzepte im Alten Israel*.

Marienberg, Evyatar. *Niddah: Lorsque les juifs conceptualisent la menstruation*. Paris: Belles lettres, 2003.

Marsman, Hennie J. *Women in Ugarit and Israel: Their Social and Religious Position in the Context of the Ancient Near East*. Leiden: Brill, 2003.

Marx, Alfred. 'Les recherches sur le Lévitique et leur impact théologique'. *Bib* 88 (2007): 415–33.

———. 'Sacrifice pour les Péchés ou Rite de Passage? Quelques Réflexions sur la Fonction du *Hattat*'. *RB* 96 (1984): 27–48.

———. *Les systèmes sacrificiels. Formes et fonctions du culte sacrificiel à Yhwh*. VTSup 108. Leiden: Brill, 2005.

Mayer, G., 'מול *mûl*'. *ThWAT* 4:734–38.

Meachem, Tirzah Z. 'An Abbreviated History of the Development of the Jewish Menstrual Laws'. Pages 23–39 in *Women and Water: Menstruation in Jewish Life and Law*. Edited by Rahel R. Wasserfall. Hanover, NH: University Press of New England, 1999.

Meshel, Naphtali S. *The 'Grammar' of Sacrifice. A Generativist Study of the Israelite Sacrificial System in the Priestly Writings*. Oxford: Oxford University Press, 2014.

Meyers, Eric M. 'The Pools of Sepphoris: Ritual Baths or Bathtubs? Yes, They Are'. *BAR* 26 (2000): 46–49.

Milgrom, Jacob. 'The Dynamics of Purity in the Priestly System'. Pages 29–32 in *Purity and Holiness: The Heritage of Leviticus*. Edited by Marcel J. H. M. Poorthuis and Joshua Schwartz. Jewish and Christian Perspectives Series. Leiden: Brill, 2000.

———. *Leviticus 1–16: A New Translation with Introduction and Commentary*. AB 3. New York: Doubleday, 1991.

———. *Leviticus 17–22*. AB 3A. New York: Doubleday, 2000.

———. 'Rationale for Cultic Law: The Case of Impurity'. Pages 103–109 in *Thinking Biblical Law*. Edited by Patrick Dale. Semeia 45. Atlanta: Scholars Press, 1989.

———. 'Sin-Offering or Purification-Offering?' *VT* 21 (1970): 237–39.

Moor, Johannes de. *An Anthology of Religious Texts from Ugarit*. Leiden: Brill, 1987.
Morgenstern, Mathias. *Übersetzung des Talmud Yerushalmi: Nidda – Die Menstruierende* Bd. VI/1. Tübingen: Mohr & Siebeck 2006.
Muraoka, Takamitsu. *A Greek–English Lexicon of the Septuagint: Chiefly of the Pentateuch and the Twelve Prophets*. Leuven: Peeters, 2002.
Nihan, Christoph. *From Priestly Torah to Pentateuch: A Study in the Composition of the Book of Leviticus*. FAT 2/25. Tübingen: Mohr Siebeck, 2007.
———. 'Forms and Functions of Purity in Leviticus'. Pages 311–68 in *Purity and the Forming of Religious Traditions in the Ancient Mediterranean World and Ancient Judaism*. Edited by Christian Frevel and Christophe Nihan. Dynamics in the History of Religions 3. Leiden: Brill, 2013.
Noordtzij, Arie. *Het Boek Leviticus*. Korte Verklaring der Heilige Schrift. Kampen: Kok, 1940.
Noth, Martin. *Das dritte Buch Mose*. ATD 6. Göttingen: Vandenhoeck & Ruprecht, 1962.
O'Grady, Kathleen. 'The Semantics of Taboo'. Pages 1–28 in de Troyer et al., eds., *Wholly Woman*.
Oosting, Berthil. *Verzoening als Verleiding: Een nieuwe toegang tot de wondere woorden van het boek Leviticus*. Vught: Skandalon, 2004.
Orlinsky, Harry M. 'The Hebrew Root ŠKB'. *JBL* 63 (1944): 19–44.
Otto, Eckart. 'Forschungen zur Priesterschrift'. *TRu* 60 (1995): 1–50.
Pape, Wilhelm. *Griechisch–Deutsches Handwörterbuch*. Braunschweig: Vieweg, 1880.
Paschen, Wilfried. *Rein und Unrein: Untersuchung zur biblischen Wortgeschichte*. StANT 24. Munich: Kösel, 1970.
Péter-Contesse, René. *Lévitique 1–16*. CAT 3a. Geneva: Labor et Fides, 1993.
Pham, Xuan Huong Thi. *Mourning in the Ancient Near East and the Hebrew Bible*. JSOTSup 302. Sheffield: Sheffield Academic, 1999.
Philip, Taria S. *Menstruation and Childbirth in the Bible: Fertility and Impurity*. Studies in Biblical Literature 88. New York: Lang, 2006.
Plaskow, Judith. *Standing Again at Sinai: Judaism from a Feminist Perspective*. New York: HarperSanFransisco, 1990.
Püschel, Erich. *Die Menstruation und ihre Tabus*. Stuttgart: Schattauer, 1988.
Ramban (Nachmanides). *Commentary on the Torah: Leviticus*. Translated and annotated by Charles B. Chavel. New York: Shilo, 1974.
Rapp, Ursula. 'The Heritage of Old Testament Impurity Laws: Gender as a Question of How to Focus on Women'. Pages 29–40 in *Gender and Religion: European Studies*. Edited by Kari E. Børresen, Sara Cabibbo and Edith Specht. European Studies, Università degli studi roma 3. Rome: Carocci, 2001.
Rehkopf, Friedrich. *Septuaginta-Vokabular*. Göttingen: Vandenhoeck & Ruprecht, 1989.
Reich, Ronny. 'The Hot Bath-House (balneum), the Miqweh and the Jewish Community in the Second Temple Period'. *JJS* 39 (1989): 102–7.
———. 'Some Notes on the Miqva'ot and Cisterns at Qumran'. Pages 414–24 in *Viewing Ancient Jewish Art and Archaeology*. Edited by Ann E. Killebrew and Gabriele Fassbeck. Supplements to the Journal for the Study of Judaism 172. Leiden: Brill, 2015.
Rendtorff, Rolf. 'Another Prolegomenon to Leviticus 17:11'. Pages 23–28 in *Pomegranates and Golden Bells: Studies in Biblical, Jewish, and Near Eastern Ritual, Law, and Literature in Honor of Jacob Milgrom*. Edited by David Wright et al. Winona Lake, IN: Eisenbrauns, 1995.

———. *Die Gesetze in der Priesterschrift: Eine gattungsgeschichtliche Untersuchung.* Göttingen: Vandenhoeck & Ruprecht, 1954.

———. 'Is It Possible to Read Leviticus as a Separate Book?' Pages 22–35 in *Reading Leviticus: A Conversation with Mary Douglas.* Edited by John F. A. Sawyer. JSOTSup 227. Sheffield: Sheffield Academic, 1996.

———. *Leviticus.* BKAT III/1. Neukirchen-Vluyn: Neukirchener, 1985.

———. 'Two Kinds of P? Some Reflections on the Occasion of the Publishing of Jacob Milgrom's Commentary on Leviticus 1–16'. *JSOT* 60 (1993): 75–81.

Rendtorff, Rolf, and Robert A. Kugler, eds. *The Book of Leviticus: Composition and Reception.* VTSup 93. Leiden: Brill, 2003.

Römer, Thomas. 'De la périphérie au centre: Les livres du Lévitique et des Nombres dans le débat actuel sur le Pentateuque'. Pages 3–34 in Römer, ed., *The Books of Leviticus and Numbers.*

Römer, Thomas, ed. *The Books of Leviticus and Numbers.* Leuven: Peeters, 2008.

Rost, Leonhard. *Studien zum Opfer im Alten Israel.* Stuttgart: Kohlhammer, 1981.

Roth, Martha. *Law Collections from Mesopotamia and Asia Minor.* SBLWAW 6. Atlanta: Scholars Press, 1995.

Rousselle, Aline. 'Observation féminine et idéologie masculine. Le corps de la femme d'après les médecins grecs'. Pages 1089–115 in *Annales ESC* 35. Paris: Colin, 1980.

Ruane, Nicole J. *Sacrifice and Gender in Biblical Law.* Oxford: Oxford University Press 2013.

Sanders, Ed P. *Jewish Law from Jesus to the Mishnah.* London: SCM, 1990.

Sarasin, Philipp. *Reizbare Maschinen: Eine Geschichte des Körpers 1765–1914.* Frankfurt am Main: Suhrkamp, 2001.

Sasson, Jack M. 'Circumcision in the Ancient Near East'. *JBL* 85 (1966): 473–77.

Sawyer, John F. A., ed. *Reading Leviticus: A Conversation with Mary Douglas.* JSOTSup 227. Sheffield: Sheffield Academic, 1996.

Schaper, Joachim. 'Priestly Purity and Social Organisation in Persian Period Judah'. *BN* 108 (2003): 51–57.

Scharbert, Josef. *Fleisch, Geist und Seele im Pentateuch.* 2nd ed. SBS 19. Stuttgart: Katholisches Bibelwerk, 1967.

Schenker, Adrian. 'Interprétations récentes et dimensions spécifiques du sacrifice *ḥattat*'. *Biblica* 75 (1994): 59–70.

Schorch, Stefan. *Euphemismen in der Hebräischen Bibel.* OBC 12. Wiesbaden: Harrassowitz, 2000.

Schreiner, Stefan. '"Wo man Tora lernt, braucht man keinen Tempel". Einige Anmerkungen zum Problem der Tempelsubstitution im rabbinischen Judentum'. Pages 371–92 in *Gemeinde ohne Tempel – Community without Temple: Zur Substituierung und Transformation des Jerusalemer Tempels und seines Kults im Alten Testament, antiken Judentum und frühen Christentum.* Edited by Beate Ego et al. WUNT 118. Tübingen: Mohr Siebeck, 1999.

Schroer, Silvia. 'Feministische Anthropologie des Ersten Testaments: Beobachtungen, Fragen, Plädoyers'. *lectio difficilior* 1/2003. Online: http://www.lectio.unibe.ch/03_1/schroer.htmn (last accessed 11 September 2003).

———. 'Die Göttin auf den Stempelsiegeln'. Pages 89–207 in *Studien zu den Stempelsiegeln aus Palästina/Israel.* Edited by Othmar Keel, Hildi Keel-Leu and Silvia Schroer. OBO 88. Freiburg, Schweiz: Universitätsverlag; Göttingen, 1989.

Schroer, Silvia, and Thomas Staubli. *Die Körpersymbolik der Bibel.* Darmstadt: Wissenschaftliche Buchgesellschaft, 1998.

Schwartz, Baruch J. 'The Prohibitions Concerning the "Eating" of Blood in Leviticus 17'. Pages 34–66 in *Priesthood and Cult in Ancient Israel*. Edited by Gary A. Anderson and Saul M. Olyan. JSOTSup 125. Sheffield: JSOT, 1991.

Seidl, Theodor, 'Rein und Unrein: (I) AT'. *NBL* 2:315–21.

Smith, Mark. 'The Heart and Innards in Israelite Emotional Expressions: Notes from Anthropology and Psychobiology'. *JBL* 117, no. 3 (1998): 427–36.

Staubli, Thomas. *Die Bücher Levitikus, Numeri*. NSKAT 3. Stuttgart: Katholisches Bibelwerk, 1996.

Stausberg, Michael. 'Ritualtheorien und Religionstheorien: Religionswissenschaftliche Perspektiven'. Pages 29–48 in *Ritualdynamik: Kulturübergreifende Studien zur Theorie und Geschichte rituellen Handelns*. Edited by Dietrich Harth and Gerrit Jasper Schenk. Heidelberg: Synchron, 2004.

Stein, D. E. S., ed. *The Contemporary Torah: A Gender-Sensitive Adaptation of the JPS Translation*. Philadelphia: Jewish Publication Society, 2006.

Stemberger, Günther. *Geschichte der jüdischen Literatur: Eine Einführung*. Munich: C. H. Beck, 1977.

———. 'Leviticus in Sifra'. Pages 429–47 in *Encyclopaedia of Midrash: Biblical Interpretation in Formative Judaism*. Edited by Jacob Neusner and Alan J. Avery Peck. Leiden: Brill, 2005.

Stol, Marten. *Birth in Babylonia and the Bible: Its Mediterranean Setting*. With a chapter by F. A. M. Wiggermann. Groningen: STYX, 2000.

Stolz, Fritz, 'אֹת *ʾōt* Zeichen'. *THAT* 1:91–95.

Tolbert, Mary A. 'Philo and Paul: The Circumcision Debates in Early Judaism'. Pages 394–407 in *Dem Tod nicht glauben: Sozialgeschichte der Bibel*. Edited by Frank Crüsemann et al. Gütersloh: Gütersloher Verlagshaus, 2004.

Troyer, Kristin de. 'Blood: A Threat to Holiness or toward (Another) Holiness?' Pages 45–64 in de Troyer et al., eds., *Wholly Woman*.

Troyer, Kristin de, et al., eds. *Wholly Woman – Holy Blood: A Feminist Critique of Purity and Impurity*. London: T&T Clark International, 2003.

Utzschneider, Helmut. *Das Heiligtum und das Gesetz: Studien zur Bedeutung der sinaitischen Heiligtumstexte (Ex 25–40; Lev 8–9)*. OBO 77. Freiburg: Universitätsverlag 1988.

Vahrenhorst, Martin. 'Levitikon/Levitikus/Das dritte Buch Mose'. Pages 325–430 in *Septuaginta Deutsch. Erläuterungen und Kommentare I: Genesis bis Makkabäer.* Stuttgart: Deutsche Bibelgesellschaft, 2011.

Van der Toorn, Karel. *Van haar wieg tot haar graf: De rol van de godsdienst in het leven van de Israëlitische en Babylonische vrouw*. Baarn: Ten Have, 1987.

Vervenne, Marc. '"The Blood Is the Life and the Life Is the Blood": Blood as a Symbol of Life and Death in Biblical Tradition (Gen 9,4)'. Pages 451–70 in *Ritual and Sacrifice in the Ancient Near East*. Edited by Jan Quaegebeur. OLA 55 Leuven: Peeters, 1993.

Wagner, Andreas, ed. *Anthropologische Aufbrüche: Alttestamentliche und interdisziplinäre Zugänge zur historischen Anthropologie*. FRLANT 232. Göttingen: Vandenhoeck & Ruprecht, 2009.

Waltke, Bruce, and Michael P. O'Connor. *An Introduction to Biblical Hebrew Syntax*. Winona Lake, IN: Eisenbrauns, 1990.

Watts, James. *Leviticus 1–10*. HCOT. Leuven: Peeters, 2013.

———. *Reading Law: The Rhetorical Shaping of the Pentateuch*. Sheffield: Sheffield Academic, 1999.

———. *Ritual and Rhetoric in Leviticus: From Sacrifice to Scripture*. Cambridge: Cambridge University Press, 2007.
———. 'Ritual Rhetoric in the Pentateuch: The Case of Leviticus 1–16'. Pages 307–18 in Römer, ed., *The Books of Leviticus and Numbers*.
Wegner, Judith Romney. 'Coming Before the Lord: The Exclusion of Women from the Public Domain of the Israelite Priestly Cult'. Pages 451–65 in Rendtorff and Kugler, eds., *The Book of Leviticus*.
Weissenrieder, Annette. *Images of Illness in the Gospel of Luke: Insights of Ancient Medical Texts*. WUNT 2/164. Tübingen: Mohr Siebeck, 2003.
Wenham, Gordon J. *The Book of Leviticus*. NICOT. Grand Rapids: Eerdmans, 1979.
———. 'Purity'. Pages 378–94 in *The Biblical World*. Edited by John Barton. London: Routledge, 2002.
———. 'Why Does Sexual Intercourse Defile? (Lev 15:18)'. *ZAW* 95 (1983): 432–34.
Werret, Ian. 'The Evolution of Purity at Qumran'. Pages 493–518 in *Ritual Purity and the Dead Sea Scrolls*. Leiden: Brill, 2007.
Wevers, John. *Notes on the Greek Text of Leviticus*. Septuagint and Cognate Studies 44. Atlanta: Scholars Press, 1997.
Whitekettle, Richard. 'Leviticus 12 and the Israelite Women: Ritual Process, Liminality and the Womb'. *ZAW* 107 (1995): 393–408.
———. 'Leviticus 15.18 Reconsidered: Chiasm, Spatial Structure and the Body'. *JSOT* 48 (1991): 31–45.
———. 'Levitical Thought and the Female Reproductive Cycle: Wombs, Wellsprings and the Primeval World'. *VT* 47 (1996): 376–91.
Willi-Plein, Ina. *Opfer und Kult im alttestamentlichen Israel: Textbefragungen und Zwischenergebnisse*. SBS 153. Stuttgart: Kohlhammer, 1993.
Williams, A. V. 'Zoroastrian and Judaic Purity Laws: Reflections on the Viability of a Sociological Interpretation'. Pages 72–89 in *Irano-Judaica III: Studies Relating to Jewish Contacts with Persian Culture Throughout the Ages*. Jerusalem: Ben-Zvi Institute, 1994.
Winter, Urs. *Frau und Göttin: Exegetische und ikonographische Studien zum weiblichen Gottesbild im alten Israel und in dessen Umwelt*. OBO 53. Freiburg: Universitätsverlag, 1983.
Wolff, Hans Walter. *Anthropologie des Alten Testaments*. 6th ed. Munich: Kaiser, 1994.
Woude, Adam S. van der. 'פָּנִים *pānîm*'. *THAT* 2:432–60.
Wright, Benjamin G., III. 'Jewish Ritual Baths – Interpreting the Digs and the Texts: Some Issues in the Social History of Second Temple Judaism'. Pages 190–214 in *The Archaeology of Israel: Constructing the Past, Interpreting the Present*. Edited by Neil Asher Silberman and David Small. JSOTSup 237. Sheffield: JSOT, 1997.
Wright, David P. *The Disposal of Impurity: Elimination Rites in the Bible and in Hittite and Mesopotamian Literature*. SBLDS 101. Atlanta: Scholars Press, 1987.
———. 'Unclean—Clean (OT)'. *ABD* 6:729–41.
Zenger, Erich. *Gottes Bogen in den Wolken: Untersuchungen zu Komposition und Theologie der priesterlichen Urgeschichte*. SBS 112. Stuttgart: Kohlhammer, 1983.
———. 'Das Buch Leviticus als Teiltext der Tora/des Pentateuch: Eine synchrone Lektüre mit diachroner Perspektive'. Pages 47–83 in *Leviticus als Buch*. Edited by Heinz-Josef Fabry and Hans-Winfried Jüngling. BBB 119. Bodenheim: Philo, 1999.
Zenger, Erich, and Christian Frevel. 'Die Bücher Levitikus und Numeri als Teile der Pentateuchkomposition'. Pages 35–74 in Römer, ed., *The Books of Leviticus and Numbers*.

Index of References

Genesis		17.9	96	36.6	30
1–9	19, 48	17.10–11	96	37.27	90
1	109, 143	17.10–12	102	38.9	107
1.11–12	34	17.10	93, 99	38.27–30	33
1.12	34	17.11	37, 93	39.7	75
1.27	35	17.12	93, 98, 99,	39.10	75
2	90	17.13–14	96	39.12	75
2.21	89	17.13	93, 96	39.14	75
2.23	59, 90	17.14	93, 96		
2.24	90	17.19	96	*LXX Genesis*	
3.15	106	17.23	93	7.2	50
3.16	30	17.24	93	8.20	50
6.17	89	17.25	93, 94, 99	12	49–54, 53,
7.2	140	18	136		54
7.3	106	18.11	134, 135		
7.8	140	19	75, 110	*Exodus*	
8.20	42	19.33	110	1.16	30
9	113	19.35	110	3.8	104
9.4	113	21.1–2	135	3.17	104
9.5	59	21.4	93	4	93–95
9.8–11	149	21.7	30	4.24–26	92, 112
9.11	96	22.17	106	4.24	94, 95
9.15–17	96	22.18	106	4.25	93–95
9.15	89	24.61	69	4.26	92, 95
10.5	10	25.22–27	33	6.12	100
10.20	10	26.3	106	6.30	100
10.31	10	26.4	106	12	98
11.1	27	26.24	106	12.1	28
11.12	27	29.5	30	12.7	112
12	34	29.14	90	12.43	28, 98
12.5	34	30.1	30	12.44	93, 98
12.6	34	31	136	12.45	98
12.12	135	31.7	30	12.48	35, 93, 96,
13.6	106	31.34–36	70		98
13.16	59	31.35	134, 135	12.49	98
16.10	106	31.43	33	13.5	104
17	91, 93, 94,	32.1	134	16.29	59
	96, 98, 99,	34	92, 94, 97	20.10	30
	101, 102	34.14	97	21.5	30
17.2	96	34.15	93	21.28	59
17.4	96	34.22	93	21.29	59
17.7	96	34.24	93	22.15	75

22.18	75, 110	2.1	39	6–7	29
22.23	30	3.1	40	6.3	59, 90
24.10	146, 148	3.2	40, 112	6.11–12	32
25	7	3.7	40, 41	6.11	31, 32
25.11	145	3.8	112	6.20	33
25.17	145	3.12	40	6.21	56
25.24	145	3.13	52, 112	7.2	112
25.29	145	3.14	41	7.6	33
25.31	145	3.17	113, 161	7.14	112
25.36	145	4	43	7.15	89
25.39	145	4.1	29	7.18	39
28.42	59, 90	4.2	30, 39, 60	7.20	39, 140
29.11	41	4.3	29, 43	7.21	39, 60, 64
29.12	114	4.4	40, 41	7.25	39
29.16	112	4.5–7	44	7.26–27	113
29.20	112	4.6	112	7.26	161
29.42	41	4.7	112	7.27	39
30.3	145	4.10	70	7.28	30
31.13	96	4.13	29	8.15	46, 114
31.17	96	4.14	40, 43	8.19	112
32.2	30	4.17	112	8.23	112
33.3	104	4.18	44, 112	8.24	112
36.4	59	4.20	46	8.34	46
36.6	59	4.23	43	9.1	37
		4.25	44, 112	9.12	112
LXX Exodus		4.26	44, 46	9.18	112
4.24–26	92	4.27	29, 39	10	31
		4.28	43	10.4–5	143
Leviticus		4.30	44, 112	10.7	46
1–16	8, 10	4.31	44, 46	10.10	139, 140
1–10	114	4.32	29, 43	10.12–13	31, 32
1–7	12, 13, 39,	4.34	44, 112	10.13	32
	42, 44, 46,	4.35	44, 46, 50	10.14–15	31, 32
	114	5	44	10.14	30, 32, 33
1–4	29	5.1–13	43	10.15	32
1	28, 42, 112	5.1	39, 60	11–26	2
1.1	41, 161	5.3	64, 140	11–16	19, 114
1.2	29, 30, 40,	5.4	39, 60	11–15	2, 7, 10,
	42, 60	5.6	46		12, 15, 17,
1.3	29, 40, 42,	5.10	46		28, 59,
	45	5.11–13	43, 112		137, 138,
1.4	46	5.13	46		142, 143,
1.5	41, 52, 112	5.15	39, 44, 60		146, 148,
1.7	28	5.16	46		150, 156,
1.8	28	5.17	39		160, 162,
1.10	28, 42	5.18	46		163
1.11	112	5.21	39, 60		
1.14	42	5.26	46		

Leviticus (cont.)

11	2, 17, 18, 142, 143, 148, 149		40, 49, 64, 81, 101, 107–109, 111, 115,	13.14	50
				13.15	64, 149
				13.17	149
				13.20	149
11.1	28		120, 122,	13.22	149
11.2	30		127–29,	13.23	149
11.4	148		131, 154	13.25	149
11.5	148	12.3	29, 36, 37	13.27	149
11.6	148		81, 85, 90,	13.28	149
11.7	148		93, 98,	13.30	149
11.8	148		101, 102	13.34	149
11.26	148	12.4	27, 37–40,	13.35	147, 148
11.27	148, 149		112, 122,	13.36	64, 149
11.29	148		146–48,	13.37	149
11.31	148, 149		154, 155	13.38	59
11.35	148	12.5	27, 29,	13.39	149
11.37	149		36–39,	13.40	149
11.38	148		112, 146,	13.41	149
11.39	149		154, 155	13.42	149
11.43	140	12.6–8	28	13.44	149
11.44–45	20	12.6–7	29	13.46	149
11.44	2	12.6	27, 30, 31,	13.47–59	69
11.46	29		39–42,	13.51	149
11.47	140		146, 148	13.55	149
12–15	146–48, 157	12.7	29, 45–47, 91, 145,	13.58	149
				13.59	29, 149
			147, 149	14	149, 160
12	1–7, 17, 19, 22, 23, 27–30, 35, 42–49, 63, 70, 81, 82, 84, 91, 93, 94, 96, 99, 101, 102, 103, 107, 112, 116, 117, 125, 127, 129, 131, 137, 138, 141, 145–47, 150–58, 160, 163	12.8	29, 31, 40, 42, 45–47, 147, 149	14.1	28
				14.2	147, 148
		12.25	146	14.4–6	112
		13–15	104	14.5	73
		13–14	2, 143, 155	14.6	73
		13	64, 67, 142, 149, 150, 157, 160	14.7	149
				14.9–10	37
				14.10	28, 31
				14.11	41, 149
				14.14	112
		13.1	28	14.18	46
		13.2	29	14.19	46, 149
		13.3	50, 149	14.20	45, 46
		13.4	29	14.21	46
		13.6	28, 149	14.23	37, 147, 148
		13.7	29, 147, 148		
12.1–5	27			14.29	46
12.1	28	13.8	149	14.31	46
12.2–7	29	13.9	59	14.32	29, 147
12.2	28–30, 33, 34, 36, 39,	13.11	40, 149	14.33	28
		13.13	149, 155	14.36	156

Index of References

14.41	112	15.4	56, 64, 67,		76, 77, 81,
14.44	149		68, 71, 103		83, 107,
14.48	149	15.5–15	56		109–11,
14.49–52	112	15.5	56, 59, 60,		144, 149
14.50	73		67, 69, 73,		
14.51–53	112		149	15.19–30	74, 126
14.51	73	15.6	56, 67–69,	15.19–26	36
14.52	73		73, 103,	15.19–24	61
14.53	45, 46, 149		149	15.19–21	104, 112,
14.57	29	15.7	55, 56, 67,		134
15	1–7, 11,		68, 70, 73,	15.19–20	42
	19, 22, 23,		90, 103,	15.19	36, 52, 56,
	29, 30, 41,		149		58–60,
	44, 45, 54,	15.8	42, 56, 68,		62–64,
	55, 58, 59,		81, 83,		66–68,
	63, 64, 70,		103, 149		71, 74, 81,
	73, 81, 84,	15.9	56, 67–69,		89, 90,
	89–91,		71, 72, 80,		103, 104,
	103, 104,		81, 103		106, 112,
	106, 107,	15.10	56, 67–69,		120–22,
	110–12,		71, 72, 149		149, 153
	115, 117,	15.11–24	79	15.20–22	71
	120–22,	15.11	56, 67, 68,	15.20	56, 67, 68,
	124–27,		70, 81, 83,		81, 122
	129, 131,		103, 149	15.21	67, 68, 71,
	133–37,	15.12	56, 67, 68,		83
	142, 143,		103	15.22	56, 68, 69,
	147, 149–	15.13–15	73		149
	58, 160,	15.13–14	37	15.23	56, 68, 71,
	163	15.13	73, 103,		72, 149
15.1–10	78		145, 147,	15.24–26	122
15.1–3	55		148	15.24	59–61, 66,
15.1–2	61, 63	15.14	40–42, 147		71, 72, 77,
15.1	28, 30, 63	15.15	46, 67, 85		142, 154
15.2–15	61, 66, 126			15.25–33	58
15.2–3	64, 65	15.16–24	57	15.25–30	61
15.2	59, 60, 63,	15.16–17	61, 62, 70,	15.25–27	62
	84, 90,		74, 83	15.25	46, 66, 68,
	103, 149	15.16	56, 59, 60,		77, 81–83,
15.3–17	60, 74		65, 66, 76,		103, 112,
15.3	55, 57–59,		81, 83, 90,		120, 137,
	62, 64, 66,		103, 107,		140, 149
	68, 82, 85,		109–11,	15.26	67, 68,
	90, 103,		149		103, 118,
	104, 140,	15.17	65, 107,		122
	149		109–11	15.27	56, 67, 68,
15.4–12	69	15.18	56, 59–61,		72, 149
15.4–6	64		65, 70, 74,	15.28–30	73

Index of References

Leviticus (cont.)
15.28–29	37	18	95, 121, 122, 142		110, 143
15.28	82, 103, 145	18.3	17, 121		22.5
		18.6	60, 90	22.6	105
15.29–30	45	18.19	52, 121, 122, 137, 154	22.8	141
15.29	40–42, 121			22.18	59, 60
15.30	46, 56, 103, 140	18.20	34, 83, 111, 141	22.27	37
				23.2	30
15.31–33	61			23.3	161
15.31	63, 76, 77, 157	18.22	110	23.12	28
		18.23	111, 141	23.14	161
15.32–33	76, 85, 106	18.24	141	23.21	161
15.32	29, 57, 65, 75, 77, 78, 103, 106, 107, 109–11, 140	19.2	2	23.24	30
		19.20	59, 65, 107, 109, 110	23.28	46
				23.29	39
				23.30	39
		19.22	46	23.31	161
15.33	59–61, 77, 103, 106, 118, 127–29, 131	19.23–25	100	23.34	30, 33
		19.26	113	23.36	37
		19.28	92	23.39	37
		19.31	141	23.42–44	33
		20	95, 110, 122, 127, 131, 137, 142	24.2	30
16	16			24.5	55
16.4	59, 90			24.15	59, 60
16.7	41			24.22	98
16.8	114	20.2	60, 122	25	94
16.14–15	112	20.8	91	25.22	37
16.18–19	45	20.9	60	25.49	90
16.18	46	20.11	75		
16.27–28	140	20.12	75, 122	*LXX Leviticus*	
16.30	45, 46, 145	20.13	59, 110	12	49–54, 53, 54
16.33	46	20.14	122		
16.34	46	20.15	111	12.1–6	49
17	113, 114	20.18	47, 48, 59, 75, 84, 110, 128, 129, 131	12.2	50
17.3–5	114			12.3	54, 59
17.3	55, 59, 60			12.4	51
17.4	40, 112			12.5	51
17.5	40	20.20	75	12.6	51, 53
17.6	112	20.24	17, 104	12.7–8	50
17.8	59, 60	20.25	140	12.7	52
17.10–14	113, 144	20.27	59	12.8	52
17.10	55, 59, 60	21.11	143	15	78–86, 152
17.11	44, 46, 113–15	22.2–6	105	15.2	81, 82
		22.2	105	15.3–14	82
17.13	60, 112	22.3	105	15.3	81
17.14	113–15	22.4	59, 60, 65, 104–105, 107, 109,	15.4	81, 83
17.24	93			15.5	83
				15.6	81, 83

15.7	80, 81, 83	10	7	32.19	30
15.12	80, 81, 83	13.27	104		
15.13	81–83	14.8	104	*Joshua*	
15.19	82	15.16	98	5	95
15.23	83	15.25	46	5.2–10	98
15.24	81, 83, 84	16.14	104	5.2	93
15.25–33	80	18.7	112	5.3–5	93
15.26	80–83	18.11	32	5.3	93
15.32	80, 81, 83, 85	19	119	5.6	104
		19.1	28	5.7	93
15.33	81–85	19.7	140	5.8	93
19.23–25	101	19.9	118	17.2	31
		19.13	118		
Numbers		19.14	143	*Judges*	
1.4	60	19.17	73	9.2	90
1.44	60	19.20–21	118	14.3–4	97
4.19	60	31.19–20	143	15.18	97
4.49	60	31.23	118		
5	106	31.24	143	*Ruth*	
5.1–4	105			3.4	110
5.2–3	67, 104	*Deuteronomy*		3.7	110
5.2	82, 104	4.10	30		
5.3	105	6.3	104	*1 Samuel*	
5.6	59	7.14	108	2.5	30
5.12	59, 60	7.15	129	2.13	89
5.13	65, 107, 109, 110	10.16	93, 99	2.15	89
		11.9	104	2.22	75
5.20	111	12.23–25	113	14.6	97
5.28	34, 106, 107	12.23	113	17.36	97
		14.7	148	17.44	89
5.30	59	14.8	89, 148	18.27	97
5.31	59	14.10	148	20.26	111, 140
6	44, 76, 147	14.19	148	21.14	104
6.2	76, 77	22.26	70	25.20	70
6.3	76, 77	23.11–12	110	31.4	97
6.5	77	23.11	110, 140		
6.6–7	143	23.13–15	110	*2 Samuel*	
6.6	77	23.15	110	1.20	97
6.9–10	37	26.9	104	3.14	97
6.9	143, 146, 147	26.15	104	3.28–29	104
		27.3	104	3.29	104
6.10	41	27.20	110	4.3	98
6.11	46	27.21	110	5.1	90
6.12	77	27.22	110	5.29	103
6.14	31	27.23	110	11	75, 136
9.6–11	143	28.60	129	11.2–5	134
9.10	59, 60	30.6	93, 99, 100	11.2	135
9.14	98	31.20	104		

2 Samuel (cont.)
11.4	135
13.11	110
19.13	90

1 Kings
20.20	60

2 Kings
4.24	70
12.10	35
18.4	124
18.21	35

1 Chronicles
10.4	97
16.3	59
23.28	146
29	122

2 Chronicles
29	127
29.5	124, 131
30.19	146
31.19	33

Ezra
2.59	106
9	122, 123, 126, 127
9.2	106
9.11	123, 131

Nehemiah
12.45	146

Job
1.5	30
1.21	34
6.6	104
6.7	131
13.14	89
14.22	89

Psalms
1.1	59
25.17	130
36.10	47
41	129
41.4	36, 129
63.2	89
84.3	89
113.9	30
136.25	90
139.15	34

Proverbs
5.16	48
5.18	48
10.11	47
13.14	47
14.27	47
16.22	47
20.9	145

Isaiah
1.5	129, 130
30.18–26	131
30.22	131
40.5	89
40.6	89
43.6	30
52.1	101
59.3	112
66.16	90
66.23	90
66.24	90

Jeremiah
2.13	47
4.4	93, 99–101
6.10	100
9.24	93, 100
9.25	97
11.5	104
17.13	47
20.15	31
31.33	100
32.22	104

Lamentations
1	137
1.1–11	132
1.1	130, 133
1.9	132
1.12	132
1.13	36, 130, 132
1.17	132, 133, 137
1.22	129, 130, 132, 137
5.17	36, 129

Ezekiel
7	122, 126, 127
7.19–20	123, 125
7.19	124
14.4	60
14.7	60
16.20	30
18	122
18.6	137
20.6	104
20.15	104
22	122
22.10	122, 137
22.26	139
24.13	145
36	118, 122, 127
36.17	117, 124
36.25	145
44.7	100
44.9	100
44.26	146, 147

Zechariah
13.1	47, 52

NEW TESTAMENT
Matthew
3.4	52

Luke
2.24	42

Acts
7.51	101

Romans
2.25–29	100
2.25	100

2.28–29	101	PHILO		CLASSICAL AND ANCIENT	
2.29	101	*Quaestiones et*		CHRISTIAN WRITINGS	
4.9–10	100	*solutiones in Exodum*		Hippocrates	
4.11	100	2.2	101	*Aphorismata*	
				5.32–33	84
1 Corinthians		JOSEPHUS		5.56	84
7.18–19	100	*Antiquities*		5.57	84
		1.191–93	98		
Galatians		1.214	98	*Genitalia*	
3.28	101	12.56	95	4.1	108
5.2	100			8.1	108
				5.6.7.8	108
Hebrews		TARGUMS			
11.11	34	*Targum Neofiti Exodus*		*De natura pueri*	
		4.25	95	12.1	108
APOCRYPHA/DEUTERO-					
CANONICAL WORKS		*Targum Onqelos Exodus*		Dioscorides	
Ecclesiasticus		12.43	98	2.75	52, 84
26.20–21	107				
		Targum Pseudo–Jonathan		Galenus	
1 Maccabees		*Exodus*		14.208	84
1.15	96	4.25–26	92		
1.41–64	97	12.48	98	Herodotus	
1.48	91			2.37	92
1.60–61	95	MISHNAH			
		Miqwa'ot		Soranus Ephesius	
2 Maccabees		8.1.5	15	*Gynecology*	
6.10	91, 95			16f IV	51
		Niddah			
PSEUDEPIGRAPHA		2.5	48	ANCIENT NEAR EASTERN	
3 Maccabees		4.3	15	SOURCES	
3.4	52	9.11	108	*Laws of Eshnunna*	
				§26	35
DEAD SEA SCROLLS		BABYLONIAN TALMUD		§31	35
11QTa		*Niddah*			
45.10	125	31a	108	*KTU*	
		31b	126	1.11.24	48
4QMMT		64b	108	1.13	48
45.10	125			1.17.I.39–42	108
		MIDRASH			
CD		*Leviticus Rabbah*		QUR'AN	
12.1–2	125	7.3	162	2.223	107
		Shem. Rabbah			
		19.6	92		

Index of Authors

Anderson, G. A. 161

Bachmann, V. 1, 4, 142
Bachmann-Medick, D. 6
Bailly, A. 52, 84
Bar Asher, M. 119
Bartor, A. 9
Bassnett, S. 6
Bauer, W. 52
Beidelman, T. O. 99
Bell, C. 11, 161
Benthien, C. 3
Bergen, W. J. 13
Bergquist, B. 113
Berlin, A. 133
Berlin, A. M. 14, 158
Beuken, W. 75
Biale, R. 38, 127
Bibb, B. D. 9, 12
Bienkowski, P. 11, 69
Biggs, R. D. 107
Blaschke, A. 92, 100
Blum, E. 8
Boyarin, D. 21, 91, 97, 100, 101, 158, 160
Bratsiotis, N. P. 89
Brenner, A. 1, 4, 94, 110
Brockelmann, C. 38, 48
Butler, J. 3, 22

Camp, C. 127
Cantarella, E. 108
Cohen, S. J. D. 92, 93, 97, 98, 154
Cooper, A. 38, 109, 126
Crüsemann, F. 9, 12, 14, 98

Daniel, S. 53
Davies, P. R. 13
Dean-Jones, L. 84, 108
Delaney, C. 107

Denny, F. M. 94
Dijk-Hemmes, F. van 4, 133
Dijkstra, M. 14
Donner, H. 35
Douglas, M. 3, 8, 18, 19, 23, 73, 94, 124, 142–44, 148, 149, 162
Duden, B. 3

Eberhart, C. 31, 42, 46, 112, 113
Ehrlich, A. B. 55, 95
Eilberg-Schwartz, H. 1, 18, 19, 91, 96, 99, 144
Ellens, D. 1, 18, 19, 30, 61, 74, 77, 85, 128, 131, 133, 143
Elliger, K. 2, 8, 17, 29, 31, 32, 37, 47, 55, 58, 60, 65, 66, 71, 72, 76, 77, 105, 128
Erbele, D. 107
Erbele-Küster, D. 1, 2, 6, 12, 13, 16, 28, 39, 52, 69, 91, 136, 138, 141
Eshel, H. 14

Fabry, H.-J. 8
Feld, G. 118
Feucht, E. 107, 108
Fischer, I. 33
Fishbane, M. 60, 67, 70
Fleishman, J. 94
Fonrobert, C. E. 21, 22, 48, 62, 65, 90, 127, 158
Frevel, C. 9, 19, 20, 161
Frymer-Kensky, T. 16, 122, 142

Gane, R. 43, 49, 56
Gennep, A. van 39, 144
Gerlemann, G. 111
Gerstenberger, E. S. 12, 13, 18, 29, 44, 106, 140, 145, 149, 157
Gilders, W. K. 44
Gispen, W.-H. 28

Gorman, F. H. 9, 41, 72, 157, 159
Gottlieb, A. 115
Grabbe, L. L. 11, 13
Graf, K. H. 10
Greenberg, B. 127
Greenberg, M. 119
Grohmann, M. 21
Gruber, M. I. 39, 118, 125

Hall, R. 94, 96
Hanson, A. E. 84
Haran, M. 10, 40
Harle, P. 49
Harrington, H. K. 14, 15, 70, 153
Hartley, J. E. 68, 104, 109
Hayes, C. E. 156
Hengel, M. 97
Hermisson, H.-J. 139
Hertog, C. G. 55, 57, 74, 75, 81
Hieke, T. 5, 43
Himmelfarb, M. 125
Hoffman, L. A. 94, 96
Holzinger, H. 8
Hostetter, E. 74
Houtman, C. 10, 31, 36, 59, 95
Huber, K. 50, 53, 81

Ilan, T. 153
Iser, W. 159

Jacob, B. 12, 37, 93
Janowski, B. 44, 46, 47, 114, 130
Jenni, E. 31, 47, 141
Joüon, P. 31, 39, 55, 57, 59, 63, 71, 74, 75, 150
Jüngling, H.-W. 8

Kaufmann, J. 10
Kidd, J. E. R. 98
Kiuchi, N. 43, 46
Klawans, J. 15, 16, 20, 69, 123, 139, 142
Klee, D. 61, 72, 117
Klingbeil, G. A. 39
Knierim, R. P. 7, 11, 13
Knohl, I. 158, 160
Koch, A. 3
Koch, K. 7, 8, 11, 12, 29
Köckert, M. 8

König, E. 59
Korpel, M. 89
Kratz, R. G. 9, 11, 12
Kraus, W. 49
Kuenen, A. 8

L'Hour, J. 16, 139, 142, 143, 145, 148
Landsberger, B. 35
Laqueur, T. 3, 4, 22, 89
Lefevre, A. 6
Leick, G. 107
Levi-Strauss, C. 116
Levine, B. A. 11, 33, 34, 44, 58, 61, 65, 68, 103, 120, 121, 128, 147, 158, 160
Liss, H. 10, 12, 13, 23, 107, 159, 160, 162
Loader, W. 125
Løland, H. 21
Lorenz, M. 3
Luciani, D. 8, 9, 28, 29, 61, 159
Lust, J. 82, 83

Magonet, J. 38
Maier, C. 21
Marienberg, E. 127, 141
Marsman, H. J. 21, 51, 95, 108, 135
Marx, A. 11, 42–44, 144, 148, 160
Marzana, M. 4
Mayer, G. 93
Meachem, T. Z. 108
Meshel, N. S. 42
Meyers, E. M. 14
Milgrom, J. 10, 16–18, 29, 32, 34, 37, 43–45, 48, 56–58, 60, 61, 64, 65, 68, 72, 74, 76, 103, 106, 109, 111, 114–16, 118, 119, 122, 128, 139, 140, 143–45, 148–50
Moor, J. C. de 48
Morgenstern, M. 152
Muraoka, T. 31, 39, 55, 57, 59, 63, 71, 74, 75, 81–84, 150

Nihan, C. 2, 7, 9, 10, 18, 19, 141, 144, 160
Noordtzij, A. 155
Noth, M. 7, 12, 17, 29, 32, 37, 38, 60, 105

O'Connor, M. 74
O'Grady, K. 19, 61, 108
Oosting, B. 160
Orlinsky, H. M. 75, 107, 109
Otto, E. 7

Pape, W. 51
Paschen, W. 118, 139, 142–44
Peter-Contesse, R. 61, 82, 145
Pham, X. H. T. 132
Philip, T. S. 1, 57, 70, 74, 85, 90, 117, 118, 123, 128, 135
Plaskow, J. 99
Pralon, D. 49
Püschel, E. 119

Rapp, U. 1, 2, 18, 49, 61, 63
Rehkopf, F. 82, 83
Reich, R. 14
Rendtorff, R. 7, 9, 11, 28, 29, 43, 44, 46, 47, 114
Röllig, H. 35
Römer, T. 8, 13
Rost, L. 12
Roth, M. 11
Rousselle, A. 108
Ruane, N. J. 2, 38, 42, 45, 119, 143, 144

Sanders, E. P. 15
Sarasin, P. 3
Sasson, J. M. 97
Schaper, J. 145
Scharbert, J. 37, 96
Schenker, A. 43
Schiffman, L. 159
Schorch, S. 48, 75, 109, 110, 134
Schreiner, S. 162
Schroer, S. 20–22, 109
Schwartz, B. J. 114

Seidl, T. 142, 147
Smith, M. 130
Staubli, T. 17, 18, 20, 85
Stausberg, M. 15
Stemberger, G. 159
Stol, M. 34, 107, 108
Stolz, F. 96

Toenges, E. 91
Tolbert, M. A. 92
Troyer, K. de 5, 17, 19, 51, 52

Utzschneider, H. 8

Vahrenhorst, M. 139
Van der Toorn, K. 119, 134
Vervenne, M. 113

Wagner, A. 20
Waltke, B. 74
Watts, J. 5, 7, 9, 11, 13, 18, 47, 159, 161
Wegner, J. R. 41, 42
Weissenrieder, A. 83, 128
Wenham, G. J. 16, 76, 112, 115, 143
Werret, I. 158
Wevers, J. 5, 51, 52, 79–83, 85
Whitekettle, R. 47, 48, 60, 74, 76, 107, 141
Willi-Plein, I. 44, 139
Williams, A. V. 17
Winter, U. 48
Wolff, H. W. 20
Woude, A. S. van der 41
Wright, B. G., III 14, 18
Wright, D. P. 16, 57, 68, 69, 73, 118, 126, 139
Wulf, C. 3

Zenger, E. 8, 9, 13, 28, 161

www.ingramcontent.com/pod-product-compliance
Lightning Source LLC
Chambersburg PA
CBHW070638300426
44111CB00013B/2159